A Mother's Work

A Mother's Work

Deborah Fallows

HOUGHTON MIFFLIN COMPANY

Boston ~ 1985

A Richard Todd Book

Library of Congress Cataloging in Publication Data

Fallows, Deborah.
A mother's work.

"A Richard Todd book."
1. Child rearing — United States. 2. Day care centers —
United States. 3. Mothers — Employment — United States.
I. Title.
HQ769.F263 1985   649′.1   85-10717
ISBN 0-395-36218-0

Printed in the United States of America

V 10 9 8 7 6 5 4 3 2 1

I have changed the names of the first two day care centers
discussed in Chapter 5 and, as noted in the text, the names of
certain individuals. All other names are real. — D.F.

FOR JIM AND OUR SONS

Acknowledgments

Many people helped me write this book. It started out as an article in the *Washington Monthly* for Charlie and Beth Peters, who have encouraged me ever since. Dick McDonough first talked seriously about expanding it into a book. Dick Todd, my editor, has steered the book around a winding course with a master's touch. To him, and to Susan Todd, I am grateful for the personal as well as the professional interest they have always shown. Ann Buchwald, my agent, has had a way of saying just the right thing just when I needed to hear it. That has kept me going.

I have gotten valuable help all along the way from Nick Lemann. There have been many others, as well, who have talked honestly, patiently, wisely, and passionately about many of the issues herein: Dominique Browning, Bill Broyles, Sybil Broyles, Grant Thomas, Margot Thomas, Frances Schenkkan, Debbie Siebert, Tom Siebert, Bob King, Karen King, Anne Redman, Ric Redman, Jack Wheeler, Susan Fallows Tierney, John Tierney, Libby Doggett, Sherry Jacks, Ros Lazarus, Si Lazarus, Carol Adelman, Ken Adelman, Chris Campbell, Carrie Hayes, Ron Hubbard of the Austin Community Nursery Schools, Beret Moyer, Maralee Schwartz, and Francie Barnard. I'd also like to thank Maria Mendes.

Most of all, I want to thank my family. I am grateful to my

parents, Frank and Angie Zerad, for my childhood. I hope it's clear how much I treasure it. My husband's parents, Jean and Jim Fallows, have given me a second family that is second to none. I hope that one day my sons, Tommy and Tad, will get from this book as much as they have given it. Our family has had a special young man, Jim Haley, live with us off and on over the past three years. I am grateful for his gifts as a teacher, carpenter, gardener, and friend, which he has shared with us and, especially, with our boys. My husband, Jim, has worn many hats while I was writing this book—husband, father, writer, confidant, cook. The list is endless. There is one hat in particular—that of editor—that he has nearly worn out. His well of patience, humor, and help has run very deep. He is special to me for these things. But he is most special because he has shared with me each and every pleasure and pain of raising our sons.

Contents

Introduction

THIS BOOK IS ABOUT mothers, fathers, children, and work. In its biases, convictions, weaknesses, and strengths, it inevitably reflects my own experience in life. My opinions grow from my memories of childhood, my years in school, and my time at work; but most of all they have been shaped by the last eight years of my life, in which I have been a mother. In addition to reflecting on my own experience, I have through those years tried to watch and understand and learn from other mothers and fathers. When preparing to write this book, I talked with child care workers, educators, journalists, doctors, and friends who lead many different kinds of lives. From this sample of men and women trying to cope with children and career, I reached the conclusions I will discuss in the following pages.

I decided to write this book because so many young families are, like mine, in the midst of working out their own equations for the proper balance between raising children and holding jobs. In part, I wrote it because I personally felt at such loggerheads when my own children were born. My desires and feelings about the way I should raise children and be a mother suddenly seemed to place me at sharp, and unnecessary, odds with the women's movement, whose campaigns to offer women the chance for stronger and more independent lives were, along with the civil rights movement, the most important social developments of my lifetime. I thought of the women's movement as my friend, and still do; yet its positions on motherhood and child rearing made it seem as if I would be failing the movement if I took the steps I thought necessary to care for my children.

At every moment in history, children have caused complications, but the conjunction of the (welcome) advances of the women's movement and the (unwelcome) economic pressures of modern American life has made child rearing an especially pressing issue in the 1970s and 1980s. The solutions we devise — what we choose as families, how the nation factors the raising of children into legislation, what attention industry and business pay to the problems — will reflect the value our society places on families. These solutions will determine whether, and how far, equality between women and men will progress, and they will define the choices our children will face when it is their turn to become parents.

It is hard to think of a subject more personal and emotional than that of children, and I do not expect that every reader will agree with the preferences I express here. I do hope, though, that I will be able to persuade readers of several more fundamental points. One is that our public discussions about raising children are becoming too abstract, theoretical, and removed from attention to the details of how a boy or girl spends the five thousand days of childhood. We often gaze at some distant goal, wishing or imagining that our children will be smart, happy, and well-adjusted adults, instead of focusing on the everyday and often mundane events that make up their childhood. I have tried to pay attention to those details, and I describe some of them here. I hope to remind readers of things we knew well as children — how it feels to go through the long hours and long days of the years of being a child.

I also believe, and hope readers will come to feel, that the life of the full-time parent (which, in most cases, still means the mother) is misunderstood and misrepresented. The full-time mother is largely seen as one who has somehow missed the point of the women's movement and the expanded horizons of the last thirty years. I know from my life as a mother that staying at home *can* offer challenges as demanding and, yes, as important as those in nearly any career. I hope it will be clear that I believe passionately in the obligation of full-time parents, especially full-time mothers, to conduct lives that are meaningful, varied, and satisfying. But I sense that the home is unknown territory to many who are involved in today's debates about children. I hope to shed some light on this territory, not with the expectation that everyone will choose to join me in it but because an understanding of its contours is essential if we are to make honest decisions about children and work.

I would prefer to remain apolitical in my arguments, and I take no partisan stance here. I will, however, examine the politics of child care, since the questions of parenthood, career, children, and child care have become so heavily politicized in the last few years. I think it will become clear that I am uneasy with the most familiar versions of both the liberal and the conservative formulas for the balance between parenthood and career. What disturbs me most about each of them is that they seem to place the real interests of children second, behind some other goal (usually fidelity to other ideological interests). I will try to suggest a kind of politics that could arise from more detailed consideration of what children need in order to thrive. Conservatives and profamily activists may like — or think they like — what I have to say about the importance of family bonds and the need for parents to sacrifice for their family's sake. But my definition of family is not as narrow as theirs, nor would I ever say (as many of them do) that women are naturally subservient to men. Feminists and women's movement advocates may be irritated by my support of nonworking women; I hope they will consider carefully the conditions under which I urge women to stay home. Child care professionals may be angry about my descriptions of what I saw when I visited the day care centers where children spend eight or ten hours a day. I hope they will bear in mind my enthusiastic support for part-time nursery schools and preschools. Like those professionals, I recognize that day care centers are a permanent, growing aspect of our society; that is why I will argue that government, business, and parents all need to do more to raise their quality.

Many women may wonder why I am writing more about

mothers than about fathers, who bear equal responsibility for their children's creation and presumably should also do so for their care. In discussing any social situation where realities depart from the ideal, we face a dilemma: do we resolve to discuss the way things should be, or do we momentarily put aside the ideal to talk about the real? I return time and again in this book to the importance of fathers caring for their children. My emphasis on mothers, in the title of this book and elsewhere, reflects my understanding of the way most American families now function, not the goal toward which they should evolve.

Working mothers and fathers may think I sound smug or cruel; it may seem that I am trying to impart guilt or blame for family situations that are often beyond parents' control. Even if I wanted to sound judgmental, however, I could not do so after meeting the scores of people I have talked with while preparing this book. My purpose in writing is not to distribute guilt or blame. It is, instead, to set forth the facts, as best I know them, about how we are raising our children, why we are working, the choices we are making, and the costs we are choosing to pay.

I begin with my own story, not because it is entirely typical — no one's is — but because it helps raise some of the issues that apply to the lives of all mothers.

I

At Work

I WAS BORN IN CHICAGO, in 1949, the second of two daughters. Our family lived in suburbs and small towns throughout the Midwest while I was growing up, first in Minneapolis, then in Chicago, then on the shores of Lake Erie in northern Ohio. My father was a traveling salesman, so most of the day-by-day work of raising us was left to my mother.

My grandparents were all immigrants from Czechoslovakia. My father's parents came to the United States early in the twentieth century, when they were young teen-agers. My grandfather was a baker, having learned his trade in his hometown city north of Prague and then transporting it to the west side of Chicago, where many Czechs, Poles, and other Central Europeans settled. Neither he nor my grandmother ever became comfortable in English; my father spoke Czech until he went to school. My grandfather taught my father to bake but, like so many other ambitious immigrants, my grandparents worked and saved so that my father and his siblings could go to college instead of being stuck in the family trade. My father went to DePaul, served on a submarine during World War II, and started his career as a manufacturer's representative after the war by selling bakery equipment.

My mother's family came from Czechoslovakia one generation before my father's, but they were no less deeply entrenched

in the Czech-Catholic community around Chicago. My grandmother played her organ in church every Sunday, as did my
mother after her for many years. My mother went to college as
well, at Mundelein, a small Catholic women's college near Chicago. There she studied music. When my father went off to war,
my mother went to work as a secretary in her father's small
printing plant and volunteered at the USO on the weekends.

By the time my sister and I were little girls, during the fifties,
our Czech heritage had become a weekend and holiday link. We
visited relatives regularly, learned the ethnic customs, memo-
rized a few Czech nursery rhymes, collected my grandfather's
recipes for baking in enormous proportions (10 lbs. flour, 2
dozen eggs . . .). But aside from this, our upbringing was in a
typically wholesome, totally Midwest American style.

There are two things about the way I grew up, and my own
family circumstances, that I always return to when pondering
the dilemmas of family, children, and work. One is that there
were two girls — no boys — in my family. There was never a
thought that we should expect to strive for anything less than
boys did. There was no brother to take up the mantle. My father
taught us how to understand an engine (or tried to; I never liked
it much), race a sailboat, and tie knots — and did so far more
seriously than my mother taught us how to cook and iron. My
father insisted I learn to play the trumpet when I really wanted
to play the flute because trumpets were more powerful and important instruments in the marching bands, which were very
serious business in high school in Ohio. Our chores included
mowing the lawn as well as doing the dishes.

This attitude seems no less liberated than anything that today's feminist writers would espouse as the blueprint for childhoods free of sexual stereotyping (except possibly that it was
my father teaching about the hardware and my mother teaching
about the domesticity). It is true that the mothers of a small
group of my friends banded together and forced us — an assortment of awkward twelve-year-old girls — into a "charm" course
for six Saturday mornings. Amazingly, I still remember the
proper way a lady dons her coat, and occasionally I think about
walking with one foot directly in front of the other rather than

with my natural cowboy gait. But those same girls were class presidents, student council leaders, club presidents, student band directors. I know of two people from my high school class who ended up as doctors; both are women. There was as much glory, respect, and prestige in being head cheerleader or head majorette as in being the football team captain or basketball star. I recall with some embarrassment that what I considered my two finest achievements in high school were being on the homecoming court during my senior year and being — at least for a time — first chair trumpet in the concert band.

The second thing that left its mark was the way my mother handled her full-time mothering. I always remember my mother being home. She was there when I was small, there when I came home from school, there when I wandered in from friends' houses after playing, there in emergencies (like when I got pecked by Blackie the crow — the nemesis of the neighborhood's young children — while on an errand to the corner store, and when my sister came running up from the creek when two teen-age bullies with jackknives were harassing the little kids). But I was as aware of her other interests as of her presence. I knew she had studied organ music in college, and her gigantic Hammond organ was the focal point of our living room. I remember turning up to full force the volume on the television once a day during the organ music theme song for some program (one I didn't watch, but tuned to for her because I thought she'd like it) so she could hear it waft up the basement steps into the kitchen where she was making dinner.

My mother tells me now that she used to play regularly at her church on weekends and some evenings while my father took care of us, although I don't remember that. I remember being worried that she refused to join regular bridge clubs when all the other mothers were doing it. She tells me she didn't want to waste her time. When I was in school all day, she began working part-time for my father's business, managing the office and doing all the secretarial work, and she was paid for it. I ask her now if she read Betty Friedan's *The Feminine Mystique* when it came out in 1963, when I was thirteen years old, and what all her friends thought about the early days of feminism. She tells me she tried to read it but threw it down in anger, and that their impression of feminism was of outrageous, brassy, big-city women — representatives of a culture that she and her friends felt entirely estranged from.

As a child, I did not think about being raised in a fairly sexually unstereotyped way and having a mother who was sure of her role at home while sure she wasn't feeling entrapped by it. But these two characteristics of my childhood were both clear enough to me to have left a sense of my possibilities and purpose now that I have a family of my own.

I left Ohio to begin college at Radcliffe in 1967. It turned out to be a turbulent era. At the end of my freshman year, Martin Luther King and then Bobby Kennedy were killed; when I was a junior there were shootings at Kent State, American troops crossed into Cambodia, and Harvard shut down before our final exams because of widespread student sit-ins in protest. Vietnam shadowed everything in all our days at college. On a personal level, girls worried not about their boyfriends as fathers, but as potential soldiers.

Throughout most of my time at college, I dated one person, a young man from California named Jim who was a student at Harvard. He graduated in 1970 and began graduate school in England; I graduated a year later, and we were married immediately afterward. We worked for several months as manual laborers on a work gang in West Africa and then went back to England to spend the first year of our married life living in idyllic circumstances outside Oxford. I worked in an experimental psychology lab, running experiments on rats, while my husband studied economics. The 10 pounds I earned each week — in those days, $24 — covered our weekly grocery bills.

In 1972, we returned to the United States, where we began five or six years of the impoverished young-marrieds' life that was so familiar from the lore of our parents' generation. We lived first in Washington, D.C., where Jim worked for a chronically broke political magazine and I bounced from one unsatisfactory temporary job to another. After two years of this, I decided that I wanted to continue to study linguistics, the subject in which I had majored in college. We moved again, to Austin, Texas, where I began work on a Ph.D.

By the beginning of 1977, I was twenty-seven years old and working on the last requirement for my degree, my dissertation ("The Syllable as a Unit of English Phonology"). We were living again in Washington, because my husband had joined the Carter presidential campaign and then taken a job in the administration. I was also pregnant; I had learned of my pregnancy on the very day Jim joined the Carter campaign. The baby was due in March.

With such limited wisdom of hindsight as I now possess, I realize that in those days I was granted a temporary reprieve from confronting the issues of children versus work. Up to this point, I had not given much thought to juggling family and work. I had assumed I would do both, and assumed it would all work out. We were at that time still living a kind of student life. Until my husband began working in the government, he had no fixed working schedule, and neither did I. We had few obligations, an easygoing social life, and modest means. It seemed that a child would slip right into our way of living; we had little sense of how few things you can count on when it comes to planning life with children.

But, as if I had written the script, my professional life proceeded according to plan for a year. There was a single, crucial fact that made this possible: Tommy, our first son, was a hard-sleeping infant. He would take extraordinary naps. For a year, I was able to settle down at my desk for guaranteed three-hour stretches both morning and afternoon. I remember one day — having worked more than I could take — standing, staring at him in his crib at 4 P.M., waiting for him to wake from his 10 A.M. nap. It seemed to me that motherhood was some well-kept secret; it was working out just fine for me and my career. I finished my dissertation just about the time Tommy finished sleeping, and life with children has never been the same since.

When Tommy was 18 months old, I began working about fifteen hours a week at a linguistics center. I had gotten to know the office while I was writing my dissertation and had even brought Tommy in with me when he was a sleeping infant. Now it seemed like a mother's dream: my bosses and colleagues were sympathetic to the needs and conflicts of working mothers. Indeed, there were many women employed there, among them working mothers. They made it comfortable for me to adjust my hours to my convenience. They were understanding when Tommy was sick. They asked after his general well-being, and mine.

To find part-time care for Tommy, I did what most mothers do — I asked my friends and neighbors for references. Tommy and I were among the lucky ones. There was a young, vivacious woman named Omeda who was, by then, a tradition in our neighborhood. She had worked as the full-time caretaker for two young daughters of a single working mother. When the girls went off to school, Omeda stayed on. She fixed up the walk-out basement of the family's home and cared for several small neighborhood children there, as well as being around for the two older girls when they came home after school.

In today's child care vocabulary, this is known as family home day care, but even that sounds too cold and institutional to describe what I came to think of as almost an extension of our own family. Omeda's was among the best of this kind of care. She was magical with the children, wholly reliable with the parents. The children were all playmates; their parents were neighbors and friends. At one point, I marveled that we knew nearly a generation of her charges, from our sixteen-year-old babysitter to the baby daughter of one of my best friends. The quarters were very modest, and by comparison the prices were high. If sitters in the area were charging $2 an hour, Omeda would probably be charging $3. If the going weekly rate were $65, you might pay $80 to Omeda. People grumbled but kept their children there. I knew, but many others didn't, that she gave reduced prices to at least one woman, a single mother who couldn't have made it without her.

I remember many, many things about Omeda, but a few stick out in my mind: I would always see her dancing with the children when she played records; a briefly evident television set disappeared quickly, never to be seen again, when parents voiced concern; the children dressed up on every Halloween and were welcomed door to door in the neighborhood on Halloween morning. Tommy was very happy there.

I felt I was making no compromises about Tommy's part-time child care that year. The compromises I was making were professional, by being a part-time worker. My erratic work schedule worked well for me and my son, but it was hard for everyone else at my office. I missed meetings; I bowed out of last-minute crises; I wouldn't travel; I couldn't stay late. In short, I was not the kind of employee who could be counted on in a crunch. Dependable, yes, hardworking and competent, but highly restricted. I was passed over for projects I would have liked because they demanded the kind of performance and responsibility that didn't mesh with my private obligations as a mother.

These may sound like minor complaints, especially to seasoned mothers who would kill for a part-time job in their field, but this was the first time I had faced the conflicting demands of children and work. They are the demands that every working parent soon faces that force her, or him, to make choices and pay tolls on one end or the other.

During that year, I was offered a full-time, year-long position, to replace a woman who was taking maternity leave. I was to be an assistant dean, in charge of undergraduate affairs for the students in languages and linguistics at Georgetown University, which was just down the road. It sounded irresistible, particularly when compared to the current frustrations I was feeling. It was clearly and definitely a one-year commitment, although I suspected, and rightly so, that it could open doors at a place that looked perfect for me. As for Tommy, he was doing well and could continue in the same environment, with longer hours. It seemed like a fine situation for him, too. So I took up the offer, full of enthusiasm and optimism.

The logistics of our household ran fairly smoothly that year. I would drop Tommy off at his cooperative nursery school at 9 A.M. (Around Thanksgiving, we had decided to send Tommy to a morning nursery school. He seemed ready, and all of his friends were going. He could spend his morning there, be walked over to Omeda's at noon for lunch, a nap, and afternoon play.) Since home, school, and work were all within a mile's range, I could be at my desk by 9:15. The staff in my office was able to cover for the moments on either end of the day that I wasn't there. So I came in a few minutes late each morning and left a little early to pick Tommy up before 5 P.M. each day.

On our best days, the most I had to feel guilty about was sending Tommy off in the morning on a bowl of cold cereal rather than the steaming oatmeal I would have loved to prepare, if only we weren't always in a rush. Tommy had always been a very active, outgoing boy. I never worried that he might be hiding his real feelings; if anything, this was a child who would need to learn to keep his moods and emotions a little more under wraps. Usually, he showed an irrepressibly lively nature that made being with him a real challenge, and most times a real joy.

But on other days, which occasionally dragged into weeks, and which we tried to pass off as "just a phase," I had more to worry about. On those days, there were signs of strain that surfaced in various ways. Tommy whined that he didn't want to go to the babysitter's; he asked hopefully whether it was Saturday today; he slowed down the whole hurried morning process, screaming when I tried to change his soggy pajamas and put on clean school clothes, pulling his shoes and socks off as soon as I put them on, and doing everything possible to postpone our leaving.

I would have loved to humor him at those moments, to let him play with his trucks and dawdle over breakfast, but there was no time and I was in no mood. We had to keep moving if he was to get to school on time, and I to work — fifteen minutes late every day as it was. I would have loved to read to him — right then, when he was asking — the book he had been carrying around since he woke up. But I had instead to put him off with promises of "later" — when, of course, he would have long since forgotten it.

Certainly, part of his balking was being two years old. And certainly, as I suspected then and know for a fact now, he would have done many of those things whether or not I worked. But what I hated was the idea that rushing was becoming the norm, replacing the sense that as a parent I should have all the time and love in the world to give. And I worried, once I knew I was pregnant again, that when our second child arrived in June, these realities and feelings would only be compounded.

After work, it was a replay of the morning in reverse. We'd try to squeeze in a visit to the neighborhood playground or a stop at the library. Before I worked full-time, we had loved our daily outings. They were our formless, shapeless, improvised times together when we'd be directed only by the weather or our own moods and energy. Sometimes we'd take a very slow walk down the street to the firehouse to visit our friendly firemen. Sometimes we'd build a blanket fort over the card table and read inside it. Sometimes we'd bake cakes and make a complete mess. I remember that these activities would go on for very long times — certainly at a slower pace and more drawn-out duration than an adult would direct, but one that seemed in keeping with the orchestration of a child. But now, our afternoon time was very different. We kept to a faster beat, trying to complete whatever it was before it got dark, before the cleaner's closed, or before our hunger for dinner did us in. Almost invariably, I'd have to cut short our outings.

I tried, like most every working mother, to sell myself on the "quality time" argument: what Tommy and I lacked in the quantity of time we spent together, we could make up in its quality. If we didn't have a lot of hours together during the day, it didn't really matter. I could arrange special moments for just the two of us, giving him my full attention after work, in the evenings, or on weekends. After the long separation, we would be so happy to see each other that we'd make every minute count. In fact, we'd make such good use of our time that we'd be on at least as firm a foundation as the families that took their time for granted and squandered it running errands and watching television. Or so the theory goes.

There is some small grain of truth to this argument. After eight hours of not seeing my son, I was truly delighted to be with him again. I remember certain things that had pushed me to the limit when I spent full days with Tommy: having him perched in his highchair calling "dinner ready?" "dinner ready?" "dinner ready?" thirty-five times in a row while I hurried to prepare his food, or the frustration of the struggles to bundle him into his snowsuit, only to strip him down to go to the bathroom, rebundle him again, and maybe do it once more before we'd make it out the front door. Such things could pass me by with scarcely a notice after a day at work. Certainly, I had more patience for these frustrations when I hadn't faced them all day long. Certainly, I could handle them with more humor when they happened once or twice, not dozens of times during a day. Certainly, it was easier to be a cheerful, even-tempered mother when I was with my son only three hours a day. But did this make me a "better" mother? Did quality make up for quantity?

In our family, it did not — and I do not think we were so unusual in finding it difficult to substitute intensity for time. On the contrary, I think we were very much like other people in other relationships that take time to develop. Not that we couldn't develop a strong and special relationship without it — as in fact we did with our own fathers, who worked long and hard hours when we were children, as many working fathers and mothers do now. No doubt there was, as there is now, something special about those "quality moments." The small moments — reading with a child curled up on your lap, a private talk at bedtime — are the same ones I relish now as when I was working. But while I was working full-time, those few moments during our time together were just not enough to make up for the separations of the day. And even those moments, no matter how well I planned for them, were not promised to us. Often, the best-laid plans for special moments we waited to have went awry with a cranky mood, an overtired child, an emergency phone call, a misplaced favorite teddy. I learned quickly that I couldn't expect a three-year-old to hold his affectionate moods until I had time to cuddle him. Neither can I expect that same child, now seven, to hold his news from school until dinner instead of spilling it the moment he comes bursting out of school, papers flying, nor can our younger son, now four, wait to be introspective and tell me what's on his mind at eight-thirty in the evening, when something is bothering him at four in the afternoon. Our best quality moments come not when we're waiting to savor them but as surprises, fleeting episodes. If I'm lucky now, I'm there to catch them.

But when time is short, the relationship is never quite complete. What we needed most in order to understand each other was a lot of experience in dealing with one another. My son, like every child, was going to spend the majority of his day (his quantity time) with someone. From whomever that would be, he needed certain things. He needed to develop the certainty that that person cared about him and could be relied on to take care of him. Whoever that person was needed to develop confidence in his own instincts about my son, and in his knowledge of his needs and reactions. I wanted that person to be me. If quality time were all it took to develop these understandings, then we could have done it in two or three hours after work each night. We couldn't, and the only mystery now is why that should have come as a surprise. If quality time were all that mattered, there would be no difference between couples who date regularly and those with the experience of actually trying to live together under the same roof. Of course there is a difference, within a couple and within a family; and that is why I found quality time to be so fundamentally mistaken a concept.

Our abundance of nonquality time together might not make for exciting reading. It consists of the hours at the park, the afternoons at the swimming pool, the routines of shopping, stops at the post office and the bank, sandwiches around the kitchen table — all the things we do every day in each other's company. But I have witnessed a thousand small instances that illustrate the kinds of things my sons and I share with each other only because we have spent quantity time together. Quality time with a child is like the highlights of dating — occasions when you're in the right mood, when things go well, when the moment is special. Quantity time is like living with someone, seeing the ups and downs that make up real life, the times that are Monday morning as well as Saturday evening.

One incident that stays in my mind as an illustration of the totally spontaneous and thus unplannable nature of quality time happened a few summers ago. I had just dropped Tommy off at morning play camp at the neighborhood school. I was about to drive off when a little boy about eight years old burst out of the school and ran down the front steps in tears. His mother was on her way down the walk when she heard him. She turned back and led him over to the steps, took his hands in hers, looked him directly in the eyes, and talked with him softly but deliberately for a few minutes, calming him down so he could go back inside happily and she could leave. What I recognized in that instant was something I'd been trying to put my finger on for months. I'd seen it many times before. When a child is overwhelmed or confused by something, there is a distinct way parents respond, different from the way I had seen any babysitter or nanny act, however loving or competent she may have been. If that boy had been my son, I would have been glad to be there for him, too, at that moment. I would not have wanted to coddle or delay his recognition that in life he would have to handle many situations without me, but I think it important that someone who knows him as well as I do steer him through a potentially troublesome situation.

No single episode seems very important as an example of this conviction of mine. But the more I'm around my children, the more such instances I happen to see and deal with. Perhaps a thousand of these episodes add up to the values and security I want to give them. They define the standard for my role as a mother. I don't have to be a supermom who sews all my kids' clothes (I can't sew), who does all the volunteer work at school (I do my share), who cooks gourmet meals (we eat a lot of spaghetti and chicken). I simply have to be around my children — a lot. To meet my standard of responsible parenthood, I have to know them as well as I possibly can and see them in as many different environments and moods as possible in order to know best how to help them grow up, by comforting them, letting them alone, disciplining them, enjoying them, being dependable but not stifling. What I need is *time* with them — in quantity, not "quality."

*   *   *

There were moments of Tommy's childhood that, when I was working, I sorely regretted missing. I recall the time late one afternoon when we went to play at a neighbor's house. My son hopped on his playmate's tricycle, and I expected to see him scoot off in his normal manner — two feet at a time, feet on the ground rather than on the pedals, moving in fits and starts. But he set his feet on the pedals, clearly a practiced and mastered skill, and zoomed off. I knew that somehow I'd missed all the trial and error, the skips and skids along the way to becoming an expert pedaler.

These were strong parental feelings that were probably of little more consequence than just my feeling bad about them. They may well have passed Tommy by unnoticed. Did he care if his babysitter and not I was the witness of his milestones? Probably not. I was distinctly aware of these milestones, but I knew they would come up and go by regardless of my presence. It was the more subtle trail of his development that I was more concerned about, the rough edges of his personality and character that his father and I knew well and wanted to have the time and chance to affect.

In our first son, it was his wildly outgoing, compelling manner (a "desperado," a Spanish-speaking babysitter called him at five months) that we worried about. The single thing that would send me into a tailspin on a morning after I'd dropped Tommy off at nursery school was seeing that the tool set, a slapdash collection of real nails, hammers, and wood, was set up as an activity for the morning. I would work at my desk just waiting for the phone call that my son had nailed someone's small shoe to the floor.

When Jim and I did our co-op duty (the euphemism to describe the requirement that parents spend a day every few weeks helping the regular teacher) at the nursery school, our suspicions were verified. If a building of blocks came crashing down in one corner of the room, I could be sure it was my son who had sent them flying; if a game of musical chairs was in progress, I could be sure to find him pushing his way to the sole remaining chair with the same vengeance and speed with which he scooped up all the colored eggs at each Easter hunt. Sitting back to give another child a chance did not come with his genetic make-up. I remember often being as mortified at his two-year-old behavior, particularly around my friends who had demure daughters, as I now am proud of his hard-fought-for and usually won self-control.

My husband and I had had enough experience with Tommy to think we knew pretty well how to handle his overenthusiasm, his lack of control, in a way that would calm him down temporarily but not stifle the tremendous curiosity and wholehearted eagerness about life that were his corresponding strengths. He has a way of engaging people and of enlivening things he touches that could be toned down but should never be weakened. We could do this when the occasion arose in the hours we saw him. But we knew well that most of the times that called for it were in the long hours — the great majority of his day—that he was away from us.

I never worried, as some working parents do, that our parent-child relationship suffered from our separations. The times he was reluctant to leave his group of buddies at the end of the day to come home with me were more than balanced by the fusses he put up when leaving me for them in the morning. He clearly loved his caretakers but just as clearly preferred us to them. I could tell he was just different with me and his father. But the fact that I and other parents are reassured by these feelings, and by research findings that back up our parental intuitions, was of small comfort to me when I considered that he was without the company of the two people he loved best and knew differently for the majority of his waking hours.

I also sensed that in my family, as in many where the jobs and careers of both parents are pursued at least in part for the independence they offer, my work was becoming a tyrant of sorts itself. Working people, by their own "success," work themselves into a position of obligation. This isn't bad in itself: indeed, this sense of obligation is one of work's satisfactions. But it can be bad when one's obligations as a worker run headlong into one's obligations as a parent. Ironically, the more "successful" the position is, in terms of prestige, power, money, and responsibility, the more commonplace and restricting its tyranny can be.

I have one friend who works as a lawyer, part-time. Theoretically, she works until about 3 P.M. every day, so she can be home to meet her older child after school. (Her younger child spends the day with a housekeeper.) In reality, those afternoons can often drag on until 5 or 6 P.M., and if it's a day when her son goes home after school with a friend or an evening when she and her husband go out, she misses time with her son nearly altogether. She is, however, far ahead of some other friends of mine, both of them lawyers, who are so often called away on business trips or weekend work that it is hard to imagine when they see their children at all. (Most of their children's time is spent under the supervision of a South American housekeeper.)

I have another friend who was a vice president of a foreign bank, working in the bank's office here in Washington, D.C. The summer her first child was three and her second child was born was also the summer the foreign heads of the bank came for an extended visit. With her daughter only a few weeks old, my friend was obliged to plunge right back into an extraordinarily heavy schedule of daytime work and nighttime entertaining, none of which she could skip, because the foreign potentates were in town. Needless to say, this was poor timing for an older daughter just greeting a new sibling and a new baby just greeting the world. But such complications do not count in the world of business.

During the year I was working full-time, I remember a number of instances when meetings would run late or appearances at evening functions were required, and I would be late retrieving my son from the babysitter's or have to leave early, before our cherished bedtime routine. Like all the women I've mentioned, I knew that I had certain obligations to the work that I had chosen to undertake, and my son would simply have to adjust.

For every working-mother story, there is certainly a matching working-father story. The husband of my friend the lawyer often travels and had to cancel a family trip with their son at the last minute because of unplanned business travel; the husband of my friend the banker is yet another lawyer, who sometimes spends weeks on the road arranging deals with far-flung partners; my own husband, when he worked that year in the White House, got home barely in time to kiss our son good-night, if we were lucky.

I am not objecting to the fact that certain jobs require these extra sacrifices from their employees. Work is sometimes like that, and the most responsible jobs often ask the most from the people who hold them. My point is that when *both* parents work, especially in nonroutine, professional positions, it's too often the case that the mother *and* the father have to cut corners with their children every day. When both parents have demanding jobs, there are more compromises and more conflicts between children and work than in families where one parent — mother or father, it doesn't matter which — is less totally obligated.

Some parents feel the pain of these compromises acutely. But after a while, the pain can start to go away. Compromise can become habit. Work can become almost an excuse for tending to grown-up affairs rather than spending time with the children. It certainly served as an excuse for the fathers of my parents' generation; after a while, we never even asked why many of the daddies were missing from the school picnics and birthday parties, because we knew they all "had to work." I think many never learned to appreciate or enjoy even parts of these events. In yet another dubious form of equality, I now see women and men behaving the way those fathers of the 1950s did. Some two-career parents stop questioning the need for all their obligations and extras — the travel, the late hours, the weekend work. They go on assuming that the children will adjust and that a little more missed time won't really matter, since it can all be made up in a week or two at the beach or on the ski slopes. They stop bothering to examine just what kind of life together their family is leading.

I know many fathers who are regularly found at their offices on Saturdays and Sundays. Most travel frequently. Most get home from their offices at 8 P.M., long after their wives have picked up the children or sent home the babysitters. When I call parents to arrange drivers for the trips my son's school classes take every few weeks, I can count on a quota of peremptory replies from people who say simply, "I work," as if this obviously exempts them from any obligation to compromise or rearrange their schedules for their children. (If more than the occasional one even said, "I'm sorry, it's difficult for me, because I'm supposed to be at work then," the impression would be much different.) "I have to go to work" and "I need to get this report done" become idioms some parents mouth all too easily as they slip into this high-gear life-as-usual.

I remember reading an article that put these concerns into focus for me. It was in *Savvy*, a magazine about successful, sophisticated women, and it described two high-powered career mothers who had, it seems, become quite comfortable in this kind of life-style, who didn't look back with even a touch of discomfort. The details of this kind of life-style, both spoken and unspoken, are telling:

> Kathryn Schrotenboer is an archetype of the new, nontraditional mother. At thirty-one she has a full-time obstetrics practice in Manhattan and is an attending physician at the most fashionable hospital in the city, New York Hospital. Her husband, an attorney, frequently works until ten or eleven at night. They have a son, three, and infant twin daughters. Schrotenboer arranged to take a month off to have her second child (which turned out to be her second and third) but the twins were late arrivals and she ended up going back to work after only a week. She routinely works ten- or eleven-hour days (an hour or two of hospital rounds on either side of her nine-to-five practice) and is frequently on call during the evenings and weekends. Her children are taken care of by full-time, live-in nannies (one for Monday through Friday, one for the weekends in case of emergency calls). Sometimes she is gone the entire night. So she and her husband are both frequently absentee parents. "The kids may miss seeing me or both of us on any one day, but not usually for two days running." . . .
>
> As for her children, Schrotenboer calls them "the most important and rewarding things in my life," but she doesn't

consider time away from them a major trade-off. ". . . And when I spend evenings and weekends with my children, I feel I have so much of them that I don't know how mothers can spend all day and all night with them."

According to the story, there was one thing about this arrangement that gave Schrotenboer pause. "The kind of trade-off she does feel bad about is being off-duty on the night that one of her patients goes into labor. 'You can't be on call every night for every patient, but I'm disappointed if I spend nine months with a patient and miss her delivery.'"

Savvy's other young mother also seemed to have worked things out just fine:

> Another mother of two very young children, with a demanding career in investment banking, describes a similar sense of conflict: "It's always hard to go back to the office after having a baby but, at the same time, I tend to leave the office late because I find it hard to take off. Sometimes I don't see the kids at all, or maybe it's just for ten to fifteen minutes a day, in which case I tell them 'I love you and miss you.' If I won't get home before they're asleep, I'll call and say goodnight."

Children are, in large part, bearing the brunt of being accommodating in all these arrangements. They say good-night to Mom and Dad on the phone instead of having books read and getting hugs. They eat dinner with the nanny instead of with the parents. They tell their school stories to the babysitter. I have seen some who spend their Sunday mornings "with Dad," waiting by the tennis court while he plays his games. Of course the children adjust; they are, by nature, quite adaptable, quite flexible. And besides, the children can't do anything about it anyway, and they are, if anything, survivors.

Because I felt that I wasn't being the kind of mother I wanted to be — that I wasn't offering my son the kind of childhood I wanted him to have, that our life was pulled to extremes where almost no margins, except perhaps an hour in the evening or a weekend afternoon, were left, and because by June a second child would join the family — I decided that at the end of the year I would not return to work or resume work at my former office or pursue the possibilities arising from that year's work.

Like almost everyone's, mine wasn't a decision that came easily or without a lot of ambivalence. I had a lot invested in my work: the years of education, years of climbing my way up, and finally a chance to work toward fashioning a position that I could keep growing with. There was the comfortable feeling of identity with the job and title, particularly in a town like Washington, D.C., where signals about such things are in the air, a part of life. There was the pay, which was enough to affect our life-style, although not dramatically. There was my long-held assumption that I could, as an accomplished woman, and should, as an advocate of independent and equal lives for women, handle both career and motherhood.

But as I measured the things I knew I would miss by quitting work against the things I thought I might gain by being home, I was more and more sure that I wanted to tip the balance the other way. These are things I couldn't have understood before our first child was born, and things I have come to understand better and better as I spend more time with our children and as they grow older.

Once I had made my decision, motherhood loomed ahead quite differently for me. This was it: I was leaving my job to stay home, all day. And, at first, it felt like a step in the wrong direction.

2

At Home

THROUGH MOST OF AMERICAN HISTORY, women's role in the work force was uncontroversial, because it was so well defined. Until World War II, the women who worked were primarily young, unmarried, and childless — or from groups that, by general agreement, were supposed to work, such as immigrants and blacks. World War II changed all that. For the first time, the typical woman in the work force was likely to be over thirty-five, married, and a mother. But although these women flocked to work in record numbers, filling theretofore traditionally male jobs in plants and factories, wartime circumstances leached much of the controversy from this sweeping change. There wasn't a sharply defined conflict between the prevailing social ideal — that mothers should stay at home with their children — and the economic and social forces driving women into the workplace. Of course women had to work; there was a war on. The former housewives who were now riveters and machinists may have entertained new ideas of their own possibilities, but the conventional wisdom was that they would sigh with relief when allowed to exchange their overalls for aprons and welcome their husbands and sons back home.

As it turned out, many women were not willing to go home when the war was over. Many wanted to remain working, and many did. The labor force participation rate for women, which had changed very little in the previous twenty years, went up sharply during the war and never really went down again. To be sure, there were quick, sweeping layoffs soon after V-J Day, probably to make clear that the jobs were supposed to belong to the returning GIs once more. But by 1952, more women were working than had worked during the war.

As the war ended, the controversies over "women's place" increased. Without the excuse of the war effort, what were women doing in offices and factories, taking jobs that male breadwinners might hold? Many of the aspirations and conflicts that gave rise to the women's movement (and the conservative countermovement) can be traced to the war and its aftermath.

Even those women who stayed out of the work force were affected by the social revolution that was under way. The element of choice had entered (and complicated) a decision that could previously have been considered automatic. Yet there was remarkably little change in the public portrayal of the interior lives of nonworking women. From the 1930s through the 1970s, the generally accepted model of the "housewife" or "Mom," as portrayed in books and movies, on radio and television, seemed to have been frozen. Evan Connell's novel *Mrs. Bridge*, published in 1959, cannot really be considered typical of anything, since it is one work of art describing a particular social situation (an upper-middle-class family in Kansas City in the 1930s), but it has always impressed me as an especially evocative image of nonworking women. In Connell's portrayal of India Bridge are countless nuances that recur in other depictions of women at home:

> At luncheons, Auxiliary meetings, and cocktail parties Mrs. Bridge always found herself talking about such matters as the by-laws of certain committees, antique silver, Royal Doulton, Wedgwood, the price of margarine as compared to butter, or what the hemline was expected to do, but since Grace Barron had entered the circle she found herself fumbling for answers because Grace talked of other things — art, politics, astronomy, literature. After such a conversation Mrs. Bridge felt inadequate and confused, if a little flattered and refreshed, and on the way home she

would think of what she should have said, and could have said, instead of only smiling and replying, "It does seem too bad," or, "Well, yes I expect that's true."

Even in the 1980s, full-time mothers are still portrayed at best as closed, traditional women whose narrow sights stop at the front door, and at worst as weak women, a group of losers who just can't cut the mustard in the big world. I read countless articles in newspapers and magazines around the country like these:

> Women like Brenda Ray and Sally Cullum describe themselves as traditional and conservative. Marrying and having a family was *always* the main goal Mrs. Cullum set for herself, she says. . . . "Some of our new philosophies are designed only for our own convenience," she says. "But traditional things are based on good sound values. In my own life I'm traditional, but I'd like to be out there doing grand things, too. I do have an intellectual conflict, but for me, it all gets back to my faith. I have my priorities in line with what the Bible says your priorities should be."

> Nobody can say that [Peggy] Saewert didn't try. Three months after Jake was born, she was back behind the manager's desk at Office Mates 5, a large secretarial and clerical placement agency that is part of a national firm. Then, grim reality set in. She had to be up before dawn, breast-feed Jake, get him dressed, get herself ready for work, leave the house at 7 A.M., drop Jake at the sitter's, drive into downtown Milwaukee and put in a demanding day. After four months on that merry-go-round, Peggy Saewert had had it.
> "I was tired all the time — all the time. Jake was sleeping through the night, but there was always something to be done. There was always wash to do, always a meal to be cooked."

> Every evening as Janet drove out of the company parking lot, her back aching from her hours at the typewriter, the urge to quit her job seemed to get stronger.
> She was on her way to pick up her nine-month-old baby, Jonathan, at his sitter's home. Then on to her own home

to start dinner, feed her son, set the table and run the water for his bath, all the while neatening up as she passed from room to room. By the time her husband walked in the door an hour later, everything would be in order — and Janet would be exhausted. She could seldom stay awake these days even long enough to watch the 10 o'clock news.

"I never dreamed I would think of being a stay-at-home mother," she says, "but I find myself feeling that I can't keep this up."

I didn't identify with the religious, traditional profile. And I certainly hoped not to identify with the portrayal of losers.

When I sat in my office the last year I was working and considered how I would feel after I quit my job, these images — of limitation, defeat, and drudgery — were what came to mind when I thought of full-time motherhood. (Recently, a forty-year-old doctor wrote in the *Washington Post* that of course she'd quit her job if things didn't seem to be working out for her eighteen-month-old daughter in the full-time care of a nanny — "But not for full-time child care!" It was not quite clear what she meant to say, except that devoting full time to children was beneath consideration.) There was nothing appealing or even comforting in the idea that this was to be my fate, that I was choosing a lengthy list of daily chores, a fusion of the self with domestic things, a contentment that approached complacency. I did not at all welcome the thought that I was throwing in the towel and henceforth might recharge myself periodically but would only go around in circles rather than advance.

Somehow it seemed unfair. I was not choosing to stay home because I liked housework but because I wanted to take more responsibility for raising my children. Yet the messages I received from much of the outside world suggested that the drone-like routine of housework was the predominant and defining fact about full-time mothers. The social history of housewives implied that postindustrial women reached liberation only when they revolted against home and hearth; the feminist movement seemed mainly to celebrate those heroines who had made their mark in business, politics, or the arts; and magazines like *Work-*

ing Mother tried to say it was all pointless anyway, since working makes for better mothers and stronger children. I felt defensive, wasteful, wasted, and bad.

I soon found myself with little time for such speculations. I remember wondering on mornings that spring when we were all rushing around, trying to get off to school and work, just what it would be like. What was I supposed to do in a few months, when I would find myself with a three-year-old and a newborn? There could be no more excuses about not having enough time to read that book to Tommy in the morning, no more reason not to indulge his dawdling over breakfast. I was going to be there precisely so we could do more together, have more time together, keep to his pace instead of mine. Once we were awake, fed, and dressed, what were we supposed to do then? And what were we supposed to do the next day, and the next? We had never had the prospect of so much time together before. We had always run out of time before we ran out of things to do.

I didn't do a very good job of it at first. I will reveal the embarrassing truth about what I did the first morning I had any free time to myself. Tommy was at morning nursery school and Tad, our second son, was napping. Do you know what I did? I scrubbed the kitchen floor, on my hands and knees, with a television talk show on in the background where women were spiritedly discussing the pros and cons of having their young children working as models in commercials. As though programmed for it, I remember distinctly thinking that the kitchen floor must be dirty, really dirty, that it had not been scrubbed — mopped, yes, but not really scrubbed — since we had moved in three and a half years before. (I have no idea now, and didn't as I bent my knees then, whether it really looked any dingier that day than ever before. And why did I care?)

A vision of myself, what I was doing, flashed into my head. I was one of those housewives in the commercials on television! This one enthusiastic foray into housework was enough to last me for all the succeeding years of motherhood. Sometimes I still have to do it, but I have never again used my own time on such unnecessary things.

And I probably took more seriously than I should have my early encounters in my new role as the "lady of the house." One was with a man I'll call Mr. Kramer, the roofer who was supervising the repair of our leaky roof. He was an oleaginous, insinuating character whose most infuriating trait was that he would never discuss "serious" matters — such as gutter placement or money — with me, the little woman. He insisted on waiting until he could have a man-to-man talk with my husband. His counterpart, the carpenter, would sometimes talk to me, but only if I convinced him that my husband was not available and made a big point of it. I probably reached the peak of my new-housewife rage when I got a telephone solicitation to renew my subscription to *Working Mother* magazine. "Perhaps you'd like to take advantage of this tremendous offer, Mrs. Fallows . . ." I explained that I was no longer working and found the articles not so relevant to my current concerns. "Ah, you're not working," the eager salesman pressed on. "Then perhaps I might interest you in some other magazines we also carry: *TV Guide*, perhaps!"

After a while I overcame my sensitivity to all this and became adept, like most at-home moms and dads, at handling such comments. As my confidence in my own decisions deepened, I've learned to laugh — most of the time — during these moments. But occasionally I suffer a relapse, like the one that happened at my tenth college reunion, when I saw my classmates who were now rising stars in law firms, on college campuses as professors, in business. And I thought: that could be me! It happens even with my own family, when each Christmas I see my sisters-in-law becoming accomplished professionals. In such moments I still feel a twinge, wondering if too much of life is passing me by.

A few weeks into my full-time motherhood, I came up with a plan. It was shrewd, I thought. I had a friend and neighbor who was a full-time mother. She was doing it in a way that looked ideal to me. She and her daughter and her house always looked like the perfect model. My friend sewed beautiful clothes for her daughter, set up a playroom in a fashion that made adults as well as children want to play in it, always had her daughter in the kitchen with her working on creations that would later

emerge in the dining room looking and smelling irresistible.
Moreover, they always went about with a good-natured, un-
hurried manner, seeming to enjoy whatever it was they did. It
all seemed to work well for her.

So all I needed to do, I decided, was to be just like her. I
planned all sorts of projects in the last weeks before I stopped
working. I made lists of things I thought the kids and I could
do: make puppets, assemble scrapbooks, sew costumes. I
thought I would paint their toy shelves, make them curtains,
clean out closets, catch up on correspondence while they
napped. It would all be a fresh start and clear the way for our
new life at home together.

Of course I should have known better. In three years I had
forgotten a lot about life with a newborn, and I had no way to
imagine life with two. The best we could do for several months
seemed like very little: feeding one or the other of them all the
time, changing wet clothes, changing wet beds, making trips to
the grocery store, going to the pediatrician, rising for late-night
tending, catching up on naps when we could. Every newborn
brings a new surprise. Tad's, unfortunately, was his sleeping
habits. He never slept. It was a cruel blow to me, especially
following Tommy, the perfect sleeper. I had counted on Tad's
nap times as reprieves, time to regroup, and I found it very hard
on the days when he could manage to make it from dawn to
dusk with only a twenty-minute catnap to refresh himself.

Once I thought we were coming out of the woods. I had
packed up both children and was headed out the door when my
husband, who by then had left the government and was working
at home, asked, "Where are you going?" "To Sears, to get some
hooks for the closet," I replied, feeling very much like a regular
person at last. We went out prepared for everything — back-up
clothes for the baby, cookies for the three-year-old, extra diapers, extra wipes, strollers, umbrellas, damp cloths, plastic bags.
When we got to the parking lot, I nursed Tad in the car to stop
his crying while Tommy ate cookies. Tad relaxed after a bout of
diarrhea, and I changed him from top to toe. By then, the wet
summer heat was building. We were all sticky and irritable. I
was sweating, feeling nauseated. Before we could make it out of

the car, a thunderstorm let loose and we were trapped. More nursing, more cookies, more changing. The storm tapered off to a gentle rain, which we finally braved to get into the store. Of course they didn't even have the hooks I was looking for.

If we weren't quite "regular people" yet, we were on the way. Slowly, over the months, I mastered the skills of my new trade. We worked out a kind of daily schedule that provided at least some moments in most days when both children would be napping. I learned to answer the phone, change a diaper, and help with Woody Woodpecker puzzles at the same time. We always managed to get everyone's teeth brushed by 11 A.M.

As these things became habits, our life at home and my life as a mother began to take on their own distinctive styles. We passed from survival and maintenance into living our own life at the pace and with the activities we enjoyed. But what I had learned by that point, from our few trial and error forays into normal life, was that there was no way I could copy my friend. She lived the way I once thought mothers were supposed to live, did what they were supposed to do. It worked well for her, but it never would for me.

So I put away our artsy crafts. I was never any good at it; the kids didn't enjoy it; we all liked to arrange and organize our supplies but then we could never think of anything very creative to do with them. I abandoned my always misguided plans for sewing clothes and costumes. It baffles me that I ever considered this; I've never sewed in my life. The machine I own belonged to my grandmother, and even a handy seamstress would have to wrestle with it. Now the boys look forward to their yearly trip to the dime store for Halloween costumes as much as I do. They may not look as cute to the adult eye as some other little custom-crafted monsters and characters, and they may look exactly like their neighbors, but it's fine for all of us. We do much better at outdoor activities: collecting things from the woods — flowers, leaves, tin cans, berries; building things with mud and sticks, or snow, or piles of leaves. We visit, visit, visit — museums often, the library, hotels to buy a Coke and ride the elevators, pick-your-own-crop farms. We often spend time in the kitchen. By now, at seven and four, the boys can whip up, from scratch, a batch of chocolate chip cookies entirely by themselves. There's nothing special or better about the things we do, except that they work for us.

Learning the right pace and style for our family has made all the difference to me and my adjustment to full-time motherhood. The one thing I knew I could never learn to live without was exercise. On days when I can run a few miles or swim forty lengths, I'm a different person all day from when I can't, so I built exercise into our schedule from the start. Sometimes we'd go to a swim club I joined expressly for this purpose. The boys would go to the nursery, Tommy with his lunch and Tad with his bottle, while I rushed through my laps. It took me twenty-five minutes, then I would gather them up, change them into suits, and we'd all play in the warmer baby pool for a while. On other days, when I couldn't swim, Jim would know and reserve a half-hour or more for me around noon if he could, or at the end of the day, and he would play with the boys while I ran off my frustrations and built-up tensions around the track.

But the most important lesson of all was that of free time. My only cardinal rule was that when I found it or made it (first with infant nap times; later with playgroups, nursery school, swapped playtimes, and at night if I didn't fall asleep right after the children), it was *my* time. Everyone has a different plan for that time (and I'll talk about that in a later chapter) and for me it has meant at first keeping up with an occasional consulting project in linguistics and, for the last three years, writing this book.

I had found a satisfaction in my professional work that is different from my satisfaction as a mother, and I wanted to preserve at least some of that. The skills I brought with me to motherhood, at least at the beginning, were much less well honed than my skills as a linguist. I had felt comfortable and confident when sitting at my desk, the very opposite of the infantile helplessness I felt as I walked my crying baby at midnight. At home, I didn't know when the good times were coming or the difficult ones would end. I didn't know if my child was "going through a phase" or if each new development was a fixed and terrible aspect of his personality. Most other mothers I knew felt some helplessness not so different from my own.

Being a parent does become easier, of course. You get better at it, just as you get better at any other kind of work. But the goals and fulfillment of life as a parent remain very different from those of life in the working world. They are less tangible: the needs of a growing child are not definable the way a job is. They are less predictable: it is harder to be sure that a solid upbringing will lead to a solid adulthood than to know that steady plugging will lead to advancement in most large organizations. They are less immediate: parenting goes on from one day to the next, while a project at work can be wrapped up and completed. It's harder to say "I'm a good mother" than it is to say "I'm a good travel agent."

But the greatest difference between a parent's satisfaction and any other kind is that it is ultimately external. The final test of whether parenthood has been successful is whether it equips a child for a happy and enjoyable life. None of us can control our children's destiny; perhaps the greatest shock most new parents undergo is realizing how much of their child's personality is simply *there*, from the start. But the only significant test of different styles of parenthood is what they mean to the children. At least in my family's case, I know it has made a difference for me to be there.

Our first son, Tommy, is a boy who would have done well as Peter Pan. He is an adventurer, a leader, a free spirit, always happy with a band of buddies. He has always had an outgoing nature that he needs to learn to rein in at certain moments. He needs to learn to draw the line between enthusiasm and delirium, to put civil limits on his curiosity, and to cultivate some small bit of generosity and kindness for his fellow man, whom he would prefer simply to overwhelm.

The special mission with this child is to guide him in learning and setting these limits for himself in a way that preserves the great gifts he has. Left unchecked, he could become a menace to society, but if simply squelched and sat upon, he would become an unhappy and frustrated child. To be his parent is to find the blend of license and discipline that his character demands.

There are many dozens of episodes in his life that illustrate what I mean. Let me mention one. When he was four years old, Tommy was in prekindergarten at our neighborhood elementary school. The class was returning from a morning's field trip to the barge and canal. The children were all excited, hungry, and tired as they ran in for lunch. I had deposited my carload of kids and was pulling away from the curb when I watched Tommy run up behind a little girl, one of his best friends, and push her down onto the cement walk. Not so bad; a little shove; they're only four years old; boys will be boys; who knows what she may have done to ask for it. The point was not this single incident, but how it fit into the stage of Tommy's life at this point.

I had watched him at length in many different situations that year, at school with large groups, at home with a friend or two. I knew that big changes in his life, a new brother and a new school, were having some impact on his life. But I knew, too, that this was the kind of thing he often did simply because he wasn't thinking how it would feel to be on the receiving end of that shove. Tommy got a quick reprimand from his teacher this time and a deserved time-out. I've seen him at such moments. He would do his penance and then forge on, unblinking. But I also knew he was susceptible to and would listen to little moral lessons. When he got home from school that afternoon, I gave him another of the thousand explanations about kindness and thoughtfulness that he, in particular, needed. And I could see by his reaction that he was mulling it over. I've heard him say the same kind of thing to his little brother lately, when he sees him inflict some similar wrongdoing.

Of course, I can't be there to witness every such incident in his life. (I shudder to think how many I've missed.) Even if I could, I shouldn't be. He needs to know that others besides his parents can set his limits. But I am absolutely certain that I know my son better, know better what to make of his behavior, know better how to deal with it, than anyone else does. The point is not that his teachers or babysitters deal wrongly with such incidents. The point is that most anyone else besides his father or me wouldn't be quite as aware, quite as concerned about this part of his personality as we are. We could take the time over this little shove to point out the lesson, to draw out his response. We would go the extra mile for him throughout his daily life to watch and wait for cues to hammer the lesson home. I simply know that once I stopped my full-time job, I had more time for my son. I was with him more often, under more varied circumstances. It gave me the time and chance to notice and act on these items of discipline, as well as to partake of the pleasures of his company.

I also have a sense of what tremendous strides Tommy has taken to get, three years later, to the point where he sometimes exhibits a magnanimous spirit. Last fall I saw Tommy and a school friend trying to play "tackle" football with Tad, then four, tagging along behind. Tad was quite a damper on these seven-year-old athletes. But Tommy and his friend fashioned a game that went like this: one of the older boys would have the ball and start to run; the other would come after him to tackle. At the crucial moment, the ball was passed off to Tad, who ran free for the touchdown. The play worked every time, and every time the two older ones cheered a very proud Tad for his goal. Tommy pretended not to notice the compliments I gave him on the arrangement, but he was listening and knew he had earned them.

Often, it's not the limits on his behavior but the horizons of his world that seem most important. Two years ago, when Tommy was in kindergarten, we lived in Austin, Texas, in a house where the back yard sloped down to meet a creek. The creek meandered around for miles, sometimes at ankle depth with tiny rapids, sometimes deepening into the size of a small swimming hole. For about half a year, Tommy and his friends stuck to our back yard and the same fifty-foot stretch of creek. Then one day they discovered they could scramble over our back fence and across the neighbor's yard, slide down a stone bank, and reach a wide rock ledge that ran right into the edge of the water. The ledge had a few small caves carved out behind it, and a soft spot that they could dig clay out of, and it was wide enough to fish from. To my eye, these natural features consti-

tuted the appeal of the place. To young boys, the attraction was
the privacy, the secretness, the slight scariness of it, the distance
from our back yard. They knew I was within shouting distance,
because I directed them to fishing poles and provided them with
buckets. What they didn't take into account was my ear always
tuned to the direction of their noise, listening for long silences
or abrupt shouts from that slightly dangerous spot. They didn't
think about my judgment, toting up each time how well each
child there could swim, or my taking responsibility for explaining to the other kids' parents why they ended up covered with
mud and had soaked their only pair of sneakers. To me, these
things were a price worth paying for the boys' ability to move
out beyond the borders of their own back yard, to stretch their
imaginations so that rock ledge became a pirates' den or robbers' cave.

My being at home gave the boys a looser tether than they
would otherwise have had. I was the one imposing the limits,
making the rules, and then taking the liberty of breaking them
if they didn't work out as well in practice as they looked in
theory. There were small judgment calls like this every day, and
I usually ruled in favor of the most liberal. I'm pretty sure,
however, that if someone else, a babysitter, had been making
the calls, I would have instructed him or her to call them more
conservatively.

Strangers often think that Tad, our second son, greatly resembles his brother. My husband and I can see the subtle differences in their appearances, and the enormous differences in their
personalities. When Tad was three years old and we were reg-
istering him for a new nursery school, one of the forms asked
for a one-word description that best summed him up. My husband and I both thought this over, independently, for some time
and both came up with the same answer: sensitive/sweet. "Sen-
sitive" has always been a dominant characteristic; "sweet" has
been less constant, coming and going with his different stages.
Unlike Tommy, who always craves companions, Tad enjoys his
time by himself. At three, he would work diligently at his careful
coloring for a good half-hour or more, blocking out any back-

ground chaos, passing by any attractive offer like games or snacks. He likes his time in the company of his father or me, whether it's running errands, working in the yard, or reading books. I've listened to his very carefully developed arguments on why children don't need to go to school — ever. "They could just stay home with their moms or dads all the time. If their moms or dads had to work, they could stay home with a babysitter. The babysitter would be there because maybe the babysitter already went to school before but was finished."

Despite this, it's also been clear that Tad has enjoyed his morning nursery school. I'm sure that his experience there has rounded out his personality, made him more independent, brought him out of his shyness, helped him make friends. I'm just as sure that he has thrived on being out of organized groups and organized activities as much as he has been.

I remember one particularly trying period the summer Tad had just turned three years old. He was in what I called his "Insistence on Starting Over" stage. When I went in to answer his calls in the morning, he would be immediately on guard. I'd bring him his shorts and T-shirt and he'd say, "No, I get them!" So I'd put them back in the dresser drawer. "No, shut the drawer!" So I'd shut the drawer. "No, put me back in bed!" So I'd help him scramble back to bed. "Now go outside." I'd leave the room. Now we were at the starting block again. I could reenter, greet him. He would be all sweetness and light. I'd ask him if he wanted to get dressed, and he would march to his dresser and find his clothes. That evening would feature a performance of similar nature, I knew, because it had happened the night before. After a bath, he would stand naked by the tub. "Where are my jammies?" he'd ask. "In your dresser drawer," I'd answer. "I want to put them on," he'd reply. "You can get them," I would say. "No, you get them." So I would get them. "No," he'd say, "I'll get them." Et cetera.

Late in the morning the mailman would arrive. If I slipped up and took the outgoing letters from the slot and handed them to him, back they had to go, in exactly the right position, so Tad could initiate the exchange and march them up the walk to the mailman's truck. When we were loading the car to go to the pool, he would announce, "I want to get the towels!" Back they went to the shelf so he could retrieve them.

It seemed very important to him, this control over the details of his participation in life. I humored him when I could, which was not always. I drew the line at lunch. We usually made it through the spreading of the peanut butter and jelly onto the bread. But the cutting stage undermined it every time. "How do you want your sandwich cut?" I'd ask. "In halves," he'd say. "Are you sure?" Sometimes I'd give him a second chance to ward off a change of heart and then wonder if I was tossing him an opportunity. So I'd cut the sandwich in halves, straight down the middle, which was what he meant by halves. "No. Actually I want it in triangles." I'd save my stamina to ride out his inevitable reaction for something I considered worth salvaging (in this case food not to be wasted, not just a retracing of steps). And then, for the fifth or sixth time that day, we would engage in our gridlock — my trying to deal with my three-year-old, and his being just plain stubborn.

I'd try to back off and have the patience to listen to Tad, to figure out why he was acting this way in this maddening stage. I'd try to go the extra mile for him, going through my repertoire of humor and bribes before resorting to cashing in some of my quota of arbitrary commands: "Because I'm your mother and I said so!" These are moments when any adult would be pushed to the brink. I sensed that this kind of situation is what I was there for. Tad seemed somehow possessed by the notion of having control, changing his mind, or not knowing his mind, then suddenly remembering he could exercise it. We were both kind of confused. It seemed to take his seeing me do something to trigger his desires. "Actually," he'd say, "actually, I want to get my jammies." As a linguist, I'd pick up on the "actuallies" of his vocabulary. That was my hint. He knew what the word meant; he used it appropriately, at a time like this in mid mind-change. He seemed to love the word and to go out of his way to orchestrate situations where he could use it.

Finding the balance between how much to urge Tad out of

the nest and how much to let him stay and roost has been constantly on my mind in the four years I've been home with him. My formulas haven't always been right for him. Sometimes that's been quickly apparent and other times it hasn't. Tad often keeps his own counsel, and it's difficult to tell just what's inside his very opinionated mind. For example, he warms up slowly to new places and people. At two and a half, he refused to join a car pool — absolutely, flat-out, scream-and-holler refused to get into any car besides his own. At three and a half, he would do it, but only with the mother of his best friend, a woman he liked because, I think, of her easy manner. At four, he would occasionally go with other friends' parents, but only if he knew them very well. (At this same age, Tommy would, I am convinced, have willingly submitted to adoption by any of a dozen families in the neighborhood.)

The same was true of birthday parties. The two-year-olds' parties were a breeze because most parents stayed on anyway. Three years old was some kind of dividing line. Tad always wanted to be sure his father or I would be there in the background. By four, he was loosening up. It seemed if he were in a particularly good mood, and feeling very brave, he'd stay by himself. And if he weren't, he'd be overwhelmed by lots of faces he didn't recognize, the confusion of the party, and an unfamiliar turf.

I know he's been slower to manage these two things, car pools and birthday parties, than most children. At first — as the mother of a first child who would from the start eagerly go anywhere, with anyone, at any time — I was puzzled and tried to force the issue, either by being cavalier or stern. But it felt all wrong; Tad balked even more and it was clearly very important to him for some reason. So I gave in. Birthday parties, after all, were for his pleasure, and car pools were for my convenience. This has meant, over the two years, that I simply slow down, plan for all the extra time he might need. It's meant a loss of free time that I would have liked to have had, thirty minutes here, a few hours there. There have been other similar slowdowns, like the warming up it takes him before he'll go alone to play at a friend's house. But this is an example of what I've been ready and able to do for him by committing so much of my time to him in these few years.

For Tad, it seems to have mattered a lot, to his happiness, to his maturing and development, that I've been able to let him call these shots. He's progressed, surely, in the last two years. I can see that he'd probably still prefer to be with me or his father (it's simply his nature), but I can also see how proud of himself he is for being so grown up when he hangs up his backpack, puts up his lunchbox, and waves good-by at his prekindergarten classroom door each morning.

Although I've learned a lot in the last seven years about being a mother, I'm acutely aware of how large a role well-intended trial and error still plays in our life as a family. I offer as an embarrassing example a recent instance in our house.

Our boys, like many boys, have for years turned nearly every toy they own into some form of a gun. Legos are built in the shapes of guns, as are Tinkertoys, snap blocks, and sticks. Wood blocks are regularly used for guns, marking pens are used for guns, and of course, fingers and hands are used for guns. I have even seen bananas turned into "submachine, quick-fire, long-range shooters." Tad, for a very long time, desperately wanted a bona fide toy gun. Tommy did, too, at age four, and somehow we high-mindedly (or stiff-neckedly) refused to break down and buy him one. Like many parents, we didn't like guns and didn't like the idea of our children playing with them.

Two months ago, however, when Tad was four years and five months old, we gave in. I bought him what he most desired, a cap gun that cost $3.98 at the dime store. It was a regular six-shooter, with a white plastic handle and a little holster. Not having been born yesterday, I also bought a second gun for Tommy.

There was no compelling reason for acquiring this gun. It did not come on any special occasion. It was not Tad's birthday, and he was not due a reward or even a bribe. It simply seemed, for reasons I have a hard time expressing, that he needed to get his way about this. Tad had been troubled lately. Something seemed to be on his mind and instead of telling us about it, he was managing to cross everyone. He annoyed his brother, was sassy and surly to his father and me, used bad words, and earned a few time-outs at school. He had seemed mad and unhappy for several days.

Tad mentioned a toy gun many times during this period — much more than usual. So I decided, with no good defense against our no-guns principle and mostly on instinct, that he should have a toy gun. I was pretty embarrassed about doing this. I drove to a dime store off our beaten path, where I hoped we wouldn't run into anyone we knew. I apologized for the guns to my friends who brought their boys to play. I attempted to control the use of the guns by imposing certain rules, such as no pointing at other people at point-blank range. My husband was at this time heading off to Houston for three days, and he brought back two more six-shooters, so the boys would have a large enough arsenal when their friends came over. Then we hunkered down to see what would happen.

The first thing that changed was Tad's mood. He seemed to shed his doldrums and become himself again. I know enough about how little I know about children not to insist that there was a cause-effect relationship. Maybe other things were going on in Tad's psyche then too. I do know, though, that he happened to brighten just as the guns appeared.

Second, the boys played with the guns nonstop for about ten days. Tad wanted to go to bed wearing his but was finally convinced to sling the holster over the headboard instead. They didn't play any differently with these toy guns from the way they had with any of their ersatz guns. Their games were about as mean and violent as they had been before, no more or less. But after a while, I did begin to notice a change. While the pretend guns had been an absolute fixation for months and months, the real guns seemed to grow gradually less interesting, like any other toy. The boys, who at first never let the guns out of their sight, began to misplace them. They left them outside and — most remarkable and telling of all — they freely traded them back and forth, between each other and with friends. I realized a few weeks ago that I hadn't seen the guns in weeks. I even dared to ask the boys about them, and they replied that the guns must be "around somewhere." And, most interesting, the level of gunplay at our house — cowboys, cops and robbers, etc. — has fallen off abruptly. In fact, I haven't seen a Lego or Tinkertoy gun since I bought the real toy guns.

Why am I telling this story? Not to recommend this specific strategy for dealing with kids and guns, and certainly not to tout guns as the ideal child's toy. All I mean to illustrate is how hard parents try to do right by their children, how often we have to operate by guesswork and in the dark, and how much of an advantage it can be when negotiating this perilous terrain to have spent "quantity" time with our children, observing and attempting to understand their changing moods.

All I really know about, of course, is my own family. But I don't think our pleasures and problems with our children, our hopes and dreams for them, are that different from other parents'. We want to give them the best we can in their childhood years — a good start, a solid footing. My sense is that there's something special that only parents can give their children, a nuance that they're someone most special, the best in the world, top dog. Parents have no scale of measurement; the rules of the world don't have to count. There are no grades, no ribbons, no order by height, beauty, or even alphabet. There are no winners or losers. Home is a very special place for children; parents are very special people. I'm looking for as many chances as I can find, during these few years that my children are young, to offer them this sense.

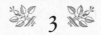

3

Dads

SO FAR I have been speaking about what family life has demanded from me and what it has meant to my children. But what about the third party to these transactions, their father?

At first glance, our family looks very traditional. My husband is the breadwinner; I do not hold a job; we have two children. But like most families, we have our own secrets and circumstances that make our life much less obvious and predictable than it may seem and, in this case, that allow my husband to take on a heavier share of the child raising than most fathers do. It didn't start out that way but, fortunately for all of us, that is how it has evolved.

Because Jim, my husband, had signed on with the Carter presidential campaign just when I found out I was pregnant, I spent most of my pregnancy on my own. My graduate school friends came over for dinner and helped make maternity clothes for me. I kept track of Jim's whereabouts through the evening news reports and hurried telephone calls from the campaign stops. Jim was around for maybe two of our eight Lamaze classes; I persuaded friends to accompany me to the others or else I went alone. Through that fall of 1976, I finished the course work for my degree. In November, after Carter was elected, we prepared to go with him to Washington. But Jim had to be there early, in January, so I packed up the house in Texas, oversaw the moving, and tried to get settled after I arrived in our new house in Washington in March, three weeks before our baby was due.

Life at the White House was hardly less hectic for Jim than the campaign had been. Jim was the chief speech writer during his two years there. Like other White House jobs, this one required him to be at the office almost all the time. He was away many evenings and weekends. He had to travel; there were last-minute emergencies. His job also had its benefits. Every few weeks, we could get seats in the president's box (minus the president, of course) at the Kennedy Center for the Performing Arts; Jim loved to play tennis on the White House court, sometimes with me; our family and relatives were photographed with the president; and on one incongruous occasion Jim and I ate popcorn as we watched a Burt Reynolds movie with the Carters and a dozen other aides.

But the performing arts (including Burt Reynolds) could not blind us to the price we were paying in our personal lives. There had been no delusions from the very start. My labor began the evening before Tommy was born, which also happened to be the day before Jimmy Carter gave his first major speech, at the UN. Because I didn't want to be alone, I spent those hours trailing Jim around the White House from one office to another while he negotiated among the factions that were squabbling over the speech. When I flew with Tommy, then nine months old, to California for his first Christmas, Jim didn't come with us — even though we were going to visit his own parents in the house where he grew up. He was, instead, traveling with Carter to Poland and India. When Tommy turned one, in the spring of 1978, we held the birthday party at Jim's office at the White House because Jim couldn't get away. And he was regularly absent for the smaller occasions: feedings, baths, walks, playtimes.

Jim did what he could, pitching in when he was home. But the simple fact was that he wasn't able to be home very much. The tone was set by the workaholics in the White House (some of them fathers, too), who made it seem wimpish to leave work before the dead of night. I knew that Jim would often steal away from his office earlier than most others, at seven-thirty or eight instead of nine-thirty or ten, so he could see Tommy for a little while before his bedtime. We would all go in together on the weekends while Jim worked. Tommy would crawl around on the floor of Jim's office, climb on the furniture, and then nap on the sofa — not so much to play as just to be in the presence of his dad.

Jim left the Carter administration after two years, as he had originally planned to do. His reasons were largely professional, but I know that he was also greatly concerned about the strain on our family life. In the six years since then, he has worked out of an office in our house. This adds somewhat to the already high level of household chaos. He gets several dozen telephone calls each day, often at dinnertime, collects mounds of junk mail, and meets visitors. But it also means that he is home, near the family, most of the time. Jim can usually arrange his working hours with some flexibility. That means he can see the boys in the morning when they get up; he sometimes drives them to school; when they are home for lunch, he can eat with them. He regularly sees them when they get home from school. (Tommy seems particularly aware of this; as soon as he arrives home from school he checks to see if Jim's car is here and, if it isn't, asks indignantly, "Where's Dad? What's he doing there? When's he coming home?") We almost always have the evenings together, for dinner and the bedtime routine of bath, books, and bed.

All this has come, I can see, at a considerable cost to Jim's working life. I have heard him turn down breakfast, dinner, and evening meetings to be with the boys; I know he'll often rearrange appointments to take the boys to school. Every night, he works until 1 or 2 A.M., or later, to make up for the daytime interludes he's spent with the boys. Many of his friends and colleagues are single or childless. As he sees them sit down for an afternoon of uninterrupted work on a Saturday or Sunday, I can tell he's thinking how much more quickly he could finish an article or book if he were similarly unencumbered. In short, he's made a trade: ambitious as he is, he has accepted less success — and money — than he might otherwise have. In exchange he has gotten to know his sons.

He knows everything about them — how to deal with Tad if he balks at the entrance to his nursery school; that Tommy is absolutely starving when he gets out of school and needs food before conversation; that Tad needs help with the socks with the stripes, which are tight; that Tommy's hair needs to be combed after he washes it but Tad's will fall into place on its own. The boys are as likely to call for Jim as for me when they fall and scrape their knees. Each night they get to choose who will read them bedtime stories and who will wash the dinner dishes and they pretty well alternate the duties, night for night, between their father and me. To them, it's no special occasion to have either of us around; we both are part of normal life.

This has meant a great deal to me as well. It has meant that Jim knows what I have done as a mother all day long. He has seen me cry on a perfectly normal morning and recognizes it comes from the fatigue, exasperation, and general state that's part of caring for a three-year-old preschooler and a three-month-old infant. He has seen the efforts I've put in at this job of mothering, from the physical demands of lugging babies, groceries, strollers, to the emotional demands of keeping company with small children for ten hours at a time. He has seen me worry about how, amid all this, I am to find time to be a person, myself, too. He has responded in ways that he could. When the boys were little, it meant he could cock an ear to their bedroom doors while they were napping and I could run off to do a necessary errand. It meant he understood that I needed some time by myself and would offer, before I had to ask for it, a regular respite on Saturday morning or an impromptu evening during the week. It meant he encouraged me to get help with cleaning or a few hours of babysitting, even though they took what seemed like a disproportionate chunk of our budget. Most of all, he displays respect for the work that I am doing in raising the boys. He considers it, in the larger scheme of things, to be more important than his own work, or any other work. And when the tests have come, I have seen him put his work second to our sons many times over.

I don't mean to preach on about my own family's situation. I realize that one of the crucial variables in our arrangement —

that my husband works at home — is quite rare. But another, equally important factor doesn't have to be rare: it is the recognition that being a parent is a serious job and that it's a job for *both* parents. This message seems not to have entered many fathers' minds.

Most men aren't yet even trying to deal with the problems of family and work the way most women are. Men aren't searching hard for the right balance. They don't agonize; they don't feel guilty. It's not a topic of men's conversation, as it is for women, when they gather. Men aren't sticking out their necks as much in the attempt to balance work and family, aren't sacrificing their work and life-style to the degree women are. Although they may say they do, men don't really understand.

Sure, it's unfair to generalize. Some men are trying, but not enough. We all know the exceptions: fathers who scrimp and save spare minutes for their children; fathers who truly share the child care; even fathers who stay home. To those, bravo! And we all recognize that change is under way. My father used to claim, with apparent pride, that he had never changed a diaper — and he was hardly unusual among men of that generation. Today, men are just as likely to claim that they are expert at it. Indeed, a wave of sensitive-father chic seemed to break in the early 1980s, but much of it seemed to be exactly that, a *stylish* attitude, implying little long-term commitment. Bob Greene's best-selling book, *Good Morning, Merry Sunshine*, is a good example of this attitude.

The book, Greene's daily journal of the first year of his daughter's life, has been much touted as the last word in paternal sensitivity. "Dear Abby" called it "what fatherhood is all about"; Erma Bombeck, "giving new insight to mothers who thought men never understood"; Phil Donahue, the "most honest and personal account of the first year of fatherhood." At first glance, all the obvious ingredients seem to be there: Greene is the Lamaze coach in the delivery room; he makes visits to the pediatrician's office; he cuts those business trips short. He walks the floor at midnight with his colicky infant; he magnanimously tolerates the disheveled appearance of his child-disrupted apartment. He talks about Snuglis and describes adjusting the baby mattress down in the crib. Greene thinks he is doing a good job as the modern father.

But Greene makes it clear he'll go only so far. He never quite gets caught between the rock and the hard place of children and work. Since his wife, Susan, has left her job (although we never learned what it was) to stay home with their daughter, Amanda Sue, Bob takes free license to resume his business as usual. He goes back to his office at the *Chicago Tribune* to check things out even while he's home on leave for a few weeks after Amanda's birth. He passes up exactly one tempting assignment, from ABC's "Nightline" (for which he does occasional evening reports) to do a story about drug trafficking, but is soon winging his way regularly to distant cities to chase other stories for them. He goes to Cleveland for two days during his first vacation with Susan and Amanda (when, incidentally, Amanda first utters "Da-Da"). He still stops off at his favorite bar during arsenic hour (twice as serious an offense as during any other hour of the day). On the eve of his daughter's first birthday, he records the episode: "The bartender — even though we hadn't seen each other much lately — quickly fell into easy conversation with me. After a while he said, 'So what are you going to do this weekend?' 'I'll be at home,' I said. 'Tomorrow is my daughter's first birthday.'"

Big of him.

Bob Greene takes us inside his apartment and shows us glimpses of what's really going on. That gives it all away to most mothers and to the outraged young fathers like David Owen, who reviewed Greene's book for *The New Republic*. Writes Owen:

> Even when Bob is physically present, he isn't altogether there. One-and-a-half months pass before he notices the small wound on Amanda's head made by the fetal monitor used at her birth. Another month goes by before he realizes that he and Susan eat different things for dinner: while she serves him grown-up food (which he eats alone in a different room), she herself eats "mushed-up fish" so that she'll have a free hand to tend the baby. . . .
> When Amanda's old enough to be mobile, one of her

favorite games is Finding Daddy. When he isn't on the road, Bob always seems to be in another room, reading magazines, watching television, listening to records, or eating something that Susan has made for him. On one of the rare occasions when he and Amanda are alone together, he gets bored after fifteen minutes, parks her in her carriage in the hallway, and goes off to make some phone calls.

Greene, and other fathers like him, may think they've made great strides as parents. But most mothers, and other fathers like David Owen, know better. Thinking about fatherhood and talking about fatherhood are only the first steps for men to take. Doing it — being there, caring for the children, making compromises for them — are the final ones.

So far I have been discussing life at home with children: what it asks of a parent and what it means to a child. Most of the illustrations I have used have been drawn from my own life with my children, since these are the episodes I can discuss most knowledgeably and honestly, but I have tried to test my own convictions against the experiences of the many different families I have had a chance to observe during my career as a parent. Although the details of my family's history may not precisely resemble those of any other family — we live in a certain part of the country, under a certain set of economic circumstances, with certain occupational advantages and constraints — I do not think that the essentials of our story are so very unusual. Like other parents, we have had to choose, learn, compromise, err, and grow.

If there is a single difference between us and most other families, it is that we almost slipped into parenthood, rather than making deliberate, rational choices about how we would balance and manage our new responsibilities. When our first son arrived, we were able to continue many of our routines for a while. I was able to finish my studies, and we could cope with my husband's more than full-time duties at the White House by classifying them as a temporary aberration. It was not until we were well into family life, with a three-year-old son and another on the way, that we realized that we had to make a change. Only then did I decide to leave my work and stay home, and we went from being a two-working-parent family to a family with one parent who works primarily, though not exclusively, at earning the keep while the other works primarily, though not exclusively, at raising the children. This transition sounds far simpler today than I remember it being almost five years ago. Then it was a process of doubt, guesswork, and anticipation, not the careful, almost contractual arrangements some parents now seem to make before their children have been conceived. But even this difference between our family and many others may turn out to be less consequential than it seems. Children do have their way of disrupting anyone's plans.

My point is that after all the variations among different families' experiences have been allowed for, certain constants remain, which distinguish the daily lives of children who have a parent home with them at least part of the time. The simplest way to sum up this distinctive quality is the sense that children are special and important — important enough to require some adjustments in their parents' desires and schedules, important enough to be indulged at some times and disciplined at others. Neither the indulgence nor the discipline can be simple or automatic, but, as I have tried to convey, each is easier when parents have a clear sense of how the child's life is going, how he or she feels and reacts and thinks in various circumstances at various times of the day.

4

Child Care: An Overview

I NOW WANT to look at children in a different setting: those who spend large parts of their day away from both parents, whether in day care institutions or in the care of babysitters or nannies. Later I will examine some of the economic and political ramifications of day care, but I want to begin, after a brief overview of the field of child care, on a more personal level, trying to describe what the child care experience is like for children whose parents do not or cannot stay home with them.

I think most parents wonder what their children do when they're out of their sight. We look at the art they bring home from nursery school; we learn their schedules. We quiz our kids about events in school: did you have P.E. today? did you go to the library? what did you do in science class? We see report cards and talk with teachers about progress and adjustments. We catch glimpses of their private lives. We get facts and statements. But we don't get the details and nuance and tone. During the hours we spend with our children, we can interpret each event in the light of thousands of similar episodes we have seen before. About their behavior, progress, victories, and defeats when they are in others' care, we know only the headline version. We can say, "Emily seems to be doing just fine," or "I think Benjamin may be having a bit of a hard time now." But we see only reflections, only shadows on the wall, without knowing for sure what cast them.

We expect all of this, of course, when children are growing up, going to school, becoming independent. It is part of the process, simultaneously gratifying and heartbreaking, that we know is necessary if our children are to begin to handle life on their own. But for parents who work full-time while their children are still too young for school, uncertainty about what their children actually *do* all day has a special gravity. From infancy, a child can easily spend ten hours a day, five days a week, in someone else's care. It quickly adds up to a childhood.

Over the last three years, I have visited a large number and variety of day care centers in an attempt to see what this kind of childhood is like. I would go during the two or three hours on weekday mornings when my older son was in kindergarten (and then first and then second grade) and my younger son was in morning nursery school. The observations I report and the judgments I make are based on what I saw there. I came to believe that not only was there a large and important difference between the best out-of-home care and the worst, but also that life was inescapably different for children who were with their parents than for those who were not.

Child care arrangements* usually fall into one of three categories: family homes, where one person cares for a small number of children in a home; individually hired babysitters or nannies for a child or family; and group centers, where large numbers of children are brought each day. According to a study made by the U.S. Department of Commerce in 1982, children under the age of five with working mothers were cared for in the following ways: 40 per cent in family homes, about half of which were operated by nonrelatives ("the woman down the street") and the other half by aunts, grandmothers, cousins, etc.; 23 per cent by the parents themselves, through split shifts or other arrangements; 15 per cent in group care of all kinds, including nursery schools, preschools, and day care centers. If the

---

*In general keeping with the terminology of the profession, I will use "child care" as an umbrella term to refer to care of children by people other than parents and "day care" to refer to group care of children in centers.

nursery schools and preschools were excluded, this category accounts for only 9.2 per cent of the total; 11 per cent by other relatives, working in the child's home; and 6 per cent by babysitters, housekeepers, or nannies. (The remaining 5 per cent were listed as "don't know" or "no answer," and presumably included the children who were left to care for themselves.)

Family Homes

Family homes constitute the largest single category of child care institutions. In America today, there are well over 1.5 million family day care homes, caring for more than 6 million children up to the age of thirteen. The children in these homes represent between 40 and 50 per cent of all children in child care, and more than half of them are in full-time care. Family home centers are everywhere — in basements, in back rooms, occupying the normal living quarters of families, spilling out into back yards. Despite their number, they are not always easy to locate. There is no formal guide to or central registry of most family homes in a given town. Some are registered with state agencies, but in 1975, the National Day Care Home Study estimated that only 6 per cent of the homes were regulated this way, and the other 94 per cent went unregistered and unlicensed. Mothers and fathers usually hear of them by word of mouth.

The very term "family home" can bring happy pictures to mind. The surroundings will be pleasant and informal. There will be a gentle, caring person, more likely than not a relative of at least some of the children, who takes in a handful of small children. Often, the extra income enables the parent to stay home and raise his or her own child. The children may range from infancy to school age, just like a real family, or they may be a group of toddlers. The parent-caretaker relations are usually quite personal, and the child care arrangements may be quite flexible, with loose hours, verbal contracts, and traded favors. The program will be less structured than a group center's; generally, home care is less like school and more like a day at home with Mom or Dad. Many parents favor this atmosphere for their infants and toddlers, and then move the children on to day care centers for the preschool years (ages three to four).

Both my sons spent time in a family home in our neighborhood. A sizable number of their schoolmates, soccer buddies, friends, and neighbors who now range in age from high school sophomores to barely toddlers were cared for at some point in the same family home. None of us referred to this arrangement as a "family home," however. We all referred to the woman who ran the home as our children's babysitter. She is a cherished institution in our part of town, who helps out mothers and fathers in emergencies and holds places open years ahead for planned babies. Parents know what she considers luxuries and shop for special presents for her at holidays. Even after my sons had outgrown the activities there, I still took them to visit her regularly.

I recognize that we were lucky. We found an excellent family home, and we were able to pay the rates, which started out at $1.50 per hour with our first son and went as high as $3.50 per hour five years later with our second. Rates for family homes are reportedly lower than rates for group centers, but these figures can be deceiving. Rates are often very inexpensive if relatives are caring for the children, but they are often quite a bit more expensive if private, nonfamily arrangements are made. In the Washington, D.C., area, group care for, say, a two-year-old may run from $65 to $125 a week. For a family home situation, it can be $110.

Not all families have such good fortune; not all can afford to pay top rates, nor can they necessarily find the kind of warm, caring person we found. Nor, in fact, do top rates guarantee good care.

One father wrote in a glossy Washington, D.C., magazine about the experiences of one family that, you can bet, was paying the going rate in the area for family home care:

> Take, for example, one woman I talked with recently — a child-care specialist at a leading local university. *She* should have had it together, right?
> Both she and her husband worked full-time, so they enrolled their baby daughter in an infant day-care center —

one of the few in the area. Unfortunately, at the age of eight months, the baby came down with an illness that required her to be withdrawn from the center. For three weeks, the family scrambled. The father stayed home one week. The mother stayed home one week. Their other daughter — age twelve — stayed home one week. Finally, after a frantic search, the mother found a Spanish-speaking woman willing to care for the infant at her apartment in Adams Morgan.

There was one hitch. Because the building management did not allow tenants to operate businesses in their apartments, the baby could not be brought through the lobby each morning. Instead, the woman said, the parents would have to drive up to a window of the woman's ground-floor apartment and hand the baby over.

Of course, the child-care specialist reacted to such a bizarre arrangement just as I or any other local parent would — she agreed. We're desperate, you see.

This story, incidentally, had an unhappy ending. The couple subsequently found out that the woman was not only taking in other children — there must have been a line of cars waiting to reach the window — but she was leaving the brood in the care of her twelve-year-old daughter while she went out to clean homes. The arrangement ended when one of the infants swallowed 30 aspirin tablets and ended up in a hospital.

I have myself seen family home centers where children wander aimlessly around with no attention from the caretaker, who was busy attending to her housekeeping chores; where all the little ones were confined in cribs or playpens, forbidden to roam or play; where there were no toys to play with; and where the only source of distraction was the game show or soap opera on the eternally babbling television. The children didn't go outside because there was no fenced area safe for them. In the very worst places, as several widely publicized cases in 1983 and 1984 made tragically clear, children suffer actual physical and sexual abuse.

Some form of state and/or federal regulation of family homes would seem to be the obvious way to insure at least minimum standards of quality. But, as with so many other aspects of social policy, from setting standards for schools to dispensing welfare payments, regulating these small family home centers has proved to be very difficult. In this politically and emotionally charged area, finding the balance between effective controls that disqualify unfit caretakers and overenforcement of petty rules that run decent ones out of business seems to be nearly impossible. Some child care advocates maintain that bringing lawsuits against family home care providers on the grounds that they are illegally using homes as places of business is really a "series of moves across the country to undermine family day care." They cite examples such as the story carried by the *Wall Street Journal* in 1982 about a family home center in Maryland:

> For about 17 years, Susan Suddath kept other parents' children in her home here. With help from her dairy-farmer husband, her teen-age daughters, her mother-in-law and her neighbors, she sometimes provided day care for as many as 20 children.
>
> Mornings, she provided a structured program for pre-schoolers. In the afternoon, she gave older children the chance to play and do their homework. Her charges could entertain themselves in her basement playroom or her spacious back yard — sometimes they took field trips to the barn to visit the cows.
>
> The children loved Mrs. Suddath. Their parents loved Mrs. Suddath. The state of Maryland didn't. It told her she would have to reduce the number of children, or close down. Deciding whom to keep, she recalls, "was the worst experience I ever had in my life." Her children didn't understand what was happening and didn't want to leave. . . .
>
> Like most states, Maryland limits the number of children who can be cared for in a single home. Its law says a private home can't take in more than four children during the school day, six after school. Above that, the home must meet standards set for larger institutions. . . .
>
> Mrs. Suddath . . . tried to get a license to care for more children, but was told the ceiling in her basement was too low in one place. Almost 6 feet tall herself, Mrs. Suddath

assured the inspector she would be the tallest person in the room. But he couldn't bend the law.

Where, then, is the line of common sense that could tell us where to regulate the gargantuan cottage industry of family home care and where to leave it alone? Do we give the unwieldy and costly task of regulating more than 1.5 million homes to the federal government? Do we let the states impose wildly varying restrictions? Should we fear that imposing more regulations will only cause even more family homes to go underground? Is it naive to assume that family home caretakers and parents will monitor themselves?

Two courses of action seem reasonable. The first is already in effect: regulating the modest number of family homes that receive federal funds. (The federal subsidies come from two sources: Title XX of the Social Security Act and the Child Care Food Program of the U.S. Department of Agriculture.) This regulation at least builds in some protection for some families. Without the subsidies, poor families can afford only the cheapest, and thus usually the worst, family homes (except for special arrangements with neighbors or relatives). Having so little choice about where to send their children, they are hardly in a position to lobby the care givers for better standards or to go comparison shopping for better homes. When the federal government requires homes to meet certain standards in order to qualify for federal funds, they put a floor under the conditions children can expect. It works for the benefit of all: the subsidies enable poor children to move over to better-quality family homes, and they enable family homes to raise standards by, for example, having to pack in fewer children to cover their costs.

Obviously, the system is not foolproof. But it puts money where it is needed, by moving children of low-income families to good facilities or improving child care operations that need improving. It is also a way of increasing the number of good-quality family homes, by offering reasonable remuneration to caretakers. Well-intentioned would-be caretakers — for example, young parents who would like to stay home with their children but can't afford it — may find they can afford now to open family homes themselves.

The greatest drawback is that the amount of funds available to family homes is extremely limited. Realistically, only a minute proportion of children in family homes will ever see any of it. To affect more children, the burden of regulation must be shifted from the strings-attached government agencies closer to home.

The second possible course of action, then, is to supplant the federal or state systems of regulating home day care with much more vigorous parent and caretaker self-monitoring. One of the inherently strong qualities of family home arrangements is the personal agreement and trust between caretakers and parents that stand as the foundation of this idea. There seems little reason for the government to interfere with the happy and sound situations like the one established between Mrs. Suddath and her children's parents. They have struck a fair balance for payment and remuneration; they have agreed that things like the height of the ceiling don't matter.

Educating parents and caretakers about the important quality factors in child care is an idea supported by Anne Bersinger, deputy director of the California Department of Social Services, who would like to see day care operators set up their own certification program in lieu of a state-run system. She suggests, among other things, that "money the state now spends on licensing [should] be spent . . . on educating parents and encouraging them to report abuses to law-enforcement authorities."

Educating parents and care givers, placing the responsibility of monitoring on their own shoulders, should, in the long run, have the beneficial effect of getting parents more involved with their children's care. Research has shown that children benefit tremendously from the link parents establish between the place of care and the home — a link that is forged by parent involvement at the place of care.

Babysitters

The Rolls-Royce of child care is the nanny, also called the housekeeper, the live-in, the babysitter, the au pair. The semantics of these different names can be confusing. There are regional variations, and there are vague boundaries of geography, income, self-image, and snobbery that separate one term from another. And like child care itself, the uses and meanings of these words are in flux. From my perspective in Washington, D.C., this is how I would describe them:

The nanny is the *crème de la crème*, top of the line in full-time child care. She was borrowed, of course, from Britain and the Continent. It's a little bit snooty to use the term "nanny" (unless you're foreign); it hints of a high price tag and conveys the idea that she may well wear a uniform. Nannies are becoming in vogue among the highly paid professionals in many big American cities. Institutes to train nannies have sprung up, and their graduates, educated and experienced, credentialed and capped, are going like hotcakes.

Then comes the au pair. To capture the appropriate nuance, "au pair" should really be spelled "oh pear"; she is the nanny's grubby little sister. She's probably from Europe (although there are networks of au pairs from the West, particularly Montana and Utah, who are making their way to East Coast cities; there they are prized for their wholesomeness). The European au pair may be interested in practicing her English; she may be the niece of a neighbor's acquaintance in Germany who is looking for a year off; she may be a village girl who'll do anything for a change. You take your chances with au pairs. They usually arrive sight unseen, preceded perhaps only by a few letters or a phone call. I know some who've been terrific (one even coached the children's soccer team to a winning season), and others who have disappeared suddenly to the Caribbean with new boyfriends. Au pairs often receive room and board and a small salary and are expected to do light housework (ironing and straightening up the children's rooms) in addition to child care.

A less exotic subcategory of au pair is the college student who lives with a family and swaps room and board for some babysitting duties, perhaps fifteen hours a week. These quasi–au pairs have more independent lives and fewer responsibilities. We have been lucky enough to have a young man live with our family off and on during the last few years under such an arrangement.

"Housekeeper" and "live-in" are terms often used interchangeably to describe the domestic jack-(rather, jill)-of-all-trades. The housekeeper's responsibilities include the housework, heavy and light, and the children. Duties vary greatly here. Some serve simply to be there when schoolchildren arrive home or to keep an ear out for a napping baby while parents are out. Others are bona fide full-time babysitters for infants, toddlers, and preschool-age children. They often do car pooling, shopping, and cooking. Live-ins have their own quarters with the family; housekeepers may live in or live out, arriving for regular full days of work. On the East and West coasts and in the Southwest, most are foreign. In the Midwest, many are black. In Washington, D.C., most are from Latin America. In Texas, most are from Mexico. Many of these women speak little or no English.

At the bottom of the list comes The Babysitter, an umbrella term that usually requires a follow-up description. The Babysitter is not to be confused with "babysitters," teen-agers who take care of the kids on Saturday night while the parents go to a movie. The Babysitter is hired for a formal position with regular, often full-time hours. She is often an older woman, one who has raised her own family, who likes children, who wants to remain active, and who could use the money. She may be a young mother herself. (In these cases, the child usually goes to her house rather than having The Babysitter come to the child's house. This does not bump her into the category of family home, however, unless she tends several children at once.) The Babysitter cleans up after herself and her charge, but unlike the housekeeper, she isn't responsible for general care of the house or management of the household.

All of these caretakers are women. There may be an occasional man in the Babysitter category, although he usually will operate out of his own home rather than the child's home, and most likely runs a family home operation. Male college students frequently appear in the quasi–au pair category. They work particularly well in all-boy-children homes.

Obviously, it's impossible to make systematic investigations of these individual caretakers, as you can for day care centers or even, to some lesser extent, family homes. The personal performance of these individuals tells the whole story here. I've seen a few outstanding ones among the ranks — those who have a special rapport with the children, a pride and dedication about their work, a real enthusiasm. I've seen many who are just putting in time on a job, trying to get from one end of the day to the other. They pay about as much attention to the children as they would to a dog or cat they were hired to watch.

Unfortunately, finding the right person is not the only difficult part of managing these private arrangements. The real challenge is keeping her. Apart from the minute proportion of professional nannies, all these jobs are temporary. None has upward mobility. The wages are modest. A family is very lucky if it keeps an excellent nanny, housekeeper, or au pair for a few years. That is not the norm. It is not unusual to have to make new arrangements every year, often under precipitous, unforeseen circumstances. I have seen my friends and neighbors run through three or four unsuccessful trials in half a year. Number one isn't reliable; she's late picking up children at school and forgets to give the antibiotic to the six-year-old. Number two is great with the baby but can't handle the three-year-old. Number three is called home to Latin America suddenly to tend a sick mother. Number four looks good so far. When all the pieces of the private arrangements fit, they can offer great convenience for the parents and suit the individual needs of the children. Life is smoother all around. When they don't, the trauma and compromises can be costly for parents and children alike.

Group Centers

If judged by numbers alone, day care centers might not seem so significant. Only about 15 per cent of the children who are cared for by people other than their parents are in centers. The figure drops to about 9 per cent when children in part-time nursery schools and preschools are excluded. By comparison, there are four times as many children in family homes.

But day care has an importance far beyond its current size. Most people who are interested in the politics of child care are principally interested in day care centers. Modern, businesslike, efficient, organized, day care is taken by both its enemies and its friends as the wave of the future. The 9 per cent of American children now in these centers dominate discussions about nearly every aspect of child care — political, educational, medical, economic, social, and emotional.

Such research as has been done on how child care affects children's development, achievement, and adjustment has nearly all been conducted in day care centers. The nation's political and economic machinery has been revved up to examine day care and consider adding to the supply. The proprietary (for-profit) centers and the child care professionals who work in day care centers have organized to lobby on behalf of group centers. Corporations, hospitals, government agencies, universities, and other groups either already provide or are being asked to provide day care centers for their employees' children. Dollar for dollar and head for head, large centers are the most efficient way of caring for children. They are the place where innovations, regulations, and developments can be most easily applied. In short, group centers constitute the leading edge of our explorations into child care. What are they like?

About half the day care centers are run for profit. Among the for-profit centers, which have been growing at a rate of 25–30 per cent annually for the last five years, only about 15 per cent are part of national chains. The vast majority are small Mom and Pop businesses. Many are located in churches, although most of those simply rent or use space from the churches rather than maintaining a more formal affiliation with them.

Day care centers usually charge more than family homes and so, contrary to popular impression, they attract a more comfortable clientele. According to the Bureau of the Census, mothers who place their children in day care centers are relatively well educated (twice as high a proportion of those who have completed at least one year of college use day care centers as those who have not completed high school); come from families with relatively high incomes (a higher proportion of women who have combined family incomes of over $25,000 per year use day care centers than those in the $15,000–$25,000 per year range, or those under $15,000 per year); are relatively successful in their work (twice as high a proportion of women in professional and managerial positions use day care as do women in blue collar and service positions); and are twice as likely to work full-time as part-time and to live in the cities and the suburbs as in the nonmetropolitan areas).

Day care centers offer several advantages to working parents. Their long operating hours mean they can accommodate most schedules — some that I have seen are even open around the clock. The big national chains, such as Kinder-Care, National Child Care, and Children's World, offer several locations in many major cities, so parents who are new to a city can make their choice easily rather than sorting through the local alternatives. While family homes, with their looser structure and more personal approach, are often more popular for parents of the youngest children, day care centers, with their more businesslike operation and more reliable schedules, are often preferred by parents of three- or four-year-olds.

But what goes on inside these centers? That is the part of the story that rarely gets told. It was in an attempt to see the day care life for myself, as well as examine the political and economic issues that surround it, that I made my own repeated visits to many different types of centers in different parts of the country.

I began looking at day care centers the way thousands of other mothers and fathers must do: I opened up the Yellow Pages to the "Day Nurseries and Child Care" listing. It's an eye-opening introduction. In Austin, Texas, a city of fewer than 400,000 people, the phone book contains six pages of listings, more than two hundred centers. Some of the names try to convey a supposed storybook charm: Angel's Playland, Candy Cane Nursery School, Buddy Bear Child Care, Little Stinkers Day Care. Some are personal extensions of the director: Heard's Smiling Face Nursery, Mrs. Hester's Nursery, Norma's Day

Care. There are chains: National Child Care Centers, Kinder-Care, Orange Goose, each with several centers around town. Others aspire to a classier, even intellectually demanding image: the "learning centers" and "academies" like Creative World Child-Care Learning Center, Beaver Brook ("the Hilton of child care"), the Windsor School ("child care at its finest"), and La Petite Academy.

When faced with such an overwhelming choice, parents searching for child care can shorten the list by resorting to local parents' guidebooks, by asking friends or consulting child care–locating services, and sometimes by using trial and error. I followed all of these steps, plus an attempt at random sampling, in choosing centers to visit.

Over a period of a year and a half, I spent hundreds of hours in dozens of day care centers in Texas, Washington, D.C., Maryland, and Massachusetts. I would usually spend most of a morning at a given center, mostly in the toddlers' and young preschoolers' (18 months to 3 years) rooms. I'd usually ask to see the other rooms, too. I visited kindergartens and some infant rooms, as well. Some centers had a policy against allowing visitors into nurseries unless the parent had a child that age. Sometimes I went as a mother, looking as though I wanted a space for my two-year-old child. Sometimes I said I was writing a book about parents and working and that I'd like to visit the center and talk with the teachers.

The directors I met were consistently helpful and open, showing me the whole center, letting me stay and watch and talk with teachers. Most directors talked with me as well. I learned not to expect that the director would be present, however. At Angel's Playland, she was at the grocery store at 11:30 A.M. and not expected back for forty-five minutes. At Noah's Ark, she was out the door for a doctor's appointment when I arrived at 8:55 A.M. and was not expected to return all morning. At Global Peach, she was on her way from one center to another at 10:45. At National Child Care she was out running errands at noon. At Kinder-Care, she was out for the day, tired after a weekend trip. One by one, these were understandable; as a pattern, they were the first of many divergences between the kind of supervision that was advertised and the kind I saw.

My first impression was that within the world of group centers there is something for almost every palate. There are large centers with more than a hundred children that look like small elementary schools and have separate, fenced-off playgrounds for different age groups and, often, a swimming pool. These centers have large kitchens from which lunch emerges on stainless steel rolling carts and one-way mirrors looking into the classrooms. There are small, homelike centers operating out of refurbished bungalows. Toddlers occupy former bedrooms, preschoolers play in converted dining rooms, infants crawl around in old living rooms. The kitchens are usually intact, and the children can watch and hear and smell their lunches being prepared. Teachers talk from room to room and hop back and forth over expandable gates that keep children contained in their assigned groups. There are church schools housed in traditional Sunday school classrooms with linoleum floors and pastel-painted walls. Some have bins of blocks, stacks of puzzles, well-scrubbed little tables and chairs, plenty of roaming space. Others have a few broken toys, a "learning corner" with some crayons and paper, a television, and rows of cribs. Almost all centers, regardless of size, have the haunting odor of ammonia wafting from the infant rooms, sometimes blanketed temporarily by cloudbursts of air-freshening spray.

There is as much variety outside. One center I visited is located in a small shopping center alongside a post office and drugstore, with easy parking. Another is on a residential side street, next door to private homes with bikes scattered in the front yards and schoolchildren running by after school. Several are connected to churches. Some are in nondescript no man's lands, just off the access lanes of highways or heavily traveled main roads passing the strip cities on the edges of town. All but one of the centers I saw (a downtown on-site center housed in a government building) have playgrounds. The playground equipment, however, varies in quality and amount; sometimes it is abundant and sometimes just adequate. One urban center has a blacktop parking lot for its playground and a ball and jump rope for its playthings. Most benefit from being located on sprawling lots where there is an unstructured, freedom-to-roam feeling. That freedom always contrasts with the rigid organization of the indoors, where rooms are marked off by barriers or by rugs or furniture groupings into formal "areas" —blocks, arts, kitchen, table space.

The philosophies of the centers vary as well. Some advertise slick tot-scale academic programs. "Give your child the Kinder-Care ADVANTAGE" urges the glossy brochure Kinder-Care distributes to parents. It describes its academic program this way: "The Kinder-Care GOAL (Growth Opportunities for Achievement and Learning) Program, designed for each stage of preschool development, helps stimulate and satisfy the child's natural curiosity. This is why Kinder-Care Learning Centers are known as the 'child care centers of school teachers' children.'"

Many parents told me they were attracted to these centers. Several said that they thought their children could get a head start in school from these academic programs and that would be at least something gained in return for the time spent away from home. But hopes like these can be misleading. At a conference for educators of young children, I listened to teachers describe the gap between what many parents were looking for in preschool experiences and what kindergarten teachers looked for when the children got to elementary school. "Kindergarten teachers are more interested in cooperation, attention, and things like that than in academics," one said. "But," said another, "so many parents [of preschool children] are looking at academics: when will Johnny be reading, counting, adding . . ."

I met one father who stays at home with his two-year-old son and runs a family home day care; he told me about the mother who came to visit him looking for a spot for her eleven-month-old infant. Her main concern was whether he'd present flash cards to the baby every day. And there was also the father of a two-year-old who was frustrated because his son wasn't getting enough "number concepts." "It's crazy," says the caretaker, who was trained in early childhood development. "They don't know what kids should be learning at that age. Even now, although

I'm not able to do the kind of teaching I should be, a certain amount of stimulation will result from my philosophy and experience. I talk to the kids. About everything. We go out for walks and talk about the dead animals we see. We go out in the garden and talk about good bugs and bad bugs."

Most centers offer a pabulumlike description of their philosophy: ". . . the best opportunities for normal growth and development, both physically and mentally . . . a loving and warm atmosphere, fostering a secure environment in which to explore." A few don't bother with any philosophy. The day's timetables in these places all tend to look the same: free period at 7:30, circle time at 9:00, activities at 9:30, bathroom and snack at 10:30, outdoor play at 11:00, lunch at 12:00, nap at 1:00, etc. etc. Some follow the schedules exactly; others ad-lib all day.

Care givers and teachers* vary a good deal from place to place. In some centers, I saw adults who looked and sounded like what every parent is looking for — warm, friendly people who hugged kids a lot, who ran organized but easy-flowing classrooms, who had time to explain, who disciplined kids in a way that reflected an underlying plan but still had the flexibility to respond to a situation. These, I knew, were the kinds of people who wrote me letters like the one I received from a woman in Idaho:

> I opened a child care center where I am the Director. I carefully chose my staff, of whom three are mothers, two holding Master's degrees. They are well paid, work only half days, and are well respected by clients. Our ratio is such that our teachers are able to build snowmen with the children at the first snow fall, explain why fights start, help the children with a good academic start and even kiss a hurt finger. . . . I lost $1,200 this past year, my first year of business, providing these children with a rich environment. . . . Many of us out here are working extremely hard

* "Care giver" is usually the preferred term of the child care professionals. I use this term interchangeably with "caretaker" and "child care worker." I sometimes use "teacher" in those cases where the function and style of the person closely resembles the more traditional classroom instructor. "Staff" is a general word to cover the employees of a day care center.

to provide children of working parents with quality care, not custodial care.

Far more often I saw less impressive types. They were not the experts, professionally trained and experienced, the caring individuals. They were the ones who met the minimum standards and not much more. They worked a full day and were paid minimum wage. Instead of offering enthusiasm, embraces, guidance, or example, these care givers would often park on the edge of a table and observe the children wandering about, intervene in fights when it became unavoidable, issue frequent reprimands, and talk among themselves rather than with the children.

During the time that I was visiting centers, scandals and allegations about sexual abuse in day care centers came thundering into the news. Like every other parent, I became instantly more suspicious, critical, and worried about these unspeakable possibilities. For all the other criticisms I have, I never felt in any of the centers I visited the slightest suspicion that anything like this might have been going on. Further, I find it difficult to imagine — with the free access I was given, usually unannounced and unplanned — how it could have taken place, particularly with regularity. I saw one incident of a young teacher manhandling a child, jerking him around by the arm. Another time I heard a story about a previously employed teacher who would lock a naughty child alone in a closet. Far more often, I saw incidents of neglect, where a crying, sobbing, and in one instance bleeding child was left alone uncomforted. Sometimes this was because no caretaker was free to aid the child; sometimes it wasn't.

Life for a child in a day care center, good or bad, is different in certain ways from other kinds of life. There is more rigidity to it. The sheer number of children that day care centers handle necessarily means organization, scheduling, and rules if the day is to have a modicum of order. Twenty or forty or a hundred children following their individual tempos, tastes, and whims simply won't do. The difference between good and bad centers here lies not only in the content and format of the schedule (time for play, time for rest, time for art) but in the way in which it is followed. For example, a good teacher knows how to ease children into activities, allow them time to follow their pace, and make a smooth and natural transition to the next activity or event. A bad teacher ignores these subtleties and mechanically follows rules for fear of not completing a project or not finishing the hand washing on schedule.

Life in day care centers is also more homogeneous than life elsewhere. The day's format is always the same. Most of the time is spent in the same building, or room, on the same playground. Variations are always "field trips" to special events or activities. Surprises and variety, whether an errand to the auto repair shop, a visit from the next door neighbor, or skipping a nap, are kept to a minimum.

The need to manage large numbers of young children, which accounts for the centers' emphasis on standardization and routine, also leads to one of the most distinctive traits of life in day care centers. The children live in an "on" atmosphere that differs from the tone of life at home. Even when care givers are most gentle and children most mild-mannered, the pressure of numbers generates considerable noise, confusion, interruptions. Children have to respond, to react, to engage the social side of their personalities almost all day long. Time alone, to be quiet, to muse, to just be there, is minimal, and usually comes only at nap time.

The next chapters are concerned with some of the day care centers I visited. I will describe the best of what I saw, the mediocre, and the worst. It should be obvious which is which.

5

All Day at the Center

THE LI'L COWPOKES Child Care Center is a sprawling one-story building — resembling the management offices found in front of large factories — on a busy side street off one of the major highways running through a mid-size city in the Southwest. There's a large parking lot extending along the front of the building and an open but dimly lit reception area inside.

The receptionist greeted me as I walked in and asked me what I'd like to see. I told her I was interested in visiting the preschool rooms. She handed me the papers — the summary of programs, the fee schedules, the contracts — and briskly led me down the hall to one of the rooms for one- to two-year-olds. She hesitated a moment as we reached the door. It was the kind of door you find in old-fashioned school buildings — heavy, solid wood with a small window well above the height of the children's heads. She stepped back and gave me a wide berth to enter, told me to make myself at home and have a good look around, and then quickly turned on her heel.

It was an abrupt withdrawal, momentarily puzzling. I had expected her to lead me on in, as she had led me down the hall, rather than drop me at the doorstep. But when I walked into the room, I instantly understood why she had left so quickly. It was the smell. My breath caught in my throat and I had to force myself to keep walking. There is an odor of diaper and ammonia that's hard to shake in a toddler room, even one that looked as clean as this one did. But here, it seemed to hang onto the rug and settle into the woodwork somehow. It was a bad smell, one you didn't get used to after a few moments. The teachers shot bursts of deodorizing spray around the room several times that morning. It would mask the odor for a few minutes and then dissipate.

The twenty-seven children were all playing in one half of the room, a space maybe fifteen by thirty feet. In the middle of the room was a large modular arrangement of black vinyl couches. Along one wall was a row of shelves with some toys. There was a big cupboard housing puppets and more toys. One of the classroom's three teachers was with the children in the play area. The head teacher was out on his break for the first forty-five minutes I was there. He came back to help during lunch and headed out again quickly for a meeting. The third teacher was a single-handed, nonstop diaper-changing brigade on the other side of the room.

I settled into an inconspicuous corner of the room and began to watch the children. Here, as in most centers, two or three kids would wander over to look at me, talk a little bit, and eventually wander off. Often, one child would attach himself to me — maybe going off for a few minutes but always coming back to say a few words, show me something, or touch me. He'd point to a shoe that needed tying, or tell me his mom brought him to school that morning, or show me his tummy.

The teacher watching the twenty-seven children tried her hardest, ad-libbing her way from one activity to the next. She put on a record and started to dance. One little blond boy started dancing along with her. A few others joined the group. Five or six gathered by some swinging cabinet doors that formed the partition between the play area and the rest of the room. One little girl sat by herself, crying softly in the corner. The rest wandered around. For about eight seconds the music played and the children danced. Then a fight erupted between two little boys, and the teacher had to stop dancing to break it up. Without her example, the dancing died off. She tried again a few minutes later but was interrupted this time by a small couple who tripped over each other. Again, the dancers stopped. She gave up records then and tried reading a story. The same few eager dancers moved right in to listen, while the rest kept on swinging on the cabinet doors or aimlessly wandering. The little girl was still crying in her corner. After a short story, the teacher opened the large cabinet and pulled out some puppets. This immediately attracted the largest crowd of the morning. All but a few rushed right over to watch the show. But the brilliance of the idea dimmed after several moments. As her impromptu story line weakened, the toddlers drifted back to their swinging doors and wandering, shuffling their feet, chasing back and forth.

I watched this "activity period" for forty-five minutes, while reading through the stack of material the receptionist had given me. The toddler portion read:

> The toddler program utilizes the independent play of the child to foster a good self-concept: a good feeling about how he looks, who he is, and what he can do. Also important for the toddler is the development of the social skills of communicating feelings and responding with some sensitivity to other children and adults. Toddlers are constantly given opportunities to improve gross motor skills through running, jumping, sliding, hopping, etc., and fine motor skills through sorting, coloring, painting, and manipulating small objects. . . .

I decided to focus on a single child for a while. Many books on choosing day care centers suggest this as a method of understanding a child's experience. I tried to pick a typical child — not the little blond boy I was immediately drawn to, a tiger who always ran to the front of the line, ready to play at anything the teacher suggested, taking his tumbles in stride, performing for pats on the head and kisses. I learned after a while that there were usually one or two like this in every bunch. This child was truly thriving. Whatever it was in his personality or chemistry that responded to this situation, that little boy had it in truckloads. It was simple to look at him and see he was having a great time. I passed him up reluctantly, just as I also passed up his counterpart on the other extreme, the little girl who spent her whole morning in or at least near tears. She would stand near the window, a little apart from the rest of the kids. She would lie on the floor or on one of the black couches. She clutched her bottle and sucked her way into a lull of contentment. If a child approached her to play, to touch, or even to look closely, she would cry or sometimes scream. She was as miserable here as the blond boy was delighted.

Instead, I picked a wanderer from out of the crowd. First, he climbed up onto the modular couch. He lay down for a few minutes. He got up and started following a friend around. He peeled off and watched the dancing for a few minutes. He watched the teacher sort out the first little fight, then wandered back to the climbing couch. Another child joined him and they marched around on the couch until one of them fell off, and then he began scuffling about again. He took a special interest in the puppets. He went back to the couches, tried the swinging doors, sat down and watched the beginnings of the preparations for lunch. I wondered what he would answer if his mother or father asked him at the end of the day, "What did you do in school today, Jason?" It was a pretty nondescript morning for him. He didn't do badly — he roamed independently, joining in when he felt like it, taking off when he didn't. He got no individual attention, because he didn't demand any. He got no special instruction, because none was offered. No one talked to him or hugged him, because there weren't enough adults to go around.

Here, as at other centers I visited, you could almost feel the morning driving itself toward the grand finale — lunch.

At one school I visited, one of a chain of Orange Goose Schools popular in Texas, I watched a particularly meticulous "getting ready for lunch" routine. There were fifteen three-year-olds and one teacher in a small classroom that was almost entirely filled with rows of tables and chairs. The children had spent the previous session drawing block pictures and had just put their drawings and crayons away. They were sitting, hungry I suppose, at long tables in little chairs. The prolonged ritual began. One by one the children took their turn at the sink. A boy would get up, walk to the sink, turn on the water, pick up the soap, wet his hands and wash, replace the soap, rinse, pull out a towel, dry, throw the towel away, return to his seat — as slowly and deliberately as any three-year-old. Then another would get up, walk to the sink, turn on the water, etc., etc. By about the sixth or seventh child, the ones near the end of the line were getting fidgety, but they were instructed to keep sitting quietly until their turn. The whole process took ten or fifteen minutes or possibly more.

At Li'l Cowpokes the preparations for lunch weren't as tedious. But cleaning up afterward certainly was. The twenty-seven toddlers were all at their tiny tables, all eating nicely, calling for more crackers, more Jell-O, more juice. Each was tied to his chair around the waist by a large swatch of cloth. It was probably a good way of insuring they didn't fall out of their chairs while they were eating, and perhaps it was only my adult sensibilities that made me uncomfortable at seeing it. When a child finished, one of the three teachers would untie her, lead her to the sink, wash and wipe away the residue of lunch, and send her toddling off to the play area to wait for the rest of the kids. It was the same play area where they had just spent the morning, except now it was unsupervised. Soon the pace quickened as more and more children finished eating and called to be let out. Several had no choice but to remain, tied in their seats, until everyone else was finished being cleaned up. The undoing of lunch for them dragged on for close to twenty minutes. The teachers cleaned up the leftovers, wiped off the tables, mopped the floor, and rearranged the tables and chairs. Then the children could start preparations to go outside to play briefly before their two-hour nap time.

Noah's Ark is a very small, privately owned day care center in a residential part of the same city. It is housed in a converted single-family bungalow and blends in with the rest of the neighborhood except for the big Noah's Ark sign in the side yard. Approaching it, you get the feeling it is a renter's house rather than an owner's: the yard could use a mowing, the shrubs and plants need pruning and tending. The play equipment in the fenced back yard has the haggard look that comes from use by a few dozen kids rather than by a family or small neighborhood group.

The director was hurrying out on the morning that I dropped by at nine. She had a doctor's appointment, she told me. She seemed slightly irritated at my showing up unannounced, but I pointed out the small sign on her front door advertising a daily visiting hour from 9 to 10 A.M. She gave me a packet of materials for parents and told me I could stay.

Once inside, most similarities to the other houses in the neighborhood faded. The living room was carpeted but empty. Perhaps a chair or two stood along the wall. The other rooms were sparsely furnished, except for the nursery — a tiny former bedroom now jammed wall to wall with six or seven cribs. The kitchen had a few highchairs, oversized trash cans, some dishes and cooking equipment lying about, cans and cartons of food, rolls of paper towels. It was the busiest room in the house.

At Noah's Ark that morning, I did what most other parents checking out a prospective day care center for their child would do: I wandered from room to room, spent half an hour here, forty-five minutes there, watching the children go about their activities. I talked with teachers when they had a few free minutes; I inspected the kitchen; I studied the bulletin boards.

I consulted the daily schedule the director had given me and decided to visit the "educational skills" period for the older children. I walked through the kitchen to the back of the house. The children were in a very small room. It looked like an addition or possibly a converted porch. There was a rectangular arrangement of tables in the center of the room and twelve children, ranging from two and a half to five years old, sitting in chairs around it. The chairs were close together, and to get from one end of the room to the other you had to squeeze between the chairs and the wall behind them.

The teacher was reading a complicated story about some animals. The youngest child, a two-and-a-half-year-old, was quickly out of his depth. He put his weary head down to rest on the table. Sequoia and Andrea, two five-year-olds, were trying to pay attention but kept complaining because the teacher and book were so far away at the end of the table that they couldn't see the pictures. Joni, a sprightly dark-haired girl, took that complaint into her own hands, left her chair, and went to stand behind the teacher, where she could see better. The teacher, an attractive young woman in her late twenties, couldn't convince Joni (whom I later discovered was her daughter) to return to her seat, and soon several others quietly tiptoed out of their places to squeeze in beside Joni.

The story line of the book was getting more complicated when the phone rang next door in the director's office. The teacher got up to answer it because the director was out. When she came back, Jason started complaining that he didn't feel well. She let the comment pass and went back to reading when the phone rang a second time. She went again to answer it. When she returned, two girls chimed in with Jason that, as a matter of fact, they didn't feel well either. I looked over at Jason, who had suddenly grown very pale. He stumbled out of his seat and toward the bathroom, spitting up on me and a few children as he passed. The teacher had not finished the book, but she gave in to the commotion at that point. I had lost the story line by then, and I assume the children had, too.

The teacher went off to clean up Jason, laid him down in the director's office, and tried unsuccessfully to call his mother. She pulled out coloring books and crayons to keep the children busy in her absence. Joni was in charge of portioning out the fistfuls of crayons into plastic trays, and she directed her best friend to pass around the trays. All but two of the children located their coloring books by their names on the covers. Andrew, the two-and-a-half-year-old, and Michele, a recently arrived five-year-old, didn't have books. They found some left over from children who were no longer at the center and started using them. Suddenly Andrea discovered that she in fact had the wrong book and little Andrew was scribbling in hers. She attempted a quick switch, which set Andrew off howling. When the teacher returned, Michele was pouting and complaining about not having her own book. The teacher, impatient by then, picked up the book Michele was using, scratched out the name "Carolyn" and wrote "Michele" over it. "Carolyn withdrew from school," she explained to me. But Michele did not look convinced. She complained a little more before starting to color. This coloring session continued for about forty-five minutes. Jason eventually returned to the classroom, looking a little better.

Next I went to the toddler room to watch "motor skills" for an hour. There were fourteen children in the room. It was probably a converted bedroom, large enough to hold that many small bodies but not to accommodate much furniture or many playthings besides. One little girl named Cookie was still in her blanket sleeper, as she was when I left at noontime that day. A little boy named Brian had arrived for his first day at the center. He had a different look on his face from all the other children — scared and amazed. He stood motionless while all the others cruised the small room, zipping around quickly because they knew the territory by heart. Walk to the two tables at one end — watch out for the corners; make a beeline for the child-sized kitchen area at the other end — remember that the stove falls over on you if you stand on its shelf like Justin just did; look through the toy box — but beware of that lid that squashes fingers; take a rest on the comfortable rug. All the other children seemed to take in these features and maneuver the hazards in a familiar, well-traveled manner. But Brian wasn't ready to try yet. One teacher, a young girl who looked no more than eighteen, held him for periods of time. When she put him down to help out Justin, who had gotten himself trapped under the sink and stove when they fell over, Brian stood motionless in his spot. He waited until the girl came back for him. A few minutes later, she put him down again while she went over to pick up Pablo, who had been pushed over by Ryan. Brian stood his ground again until she returned. Finally, at ten-thirty, exhausted from his watch, Brian fell asleep on the wooden part of the floor, clutching his bottle, while the other thirteen toddlers stepped over and around him.

Since these toddlers were well into their "motor skills" hour at that point, I asked the other teacher what skills they were going to work on that day. She told me she was just "helping out" and didn't know. Her "help" was minimal; the only time I saw her get up from her perch on the end of a table was for Dusty, a little boy who had been fighting sleep all morning and was finally giving up. She tossed him a blue blanket and he clutched it tightly, rolled himself into a ball, and nodded off on the middle of the rug. I asked the first teacher about motor skills. When she gave me a blank look, I took out the daily schedule the director had given me earlier and pointed out that this was the time slot reserved for her group's motor skills. It all seemed to be news to her. "Oh, motor skills," she finally said, looking up at the color chart taped high on the wall. "We teach them red and blue and yellow," she said, pointing to the chart. I gave her a puzzled look and she tried again. "Motor skills," she said and walked over to one of the tables and picked up a toy car. "I might roll this little car back and forth on the table and ask them what it is." "Motor skills?" I asked. "Yes," she answered.

There were five infants in the Noah's Ark nursery room that morning. I stood watching as their teacher prepared to get them out for a crawling period in the empty living room. This was the only exercise I saw any of the children get that day. Despite its being a gloriously warm January day, with the temperature in the mid-seventies, the teachers told me it was too chilly to take the toddlers outside.

There was a crowded bulletin board in the nursery room. As in many day care centers, it offered a channel of communication between parents and day care workers. At this center there were a variety of messages on the bulletin board. Some were brief: one note card read simply, "Rochelle: feed on demand." It was signed by Rochelle's mother. Some gave brief descriptions of baby's likes and dislikes, usually nap times, favorite sleeping positions, tricks for comforting. One very long and poignant message read: "When Jessica wakes up from her nap, she wants her pacifier very much. Try not to give it to her, and amuse her in another way instead — playing, rocking, singing. But if she won't be comforted, give her the pacifier for a little while, and then try to get it back when you can. Use your own judgment." There were similarly detailed instructions for Jessica's feeding, bottling, putting to sleep, crying.

I asked the teacher how she could manage to learn the habits and rituals of so many infants. She was a conscientious and capable caretaker who did manage to hug and love each of the infants who were crawling all over her on the rug in the living room later that morning. She said that you quickly get to know a child's habits. You take some cues from the parents' descriptions at first, but you don't have time to follow all the steps. "Your own judgment" means that when Brian is screaming or Tessa needs to be changed, then you have to give Jessica that pacifier because you can't play with her or sing or rock her to distraction just then. And anyway, she told me — as many other caretakers told me about similar notes at other centers — Jessica's mom put that note up there when she first brought her in several months earlier, and it didn't matter anymore.

As I left Noah's Ark that day, I ran into a young mother on her way in to pick up her child. We chatted for a few minutes. Her son had been at this center for several months. "It must look pretty bad to you," she said, and then added, "but you get used to it after a while."

The Austin Community Nursery Schools have always been ahead of their time. They were started in 1940 by the American Association of University Women with New Deal funds for low-income families. They are still providing care for such families today; only children whose combined family income falls below the forty-seventh percentile in Texas can apply. The parents pay according to a sliding scale, some as little as $50 per month in an area where competitive rates are easily three and four times that.

The teachers fare well here also. Working conditions are rivaled by none: staff-child ratios are better than the minimum standards. Each class has two teachers. Although their wages are low by most other professional standards, in the day care industry, particularly in Austin, they are the best. Some years the teachers even receive cash bonuses. Teachers attend ongoing training sessions — sometimes lectures, sometimes seminars, sometimes conferences — all of which are provided by the center. Each classroom is allotted a sum of money for yearly special purchases at the teacher's discretion. Even the food is good.

The secret, of course, is money. ACNS is a nonprofit day care center. Its funds come from the federal government, the state of

Texas, and private local donors, such as banks, clubs, and individuals. Its board of directors is made up of parents, community leaders, day care staff, and members from the American Association of University Women. Its philosophy is that it doesn't aim to grow. In an era when federal funds for day care have been so drastically cut and when an estimated 5 million children under the age of ten, including 500,000 preschoolers, come home to empty houses in the afternoon, the conditions at this center may seem almost overprivileged. But ACNS does demonstrate that high-quality care, though costly, is possible to attain.

There are two branches of the Austin Community Nursery Schools, one north of the center of town, the other south. One is housed in a church building, a modest, barely adequate facility where the administrative offices are in a separate, one-room portable building. The other is in a specially designed doughnut-shaped building that surrounds an inner courtyard, with each room opening out onto a part of the adjacent playground. To boot, it is directly across the street from a public park. I spent time at both these centers. Despite their physical differences, the feelings and attitudes of both seemed much the same.

Free-play time in the three-year-old class represented a typical slice out of the children's day and demonstrated typical caretaking by the care givers. There were twelve children and two staff members in the class one cool April morning when I went visiting. The children were moving about at will among the activities in the room: a crafts table, a housekeeping section, a sand table, one table filled with puzzles and another with small building blocks. Two little girls were in the housekeeping area. They were doing pretty well by themselves, looking in cupboards, fiddling with the equipment. One of the teachers went over and, obviously trying to set them on a track rather than letting them drift aimlessly for too long, asked the girls, "Will you set the table for me? I'll be right back." They busied themselves enthusiastically with the task, putting the utensils and dishes in all the correct places. Then they dressed themselves in some "mother" clothes from the dress-up section, returned, and started feeding their dollies. The teacher returned. "What are you serving?" she asked, joining them. "Orange juice? How? In a pitcher or in a pot?"

One little boy across the room hammered endlessly on a shoe bench with a small but noisy hammer. After a while, a teacher went over and explained that "Grandpa didn't bang-bang, but he hammer-hammered." The little boy seemed to understand, but I didn't, until she explained to me that this was a reference to a story they had been reading. She gently suggested putting a cloth under the bench, which would make his hammering softer, like Grandpa's. He agreed.

The teachers kept harkening back throughout this play period to stories the children knew. At the sand table, for example, a little figure became a goat from the Billy Goats Gruff. Or the teachers encouraged the children to practice their newly developing skills — learning colors and shapes at the block table, names and figures on the puzzles and, of course, manners in the housekeeping area. The adults moved quickly but quietly from one activity area to another, keeping mental tabs on each child, talking, guiding, but not interfering or regimenting. They made it look so easy.

I saw the same thing in the free-play period for the two-year-old class. Several children were playing at the water table, blowing bubbles through straws, pouring water from glasses through funnels into bottles. Another group played lotto, the care giver asking one child after another to name his picture. Some of these activities were clearly hard and tiring for the children; the lotto, especially, seemed to require great concentration. The children would occasionally drift back and forth from one activity to another, but they were always under the watchful eye of a teacher who made sure everyone had something to do.

The session went on for fifty minutes. By the end of the first fifteen minutes, I knew the names of more than half the children, just by listening. "Yes, Billy, that's like the biggest billy goat." "Amy, will your dolly drink a little more juice?" "Come join us at the block table, Carlos." After twenty-five minutes, I knew all but two of them. This was, I eventually learned, a true phenomenon. No other center I saw used first names with the frequency that these two places did. In many centers, "teacher," "little girl," "little boy," and "hey" were the norm.

Toward the end of the period, one of the caretakers began quietly singing the clean-up song. The children began listening to her instead of the Sesame Street records that had been playing softly in the background. They began singing along with her. She coaxed a few reluctant ones to help "clean up, clean up, everybody do their share." When a child finished his share, he drifted over to sit on the carpet in the corner and sing songs with one teacher while waiting for the rest of the children and the other teacher helping them to finish their tidying up.

These waiting periods — the transition from an activity time to lunch, or from washing up to going outside, or from taking off coats to settling into the story time — are one of the inevitabilities of life in day care. The larger the number of children, the more the staff must try to do things on a schedule. Preparations are detailed and slow. Often, a teacher can deal with only one child at a time, leaving the rest to themselves.

ACNS coped with these transitions better than any other place I saw. Partly this was because the teachers had prepared and trained the children: when they said it was time to go outdoors, the children fetched their coats by themselves and simply went outside their classroom door to the fenced-in playground. I never saw them waiting idly in line for instructions on where to find their sweaters, how to button their buttons or zip their zippers. They didn't have to wait until everyone was ready before any of them could move on. The staff worked smoothly to negotiate the transitions. Unlike many other centers, where teachers would chatter and gossip back and forth to each other all day, the only in-class communication I heard between these women was a small comment, "It's time to go outside now." Then they would glide like a pair of skaters into a duet performance — one to the active preparations for the children ready to be out the door, the other gathering up the stragglers and encouraging them on at their own pace.

I watched the expert handling of a waiting period by just one teacher one morning at the ACNS school on the north side of town. In a toddler room, there was a wooden rocking boat big enough to accommodate four children. There were seven children in the room that morning, and once one child decided to rock on the boat, the other six thought it looked like a great idea. I had seen many similar instances, where the solution would be for four children to rock on the boat for five minutes while the other three children looked on, waiting their turn like impatient diners hovering over occupied tables. But here the teacher simply and effortlessly led the other three children to a table, pulled out some puzzles, and began playing with them along with the children. The boaters were happy. The puzzlers were happy. This episode was not so remarkable in itself, except that I had so rarely seen waiting handled in such an obviously practiced way.

If there were a trademark of ACNS, it would be the direct, one-on-one dealings the adults tried to have with the children. I was in a toddler class one morning, watching the children get ready for their story time. One teacher had set out twelve small squares of carpet in a circle. She sat with the children in the circle, holding a large set of picture cards that illustrated a story played on the record player. The session began with all the earmarks of disaster: one small boy bit another. The biter was in worse shape than the wounded child, and one teacher led him, screaming, off into the hall to sit for a while. The other teacher began the story, but no one could hear for the screaming. She quietly got up, closed the door, which at least muffled the sound, and started the record over. Then she began showing the cards — holding them high and aiming them from one child to the next, drawing them out of the commotion of the biting incident and into the story line with riveting looks at one, then another, then another. She refused to acknowledge the screaming outside the door, knowing that the other teacher would have that child on her lap, doing all that could be done at the moment. The children, following her lead, soon left the incident behind and seemed almost magnetized by the way the teacher held the cards, held their eyes, and almost made them listen and look.

When the story was over, the kids broke up into groups to go to different activities they chose themselves. The biter returned then and chose, of course, to listen to the story he had just missed. While one teacher played the record again, I watched the other teacher doing something I had seen in only one other center I visited. She engaged the children. She didn't dump out a bin of blocks and assume the children would settle down to building something. She picked up blocks herself, talked with the children about them, discussed what they might build, helped stack a few. When the children were off and building on their own, she quietly slipped away to another group. She helped them paste their collages, talked about their designs, sat to drink a cup of imaginary tea. It all seemed so obvious, so easy. Yet I know from playing with my own children and from watching dozens of other teachers in other centers that she was performing some magic. These two teachers kept twelve three-year-olds not just busy, but engaged, for forty-five minutes.

I couldn't help but contrast the experience that morning with another I had just seen at a small center across town. This center was located in a tiny converted bungalow. It was one I had heard rave reviews about; I was friends with at least two families who sent their children there.

During a similar activity period, I watched two groups of toddlers. In one room, six or seven children were sitting with blocks. In an adjoining room, three more sat amid a pile of musical instruments — toy drums, small horns, cymbals, and bells. The two young care givers could talk back and forth from room to room, which they did without interrupting themselves to tend their children. The "music" teacher made no attempt to show the toddlers how to handle the instruments or even explain to them what they were. The children spent all their time trying to poke the horns through the openings in the large, expandable gate that encircled and penned them all in. The caretaker in the block room was not talking colors or shapes or forms. She was talking to the other caretaker: "Only fifteen minutes till we can start getting ready for lunch." Her children didn't build, or sort, or even pay much attention to their blocks. What I watched at this center was far from the well-guided, absorbing play I watched at ACNS. It was, unfortunately, another, more familiar scene — one that I witnessed time and again as I visited different centers; it was simply filling time.

Some parents are attracted to ACNS by its "academic" component, which it offers in moderation. One mother of an eighteen-month-old told me, "The first day Davey came home from ACNS he was singing the alphabet song. We were hooked on the place right then." Or they select the center because it offers all the extras they went shopping for: convenient hours, affordable rates, good locations, friendly staff, attractive facilities, excellent equipment and materials. But even this, a list of tangible benefits, understates the true, intangible value of these centers and sells them short. Their best feature is an attitude and tone difficult to advertise but crucial to the happiness and security of the children: this is a place where children are respected, where adults try to understand each child and help him or her grow up.

6

Kinder-Care

KINDER-CARE LEARNING CENTERS are easy to spot. Like golden-arched McDonald's, they somehow all look the same, despite differences of detail. Often located on the inbound side of major thoroughfares of America's cities, each center is a small brick building topped by a schoolhouse bell. There are nearly eight hundred Learning Centers all around the country today, caring for 100,000 children, from infants full-time to twelve-year-olds after school. Kinder-Care is barely older than the children it cares for; it was started in 1969 by Perry Mendel, a Montgomery, Alabama, real estate developer who saw the business implications of the ever-increasing numbers of new babies and working mothers. Today, *Fortune* calls Kinder-Care's commercial success "truly impressive."

I visited Kinder-Care Learning Center #136 in Austin, Texas, several times in 1983. It sits on a major traffic artery, nestled in with a car wash, a pizza parlor, and several moderate-sized apartment buildings. There's a large parking lot out in front that runs directly up to the windowless brick face of the building. When I stepped inside the door for my first visit, closing out the din of the traffic, I found myself standing in front of the director's desk. At eye level right behind her head was a sign hanging on the wall: "Ask about free tuition." It was the sort of sign I had seen in health clubs and dance studios. Clearly, this place meant business as well as child care.

The director's office was empty that morning, but I could hear the noise of dozens of preschoolers beyond the door. I walked into the main room and followed the adult voices to the kitchen just around the corner. The cook and the director were busy with a cornucopia of Valentine goodies that parents had dropped off with their children that morning for the big party. No holiday goes unnoticed in day care centers. There were groaning boards of cupcakes and cookies. There were paper hearts strung from the ceiling and rows of large paper envelopes, each with a child's name on it, taped onto the walls awaiting the stuffing of Valentines. There were cutouts and standup displays of various Valentine paraphernalia on cupboards and tables.

I explained my mission to the director — that I was writing a book about parents, children, and work, and I would like to look around the center and talk with her. She was immediately accommodating, loading me up on Kinder-Care literature for prospective parents, taking me on a small tour of the building so I could feel my way around.

It's easy to get a feeling for Kinder-Care. They design their buildings on an open-classroom plan with sections for different age groups marked off from one another by furniture or rugs. You can walk a few steps to the right or left and take in the whole building. You can see the toddler group playing in their activity area, and you can see the preschoolers sitting at their tables. The only thing you have to hunt for is the nursery, a separate room in the center of the building with its own walls, doors, and windows looking into the other classroom areas.

It's also easy to get a feeling for the program at Kinder-Care. The abundant parent literature describes the combination of education and personal touches that Kinder-Care theoretically promotes:

> The Infant and Toddler room at Kinder-Care is designed
> to provide early learning experiences as well as security.
> Colorful mobiles and wall decorations offer visual stimu-

lation. Safe educational toys are provided for pushing,
pulling, grasping, stacking, and tossing. There's daily opportunity for lullabies, nursery rhymes, and personal communication between a trained, caring staff member and the
child. . . .

At two, when your child shows signs of readiness for
toilet training, this interest is approached with love, understanding and patience. Parent and staff cooperation and
appropriately sized equipment help establish proper toilet-
ing habits. . . .

To satisfy the natural curiosity of your four year old,
Kinder-Care offers "Happily Ever After," a program designed to strengthen pre-reading readiness skills in prepa-
ration for kindergarten.

Kinder-Care's two- to five-year-olds follow a regimen called
the GOAL Program that comes straight from company headquarters. Weekly themes and daily activities are suggested for
teachers to follow. The director told me that teachers are responsible for designing their own lesson plans from these guidelines and that the results are overseen by the director herself.
Such curriculum aids can be a big help for the many inexperienced, just out of school young people who become teachers at
Kinder-Care.

Many parents find this standardized, school-like approach
appealing. I talked with a woman whose two daughters had
been in the Kinder-Care center for the last five years. Her older
daughter entered at age two and stayed on in the after-school
program through the middle of first grade, when her parents
pulled her out for economic reasons and gave her a key to hang
around her neck for those afternoons when her father could not
meet her at home. The mother was convinced, as are many
parents of children in day care centers, that the early academics
at Kinder-Care gave her daughter a boost. Kindergarten was a
breeze for her. She knew how to act in class, had worked on
academic skills. "It's served her well so far," said the mother.
"She's doing all second-grade-level work now in the main subjects, although she's just in first grade."

I spent a good part of my first day at the Kinder-Care nursery.

It was a large room with rows of cribs (perhaps fifteen or twenty) along three walls. They all had clear acrylic footboards, so that infants who were awake could peer out at the activities going on in the center of the room. There wasn't too much going on that morning. Miss Lillie, an elderly caretaker and by far the senior staff member, with seven years' experience at this center, rocked and fed one infant while tending to sixteen-month-old Emily in her highchair.

Emily had a tray full of Rice Krispies before her. "That's one of the few things she can eat," explained Miss Lillie. "She doesn't eat much, and I was trying to get her to eat some more." Emily watched me hopefully as I approached, straining to get out of her seat. She had the look of a toddler who wanted to be on the move, not sitting in a highchair picking at cereal, and after ten or fifteen minutes Miss Lillie set her free. Emily headed straight for the nursery door that led out to the older toddlers' area. The door — on her account — was hooked shut. Emily had begun making transition visits to the toddler area (she would matriculate there at eighteen months), and she clearly knew that more interesting things were happening there than in the nursery with the infants. Emily had been in the nursery for ten hours a day, five days a week, for the past thirteen months, and she wanted out. She had another six weeks to go.

I made a few return visits to the Kinder-Care center. The last was several months later, at the end of July. I wanted to talk with the director again, and to get a feel for life there during the summer months.

I walked into the office hoping to find the friendly director I'd gotten to know over the winter. But she had left a few months back, I learned, to go to work for the city's electric company. "She didn't like all the hassles, and the pay was better," her replacement told me.

Turnover is so crucial a factor in the performance of large day care centers that it deserves mention here. Although Kinder-Care is a large national chain, the directors of its centers are essentially struggling small-business men and women. They spend much of their time and energy trying to cope with paperwork and balance budgets. When enrollments dip, directors scramble to meet the budget by snipping off a few hours here and a few hours there from the "full-time" staff's working days. Under these circumstances, it is very hard to maintain a stable, satisfied work force, and even the most diplomatic of directors face the reality that most of their employees are on the verge of quitting for some better job. The salaries are in the minimum-wage range to begin with, and when the working hours are reduced, the bond of loyalty between staff and center, never very strong, practically disappears. "I've been here for seven years, and I'm the only one stupid enough to stay around," Miss Lillie told me. Parents at Kinder-Care are aware of the pressures on the directors, and they watch them struggle with it. One mother told me, "One director was willing to take it out of her own pocket. They scrape for decorations, materials. They skimp on meals — meat loaf may be posted but macaroni with bits of meat is served. Or they serve water instead of milk." Not all directors were so dedicated, however. Recalled another mother, "There was a very bad director for two years who would hold Tupper-ware parties at school. She'd pressure the parents to order, ask them on the side, cart the stuff around in her school van."

One of the mothers commented on the variety of teachers she had seen pass through Kinder-Care's door. Her older daughter "lucked out," she said, with an excellent and well-trained teacher for her "pre-kindergarten package": "That one was very open, really worked to present the concepts in math and language. She really got into them. A few teachers were very detached, a few very strict disciplinarians, a few aren't and they don't last very long." Most of the teachers this mother had seen had finished high school but nothing more. "You can tell by their verbal patterns," she said. The children imitate them, and their speech habits "are rough to break, out and out wrong. It's tough to correct that in the children, and that's been a struggle." There was one teacher in particular who was really "bad news," that mother told me. "If a child was bad, she would take him down to a small room that was paneled above the kids' head level so they couldn't see out the window of the room. She closed the door." It took a little while for parents to discover what was going on. "The kids are impressionable enough," she recounted. "If the teacher tells them not to tell something's wrong, they won't. Parents have to devise their own networks of information, build their case, and present the facts to the director to demand change." The horrified parents did this, and "that teacher lasted two weeks, tops," said the mother.

The day I returned to visit was a blast-furnace-hot July Texas day. There were twelve babies in the nursery. All but one were in their cribs when I arrived. About half of them were sleeping; two or three were sucking their thumbs, staring through the transparent footboards. A few were alert, standing watch for any sign of activity. One little boy had tossed his socks out of his crib onto the floor. I picked them up and put them back in, but was told, "Oh, don't bother, he'll just toss them out again." And so he did, in a vain effort to get a game going. But no one would play.

I looked forward to asking about Emily. Miss Lillie — who was, miraculously, still at the center — couldn't put her finger on which girl I was referring to. "I'm not sure which one it was. They all do that after a while," said the caretaker who had, until a few months before, been the constant presence in Emily's life for the previous fifteen months.

Midmorning I went outside to watch the toddlers play on their playground. It was very hot already, in the high eighties, and the burnt-out grass was receiving no respite. The two teachers — young, overweight girls with little energy for playing — sat pressed along the side of the building in the only shade on the treeless yard. "Go play," they'd instruct a wandering child who happened along and interrupted their gossip. It looked as if raccoons or dogs had gotten into yesterday's trash; there were bits of torn newspaper and plastic blowing around the yard. A few of the children were climbing on the wooden equipment, and a few others were chasing bits of the flying trash. The sounds (traffic whizzing by out front, the car wash whooshing away next door), the smells (a vague odor from the garbage), and the stifling heat made it a recess no one was sorry to see end. "C'mon, kids, time to line up. C'mon, let's go inside," yelled the teachers.

The twelve toddlers were herded in to get ready for lunch.

After an orderly procession of handwashing, they sat at their little tables for twenty minutes awaiting lunch. "Put your heads down and your hands under the table," one teacher instructed, trying to control their mounting impatience. Of course, none could comply for more than a few seconds. They fidgeted. One tipped her chair over backward. A few sneaked contraband toys under the table. Finally, as the children were still waiting, one teacher turned on the record player, which caught their attention for a while. The teachers then busied themselves setting up cots in the play area for nap time after lunch. They didn't see one of the older toddlers who kept hitting the littlest boy, a newcomer whom everyone referred to as "baby." Another little boy sat singing, "Where's Daddy and Mommy, where's Daddy and Mommy?" The teachers said he sang this song every day.

Lunch finally arrived on a steel cart from the kitchen. I ate with the children. There was half a hot dog — cold — carrot sticks, graham crackers, applesauce, purple Kool-Aid, and Chee-tos. "No, Angelo. No, Amy," cried the teachers after the plates were dished out. "Don't eat until we say grace." "God is great, God is good, let us thank him for our food. Amen." The hot dog buns appeared later, after most of the children had already eaten their hot dogs. But the children didn't seem to mind; they put ketchup on the buns and ate them anyway.

While the children were finishing lunch, I looked slowly around the toddler area. Posters identified the functions of the different corners. The "home living" section had broken kitchen apparatus; "science" was a lone paper fish mobile; "music" was a record player; "creative art" was paper lanterns the children had made; "library" was posters from six books; "manipulative" was a big square cushion with broken zippers, laceless rows of holes, broken snaps, and missing buttons; "construction" was a set of scuffed and caved-in cardboard blocks. There were a few miscellaneous sets of pegboards and a few bins of toys.

The director told me she knew the place looked bad. "There was just nothing here," she said about the center when she arrived. "I don't know if maybe it just walked off." She had managed to talk her way into getting $2,000 for supplies after a visit from some company heads. So far, however, she had received only some kitchen equipment, and they were talking about redoing the front face of the building and putting up a new Kinder-Care sign out front.

Another Kinder-Care Learning Center — one I'll call #976 because, like all Kinder-Care centers, it is identified by number — operates in the suburbs of Washington, D.C. The center's location is attractive — on the edge of carefully developed, winding residential streets with names like Windy Ridge Way and Possum Corner, and right next door to the landscaped neighborhood swimming pool. The building looks open and welcoming: there are floor-to-ceiling windows offering a woodsy view and lots of bright colors — yellow walls, orange bookcases and cubbies, yellow and orange linoleum floors. Professionally lettered posters and ceiling hangings are interspersed with the children's art. In this Kinder-Care center, unlike the one in Austin, there is no shortage of playthings: many bins of plastic building pieces in the three-year-olds' area, toys in the two-year-olds' area, games for the older Klubmates (six- to twelve-year-olds who attend the after-school and summer programs). There is a feeling of opulence here: outside is plenty of sturdy play equipment, inside is a neat storage area with drawers marked "Holiday Decs," shelves of project supplies, and a hundred huge tins of prepared food: African Pineapple Tidbits, Mandarin Orange Broken Segments, yellow cling Peach Chunks, ready-to-serve diced boned chicken, 101 All Purpose Sauce, apple juice, grape juice, pork and beans, Spoon-Redi artificially flavored vanilla pudding.

I had arranged an appointment with the director a week before, but she wasn't in when I arrived and wasn't planning to come in that day. I was shown around the center, which was laid out roughly along the same plan as the Kinder-Care I had seen in Austin. There was no infants' nursery here. The two-year-olds occupied the room in the center of the building, and the older children were in marked-off areas around the perimeter. I settled into the three-year-olds' area as they were sitting in a circle singing an animated song about a baby bumblebee.

There were thirteen enthusiastic participants and a young teacher I'll call Miss Patty, who sang and demonstrated all the proper hand motions. The children looked perky and, on the whole, better dressed than I had seen in any other center so far. They were clearly from families that could afford Kinder-Care's posted tuition ($61 per week for the two-year-olds and $58 per week for the three- to five-year-olds) plus nice wardrobes. One little boy in blue shorts, a striped shirt, and a baseball cap, called alternately Charles and William Charles, was getting himself into hot water for the first of several times this day. I'm not sure what small commotion he was causing this first time, but it warranted a warning from Patty, their teacher. "Would you like time out, Charles? Then be good," she said.

After several minutes of singing, it was time to prepare for snack. "Okay, let's see, who's sittin' up nice and straight?" asked Patty. "Emily!" Emily, a curly-haired girl in a pink and white flowered dress, started the procession to the sink to wash hands. The children line up to wash hands, one by one, some patiently, some squirming, many times a day. That's one of the bylaws of the Kinder-Care operation: wash hands before snacks and meals; wash hands after coming in from the playground.

Charles was not handling the wait well. "Okay, Charles, over here. You know what you just did," said the teacher. (He had slapped another child on the face.) Charles marched over to where I was sitting on a small red chair off to the side of the three-year-old area. "Move! Move!" he said to me. I realized then that I had inadvertently been sitting on the time-out chair all morning. Now Charles bumped me out while he sat to be punished.

Emily passed out napkins to all the places at the small tables. The second caretaker, a young woman I'll call Lynn, handed out paper containers of canned pineapple and peaches and cups of milk.

Finally, twelve pairs of hands washed, everyone seated and served, the children all said grace. This is a second bylaw of Kinder-Care operations: grace before all snacks and meals. Many times a morning you hear the choral recitation from one corner of the open-classroom building or another: "God is

great, God is good, let us thank him for our food. AAA-men."
Sometimes they chant the variation, as they did this snack time:
"We are thankful for our food. AAA-men." Everyone started in
on the fruit except a small boy seated at the end of the table
who continued, hands folded, in a lengthy silent prayer. He
glanced at me watching him every few seconds.

There were many small accidents during this snack time,
mostly spills and dribbles. The three-year-olds were expected to
be responsible for themselves and the condition of their seats
afterward. "Jeannine, Clara," called one teacher, setting the
harsh, loud tone of command and authority so different from
the one I had heard at Austin Community Nursery Schools,
"you're gonna knock your milk over and guess who cleans it
up? You're old enough to play at the table, you're old enough
to clean your own mess." Charles, having done his time on the
time-out chair, returned to have his snack, then wandered from
the snack tables back to the play area well before the others. He
was soon called back. "Who sits here? Charles! You've got a
mess to clean up here!" Over at one end of one table, several
children dissolved in giggles. One boy with a white milk mus-
tache yelled out, "Yucky! Yucky!" The rest burst into more
giggles, and he repeated his performance for more applause.
"I'm not making a mess," said a little girl proudly. "I know,"
said Patty, "you're not doing much of anything, little girl. Eat
some fruit. Eat!" She turned around. "Gregory, eat! And drink
your milk!" As snack time ended, Patty tried to speed things up.
"All right, it looks like everyone here is finished. Drink your
milk. Clean it up and leave." The children wiped up the floor
with paper towels and marched back to the free-play area. Five
girls clustered at the sink, soaping their hands and arms into a
frothy lather, laughing and screeching. "Wipe! Go!" com-
manded Patty, like a boot-camp drill sergeant.

The children next went to play in the carpeted area where
they had gathered earlier for songs and stories. They were having a combination session of art project and free play. While the
two teachers called groups of four children over to two tables
to make paper ladybugs, the other children played wherever
they wanted. The ladybugs, when finished, were to be hung

from the ceiling next to the paper apples and butterflies. The first group's ladybugs were complete, and Lynn called for a rotation in shift. "Who's left to go!" she yelled out. "Kevin! Jamie! Suzy! C'mere. Sit down over here. Jamie, come here!" ("What's wrong with him?" Lynn whispered to Patty about Jamie.) The second group sat down, ready to start pasting small black circles and black antennae onto the red ladybug shape. "Boys and girls, you have to wait for instructions. You don't just do what you wanna do," chided Lynn as Jamie started in on his work.

As I looked up at the finished apples and butterflies that hung from the ceiling, I realized that the quality of the product reflected this close scrutiny of the teachers. It was the product, not the process, that seemed to matter. "Pick up a circle. Put paste on it. Jamie, you gotta turn it over so it'll stick. Here — " Lynn picked up Jamie's circle and pasted it on for him. Kevin picked up a strip that looked like it was an antenna or a leg. "Did I say to do that, Kevin?" Lynn asked. "Okay," she continued, "pick up another little circle. Jamie, what are you doin'? I didn't say that. Take that one off. Jamie, take it off." After several minutes they were all finished. "Let me see your ladybug, Jamie. Very good!" said Lynn. Jamie smiled, all dimples, and Lynn said, "You can go wash your hands now."

As the children walked back to the carpeted area, one girl asked about Jason, who was not at the center on this day. "He's resting at home," said Patty. "Why?" she persisted. "He had to go to the hospital," said Patty. With that, interest was piqued, and several children began talking about Jason. There was more animation and more spontaneous discussion about Jason and his problem than I had seen all morning. "Why?" They pressed Patty for more details. "He got hurt. Remember?" she asked. "We talked about it." "Why?" asked another, who must not have remembered. "Did he get bit by a ladybug?" Patty glanced quickly over to me. "He got hit with a baseball bat," she said. "Did he throw up?" asked the same girl. "Yes, he threw up . . . in school," said Patty. I didn't know from this if Jason had his accident in school or not, and as I sensed everyone's discomfort, I didn't ask.

The next item on the children's agenda this morning was a

walk to the duck pond near the center. The teachers were eager to get on with this and hustled the children along to their bathroom lines and washing hands lines again. Everyone scurried to neaten up the free-play areas and to fetch ice water and a blanket for the trip to the pond. Charles and Emily began scuffling. "All right. It's time to clean up. It's not time to play," scolded a teacher. Charles proudly carried a basket of blocks back to its storage area and finally earned some praise from the teacher. There was some confusion and scuffling over on the carpet. "You listen to me!" yelled Patty, as she jerked a little boy by the arm. "I didn't tell you to do that!" Then a girl came up to Patty. "Miss Patty, she spit on the rug," she tattled. The culprit got a quick sentence — "She's staying in" — and then just as quick a reprieve as Patty realized this would mean an adult would have to stay with her. "You go sit in time-out," she said, commuting the sentence.

This morning, I guessed, had been a routine one for the three-year-olds. Posted on the bulletin board for the parents to read was a report of a previous morning's events that sounded nearly identical. "What We Did: Today we started off by singing some of our favorite songs. Our voices are getting stronger and better everyday! Next, we really got our hands 'into' our art work and made 'preppy' pink and green handprint pictures. It was really fun! Later we took a walk to the duck pond and saw two ducks that stayed close to us while we talked to them. After afternoon snack, we went outside and had an icewater party under a tree and listened to a story."

I went out to the playground with the two-year-olds. There were several pieces of climbing equipment — an elevated house, a climbing tree, tire swings. The ground was mostly dirt, wet and messy from recent rains. But today was a beautiful, sunny day. While the teachers clustered in the shade, the children were, for the most part, playing happily. Six or seven exercised on the climbing toys; groups of two and three played games they had concocted themselves; a few younger ones worked the dirt over in the corner of the lot. One blond two-year-old had been crying for a long time, his shoulders shaking, his clenched fists pressed to his mouth. A young teacher comforted him, put him down, let him stand a while, picked him up again. She seemed unsure about what to do to cheer up the boy. Another two-year-old in blue overalls named Stephen came over to stand vigil next to him. His hands were in fists next to his mouth, too, but he wasn't crying.

After about ten minutes, Stephen worked up the nerve to wander away from the teacher and over to the children digging in the dirt. He sat next to a child who had collected dirt in a paper cup. They seemed on the verge of playing together or side by side. Just then one of the teachers came over to the child who had collected the dirt, took the paper cup, and spilled the dirt out. The child wandered away and left Stephen by himself. An older girl walked over to him. She was carrying a tiny book and began "reading" to him. Then she told him to come along and directed him to come sit next to me by the fence. The other little boy was still crying and had now wet his pants and shorts. One teacher took him inside to change him and six others tried to follow them, only to be shut out or, if they made it in, quickly shooed back outside. The teacher in charge of the Klubmates' program, a young man with the gruff voice and husky build of a star high school football player, hung on the fence gossiping with two young women teachers. Stephen came to sit next to me again, this time by the side of the building, and said, "My momma come soon."

The two-year-olds had been on the playground for quite a while, and they were beginning to get hot in the summer sun. The teachers decided to take them in and lined them all up to go to the bathroom. "No playing," said Toby, one of the teachers. "Time to use the bathroom." There were thirteen two-year-olds, so the process of going, one by one, to the bathroom and washing hands afterward was slow and painstaking. In the background, a second drama was being played out. One little boy started in, "I want my mommy." A second followed suit. A third boy sat by himself at one of the tables crying softly, "I want my mommy, I wanna go to Mommy's house." A fourth boy walked over to the teacher. He shouted, "Mommy!" "Yeah, Mommy's coming," said the teacher. "Daddy!" "Yeah, Daddy's coming, too," she said tiredly.

All the calling for mommies quieted down, except for Stephen and another boy, as the teacher began reading a story to the children. The story was about a boy and a goat traveling from Russia, and it was clearly written for children considerably older than two. The teacher read like a young schoolchild: her words came out in staccatos, at most a phrase at a time; her voice lacked any animation; she missed several of the harder words. Even I could barely follow the story line. A few of the children clustered right in front of the teacher seemed mildly interested in the pictures and commented from time to time on a boat, or a cat, or some other thing they recognized. Only her occasional interpretations kept them going: "You see the people on the boat?" But most of the children were looking elsewhere and thinking about other things. Several of them could see only the teacher's back; her body blocked the book from their view. Every few pages, she interrupted herself, trying to keep the children in line. "No kicking. Keep your hands to yourself. Yes, Mother's coming, okay? Yes, your mother's coming also. No, no hitting. Be quiet." Stephen began wailing incessantly for his mother, so the second teacher took him out of the room for a short walk.

After the book, the children played a little while and began to come over to their tables for lunch. The screaming and crying from the two little boys had become exhausting to us all. The children must also have sensed the disruption. Several kept watching Stephen, although one little boy named Roopa got so tired waiting for his lunch that his head kept drooping into his empty plate. The caretakers seemed a little embarrassed in front of me. "I guess you can tell which ones are the new ones," one commented to me. I pointed them out, of course, as the criers. I was relieved to hear that the excessive crying was probably because the children were new. But one of the teachers told me later that this center got new children almost every day.

Stephen just wouldn't quit his crying. "I want my mommy. Momma comin'?" Usually one of the teachers answered, "Your mommy's coming soon." If they didn't answer, Stephen looked at me, and I told him the same thing: "Your mommy's coming soon." The assistant teacher had told me Stephen's mother was coming at noontime, for which we all felt very grateful. One or two mothers arrived to take away their children, but not Stephen's mother. The sight of a mother, any mother, sent him into an even deeper tailspin. The spaghetti and peas finally arrived. "God is great, God is good. . . ." These little children needed a lot of help and prompting with their grace. Toby helped Stephen with the first bites, hoping to distract him with food. He ate, but took time between bites for a little more crying, and bits of food dropped from his mouth. At this point, a small boy named Bradley, seated next to Stephen, picked up on the adults' cues and started saying to Stephen, "Mommy be back, Mommy be back," in a quiet voice.

After lunch and cleanup, the teachers began to set up the plastic Kinder-Care cots with sheets and blankets for nap time. At the sight of this, Stephen began to change his line. "I don't wanna sleep. I don't wanna sleep." We kept assuring him that his mommy would come in a few minutes. One by one, the children were called to their cots and all went willingly, tired from the morning's events. Stephen stood next to me, still pleading, "Momma comin'? Momma comin'?" I asked the head teacher what time Stephen's mother would come, as nap time was fast approaching and all the cots were almost filled. She glanced at her watch and said in a resigned tone, "If she was comin' she'd be here by now." At that point, I felt nauseated: we had all betrayed this child. The caretakers told Stephen he had to go and lie down on his cot. I left the room and walked around the building a few times, glancing in the doors and windows at Stephen's cot as I passed. He was thrashing and tossing around, crying as loudly as ever.

7

More Days, More Centers

THE ROSEMOUNT DAY CARE CENTER is in Adams Morgan, the most racially, ethnically, and economically mixed section of Washington, D.C. It is housed in a huge, rambling building, formerly the House of Mercy, owned by the Episcopal Church. It is located up a small hill on a dead-end street near the edge of Rock Creek Park. Enormous trees sway over the orange tile roof. Heavy, ornate wrought-iron bars cover some of the windows — all suggesting the grand old elegance of some former era.

Inside, a receptionist sits in the open entry. Here is the same feeling of bygone grandeur — high ceilings, double staircase, French doors. They contrast sadly with the make-do shabbiness of the current furnishings and decor. On the day I visited Rosemount, I met the young director of the infant-toddler program, and she led me off to the left, through the double doors, to the youngest children's wing.

The infants and toddlers, thirty-two of them, spend their time in four rooms off an L-shaped hall. Three of the rooms, each with a Dutch door or glass doors that allow for openness or privacy, open onto a common hallway. The hall is large enough and bright enough to double as a play area. Indeed, there are some large pieces of climbing equipment, tables, shelves, baby walkers, and a brightly covered single-size mattress for climbing or resting, all housed in this hallway. Still, plenty of space for roaming is left over. A child-size Raggedy Ann doll sits comfortably in one corner on a large yellow pillow chair. The fourth room, where the oldest of these children are centered, is around the corner of the hall. It is divided from the rest, at least today, by makeshift partitions to enable the toddlers to roam about at will without stepping on the babies or crawlers in the main hallway.

The smallest infants occupied a suite of two rooms linked by a small central kitchen area. From the hallway (the only place I was allowed to be as an observer) you could see only the front room, a small yellow room with a brown rug. The back room was the sleeping room, where napping babies could be away from the activity of the rest of the children. A crib-size mattress lay on the floor, along one wall of the yellow room. One tiny girl named Alexandra, in a white bubble suit and bib, spent several minutes trying to scale the mattress, perhaps so she could see herself in the mirror that hung lengthwise at infant eye level next to it. There were several other babies in the room.

In a casual glance around the Rosemount center, I might guess that half the caretakers were black and half were white. In the infant room, an elderly black woman gently rocked a small boy in a green and white striped shirt. Watching the woman throughout the morning, I could see that she didn't have the kind of energy needed to get down on the floor and play with the children or to handle the more physical tasks of caring for them. But she was there with the time and patience to rock and cuddle those who needed coaxing to sleep. I later learned that all the rooms at Rosemount have a "grandma" or "grandpa" to help in this way. These older men and women did have something unique to offer — be it patience for the infants or a kind of quiet comfort and security for the toddlers. On another day at this center, I watched a "grandpa" lagging behind the rest of his group with one small boy, a real straggler, who needed his shoes tied, then this and that small attention. The "grandpa" was able to give him the special time he needed just then — an important contribution that the regular caretakers and teachers, simply for want of time and the demands of so many other children, couldn't make.

The head teacher in this infant room was Aileen, a recent college graduate in blue jeans and sandals who had been at the center for about six months. She stood pasting photos of the children up on the wall next to the changing table. Later in the morning, I watched her study the photos as she changed babies. A bald baby girl in an orange terrycloth sunsuit tootled around in a walker, zooming first over to the toy shelves to grab a few things to chew on, then back to the third caretaker, a heavyset woman in bright green pants and tunic. The baby tugged at the woman's tunic for a few minutes until she was joined by a boy, this one able to walk by himself. The two small friends, wandering a few steps back and forth and around in the small open space of the yellow room, played with books and rattles and the toys sitting on the tray of the walker.

The eight children and three caretakers in this infant area don't keep to any regular schedule. The head teacher explained that the children are so small that it's hard to insist on common nap times. But also, she said, it's more the personal style of this group of care givers to do it this way. The care givers staggered their duties, constantly tending whoever happened to be awake (and someone always was). They moved around with the deftness and familiarity of people who were easy to work with and who were used to working with each other in a small space. They seemed to know, from practice, where to move: two steps to the right, one to the left, to dodge the many mobiles that hung down low, within the youngsters' sight line, throughout the room.

On the wall were the schedules for this week's "program" for these infants.

> Alexandra: Continue to encourage to sit up by placing in sitting position propped with pillows. Do leg exercises on rolling pillow. Play games with scarves. Continue to encourage to rock back and forth on hands and knees. Play rhyme game. Talk to her.

Kenny: Give opportunity to crawl around in hall and pull up where he has more space to move. Play hide and seek with object and cloth. Give opportunity to play with pots and pans. Play imitating and rhyme games. Talk to him.

Caitlin: Give opportunity to crawl around in hall and pull up on things. Play hide and seek with objects. Play peekaboo. Play rhyme games. Give opportunity to play with pots and pans. Read books. Talk to her.

Partway through the morning, Aileen opened the bottom half of the yellow room's Dutch door so the children could wander out into the main hallway to play. They all zoomed out, the child in the walker clearly delighted with her newly expanded horizons, the rest toddling quickly toward the climbing equipment or the farthest frontier, the double door that connected the hall to the reception area. A little curly-headed girl wearing a pink shirt with "girl" written across the front and tiny gold rings in her ears was pushing a toy shopping cart around. She abandoned that to crawl into a stack of giant plastic cubes. If she was older and could talk, she would undoubtedly be pretending she was in a rocket ship, or a fort, or a house. In and out, in and out she climbed. Then she went after a toy rocking horse, knocked it and herself over, and cried for a minute or two. She wanted to stand up again, so she went through her particular routine: down on all fours, bottom in the air, pushing with her hands and arms until she could stand. One care giver sat on the mattress, gently roughhousing with a baby and singing to him. Aileen played peekaboo through the glass hole in the climbing equipment with a little boy named Esteban. She was also holding a tiny infant, one too small to keep himself upright. She propped him up against the window to play the game with Esteban; he clearly thought this was the funniest thing he had ever seen. Aileen was tireless with the children. She had a limitless repertoire of songs, games, and ideas to take the children through their morning. She seemed to know when to switch to patty-cake or lull them with a song, to excite them with a funny game or quiet them with an impromptu story.

The decorations in the hall seemed for the benefit of the adults rather than the children. The walls were covered with lots of Spanish artifacts: colorful native skirts from Mexico, a stuffed llama from the Andes, photos from the mountains as well, and a message to parents that read: "Parents: you are the first and the most important teacher your children have." Attached to it were some funny, old illustrations that looked like propaganda from the 1950s, showing how parents do various things with their children—read to them, play games with them, feed them.

During that morning, while several crawlers were out playing in the hallway, a young couple with their tiny baby, perhaps two months old, came to see the center. (I saw more visitors at Rosemount during my time there than at any other center. Each of the families I saw had infants in tow. One mother was still quite chubby from her pregnancy.) The father, in sandals and a backpack, carried his baby (I couldn't tell if it was a boy or a girl), who was wearing a red and white bubble suit. He looked like a student, or a musician, or someone who works at home. The mother was dressed as though for an office job. They both had expectant and rather nervous looks on their faces. I watched them trying to soak in the atmosphere — looking, as I had done, at the walls, into the classrooms, at the babies on the floor, at the care givers, and at me, another visitor. They looked like they wanted to be pleased with what they saw, but they were wary at the same time. The father, still holding his child, sat down on the mattress with another care giver and baby, telling his child about the things in the room, pointing out the other babies. After a few moments, the parents slipped into the administrator's room at the end of this hallway. The baby stayed out in the hall with all the rest of us, although the parents could hear him and see him if they got up and looked through the glass. Their baby was happy enough at first and then realized his parents were gone. He let out some shrieking cries that brought his father to the glass and, eventually, back into the hallway with us.

While the visiting parents were in talking with the infant and toddler director, she probably told them some of the same things she had told me earlier about the center. It has 135 children, ranging in age from six weeks to five years. The children come from all over — as close as northwest Washington, D.C., and as far away as the Maryland and Virginia suburbs of Rockville, Alexandria, and Mount Vernon, fifteen or more miles from the center. The children come from all kinds of families, too, from different races, ethnic backgrounds, and economic circumstances. There are children of lawyers and doctors, who pay the full $100 a week for infants ($75 for toddlers, $65 for preschoolers), and children of domestic workers who may be eligible for funds from the Department of Health and Human Services and pay on a sliding scale, perhaps $12.50 a week.

The center is a private, nonprofit operation. In addition to the money it receives from tuition, there are fund raisers, help from the House of Mercy and the Episcopal Church, and food subsidies from the Department of Agriculture. The Rosemount staff is very nutrition-minded about the breakfast, lunch, and snacks prepared there, the director made a point of saying. They include lots of fresh vegetables, rice, beans, and cheeses on the menu. The center offers free vision, hearing, and dental screening for the children and a variety of consultants on family affairs and mental health for the parents.

The staff at the center varies in age, experience, and background. Some have been here a year, some as many as six or eight. There is ongoing training for the teachers, the director explained to me. They used to close the center for one week during the year for cleaning and teacher training. But with cutbacks in government subsidies, they've had to reduce that to one day, she said with a small laugh. Now, they manage to squeeze in four solid days of teacher training on a rotating basis, without closing the center, and they have unit meetings weekly. These might be films, talks, or advice from social and health workers.

Toward midmorning, things were beginning to get a little wild at Rosemount. I reminded myself that sheer numbers of children could make this happen, no matter how organized or how controlled a program was. There were thirty-two babies in all four sections of the main hall, and it was getting noisy. I peeked around the corner and found the source of the noise. In the older toddlers' section, seven toddlers clad only in underpants (on their way to or from the sprinklers, I believe) — half of them in training pants and the other half in diapers covered with plastic pants — were marching through a makeshift obstacle course. They were noisily cheering each other on along a row of plastic shapes, across a plank, up and down the slide at the end. The infant and toddler director walked by and called, "This is lovely!"

After their games, the older toddlers, ages eighteen to thirty-three months, marched around the corner into the main hall and past the babies on their way to the outdoor playground. "Watch out for the babies. Let's wait for the other canaries," called the teacher. (I assumed "canaries" was their group name.) A little girl named Jessie stopped to kiss a baby before heading outside to play.

Once the older children were outside, things began to quiet down again. The teachers remarked that they were glad that lunch today was spaghetti because all the children would eat that. The girl with the gold earrings toddled over to the French doors that separated one of the older children's classrooms from the hallway. She pressed her mouth and nose against the glass, possibly looking for the children, but this group had been out all morning. It was getting on to lunchtime by now, and eyelids on the littlest ones were drooping. They were carried, one by one, back to the yellow room for their routines of lunch, change, and nap.

The parents were out of the director's office by now, and looking around the hallway and rooms once again. I watched the father study one of the care givers, a very heavy woman who was wearing a tight blue T-shirt. It said "Tommy and Joanne" on the front and "I Love Tommy" on the back. I wondered what these parents were thinking this morning. For half an hour of their time here, it had been very loud and raucous; for another half-hour, it had quieted down. They had a long talk with the director, but they hadn't had much time to spend soaking up the feeling of the center or observing the kinds of things their baby would be doing here for ten hours a day. They looked no less expectant or wary than they had when they came in an hour before. Their baby was very young; I was sure it was their first. The mother asked if it would be possible to come over again and just observe for a few hours.

Next to the yellow room was the blue room. It was a corner room, much larger and airier. The light curtains over the tall windows were tied in knots at the bottom. Cutouts of big duck shapes were pasted up on the wall. Full-size cribs and port-a-cribs lined the wall. There was a large play area in the middle. Off to one side in part of the room with a linoleum floor were two small tables, six little chairs, and a changing table.

The woman with the "Tommy and Joanne" T-shirt arrived in the blue room, pushing a stainless steel cart with the lunch. Besides spaghetti (which looked and smelled delicious — I was hoping I'd be invited to lunch here as I had been at several other centers I'd visited), there were peaches, and milk to drink. Some of the toddlers could manage lunch themselves, spooning up bites of spaghetti from their heavy-duty plastic plates. Others were fed by the teachers.

As I studied the teachers' work schedules, the older toddlers began returning from outdoors. "I like the way you're walking. You're doing a great job," their teacher said encouragingly. Everyone was tired by now. The babies in the yellow room were moving slowly, rocking, playing with mobiles. The toddlers, full of spaghetti, were settling into their cribs for a nap.

The Pilgrim Congregational Church sits in the heart of Dorchester, Massachusetts, a working-class suburb just south of Boston. The street that runs in front of the church, Columbia Road, is very noisy. I saw nearly every kind of vehicle passing: buses, garbage trucks, taxis, private cars, limousines, a truck filled with frankfurters, mail trucks, ambulances. Jackhammers pounded away in front of the church; the pedestrians marched by in a constant parade — mothers pushing babies in strollers and holding toddlers by the hand, men heading for the bank down the street, busy people stopping in at the drugstore on the corner. A large placard was propped up in front of the church. It carried bold red letters spelling out LUNCHEON, with an emphatic NOW! added across the bottom.

Inside, the church was a hubbub of activity as well. In the entry to the dark stone building were several large cardboard boxes filled with bags of pita bread, bagels, and homemade egg bread for the taking. And there was lots more: a swiftly written note advertising Nikes on sale today, an announcement for the AA meeting, directions to the thrift and gift shop, and up the step to the right, the church office. The Pilgrim Day Care Center, the secretary told me, was in the basement.

It was warm and sunny outside, the first such June day after a week's deluge of rain, so I walked with some reluctance into the chilly church basement. It was the kind of chill that adults notice with a shiver immediately but that children, who rarely seem to mind the cold, often don't. But today, however, even the children were asking for their sweaters.

There were eighteen children seated at three small tables in the middle of the largest basement room. They were eating breakfast, supplied at least in part by the U.S. Department of Agriculture's food subsidy program for day care centers: raisin bran in yellow bowls, yellow juice in small plastic glasses. There was little sunlight in the room, only what filtered through a few small windows higher up than even adults could see out of. The lights were dim. The linoleum floor was like those in countless church basements I have seen, complete with a shuffleboard game tiled in on one corner. The walls of the basement were painted to affect a mock English Tudor decor, white with wooden beams. The two small classrooms off the main room were decorated in the same way, made to look like the fronts of small Tudor houses, with shutters and peaked roofs.

The center had the look of a place past its prime. There were some high-quality, industrial-strength climbing toys in the corner behind the tables and chairs — a slide, a tube to crawl over, and hand-over-hand bars — plus the expensive housekeeping equipment that you see in pricier centers. But all these durables had the look of things purchased in flush times many years ago, when Head Start was thriving here. There were few signs of replenishment. The less sturdy toys were shabby. Along the wall behind the tables sat stuffed but threadbare teddy bears, twelve in a row on three wooden beds under a row of six old purses used for dress-up. Broken toy telephones sat on the toy stove. All the decorative materials were homemade — the alphabet cards, the posters, the signs. The teachers had obviously done their best to dignify the room. The small tables were set with pots of paper flowers placed carefully as centerpieces and the individual places had napkins. "We're not one of the best," one teacher told me. "We make do."

Sam, the white-haired, mustachioed cook, walked over from the big kitchen across the hall to do a head count for lunch. He hurried back to his hissing pressure cooker. One small girl, probably four or five years old, wearing a patch over the left lens of her thick eyeglasses, spilled her juice. "Bravo! Bravo!" chanted the other children on cue. They sang it in an almost friendly singsong way that didn't seem to tease the victim but rather to distract her from the messy embarrassment she had just created. "Oh," comforted Joanie, the Boston Irish matron who walked around carrying a roll of paper towels to wipe up after emergencies like this one, "you spilled your juice on your nice pants."

I sat off to the side, trying to look inconspicuous. But I knew I didn't; all the children took turns staring at me. The children had been eating breakfast for about twenty minutes, and they were beginning to get a little restless. As they finished, they carried their yellow bowls, their spoons, and their glasses back to the stainless steel cart and stacked them in the proper columns. The children seemed to me to be very well controlled, very restrained in this small, close area, and I wondered if it was because there were only six boys among the eighteen children present. (As a mother of boys I am allowed to say these things. Girls are gentler than boys. The enormous difference was brought home to me clearly on the occasion of our second son's fourth birthday party. By coincidence, all his boyfriends were sick or out of town, leaving him and his brother to handle an all-girl party. It was a wholly different experience from the mostly boy parties we had been giving for the past seven years. The girls were orderly, well behaved, composed, and quiet. They came to the table when I told them it was time; they queued politely for their turn at whacking the piñata; none of them spilled anything. I wasn't quite sure they were having a good time.)

A small girl named Patricia walked into the room by herself

as breakfast was winding up. Her mother had dropped her off, a few hours late, at the front door of the church. All the children greeted her, chanting her name: "Hello, Patricia. Hello, Patricia." But she had a glazed, sort of faraway look on her face and didn't respond. Doreen, one of the three caretakers, tried to talk with her privately for a few moments but she couldn't seem to penetrate either.

Carmen, the youngest teacher of the three, buzzed around as the children finished up their breakfasts. She was dressed in a bright red sweater, wheat-colored jeans and flashy high-heeled shoes. She was pencil thin but had a softness that seemed to come from her warm doe eyes. The kids warmed up to her hugs and kisses immediately. Carmen nattered on in all kinds of different languages to the children. "Frio, muy frio," she called, reaching for sweaters. There were six or eight Spanish-speaking children, five Haitians who spoke French, several small black children, and one Anglo. Every single little girl wore brightly colored ribbons, or clips, or a headband in her hair. Melissa, Charlene, Yajaira, Sarah, Michelle, Elizabeth, Annette, Jeannette. A few were in frilly socks, patent-leather party shoes, and ruffled dresses. The rest, and most of the boys, were in more practical clothes. A few had matching shorts and shirts, but most wore a more grab-bag assortment of hand-me-downs and well-worn things.

The children were still sitting in their breakfast seats at the small tables as the group time began. Joanie conducted a very structured session. Like the other two care givers at Pilgrim, Joanie seemed to be a naturally tender and loving person. An observer could quickly sense the affection all three had for the children, and vice versa. But the women seemed not to capitalize on this very special gift and instead tried to conduct a more formal program — as teachers would — in a way that they probably thought befitted a day care center. The women were at their best during the informal moments, at lunch, on the playground, at nap time. They were weakest during these "lesson" times.

There was nothing very exciting about this morning's lesson. Joanie asked the children, "Is there anything different today?" It was quiet for a minute until one shouted out, "Summer!"

No. "Patricia!" another called out. Doreen, the other teacher, prompted: "Someone new, someone visiting." A little girl finally looked at me and got the idea. "She wants to visit," she said. "Very good, she wants to visit."

The children were instructed to "show off" on my behalf. They started singing nineteen rounds of "Mrs. Perky Bird" (or perhaps it was Mrs. Turkey Bird; each child seemed to have his or her own lyrics): "My name is Mrs. Perky Bird, Perky Bird, Perky Bird. My name is Mrs. Perky Bird. Who are you?" Schiller! or Pierre! or Stephen! or Carolyn! Rakiya! Frantz! They continued with a multilingual concert of "Buenos Dias," "One Little Bird," and "Frère Jacques." Finally, the teacher sensed the lag and got ready to switch routines. Time for a little exercise. Everyone stood up beside his or her chair for a little stretching. Arms up and down, breathe in, breathe out.

It was beginning to seem like a long morning to me. I'd been sitting on one chair in the cold basement for about an hour and a half now. The children, having been seated when I arrived, had been here far longer. I found my mind wandering to the sunny outdoors and felt bad to be cooped up with these familiar routines on the first great day in a long time.

Doggedly, the teacher started again, determined to get in some verbal exchange with the whole group. She sat them down and tried to interest them in a conversation about someone's weekend visit to a farm. But the age span was too great, there were three-, four-, and five-year-olds here, and only a few of them were keeping up with the impromptu lesson on farms. A policeman walked in on what must have been his regular rounds. There were lots of passers-through in this busy place, and all the children turned their heads in each visitor's direction. "Hi, policeman. Hi, Joe! Hi, Joe!" several children shouted. The teachers were working very hard to keep the children engaged, but this diversion was too much for them.

Finally (it had seemed like an eternity), the teachers broke the children up into three smaller groups and led them into their own classrooms. I followed Carmen and her four- to five-year-olds into their tiny cell. It was a very small room, maybe only ten feet by ten feet. There were just a handful of small chairs in the room, some books on the shelves, a calendar and a few other things hanging on the wall. It felt like a large closet. Before getting down to business, Carmen had to tape up a dangerous-looking splinter that was poking out of one of the small chairs. For ten long minutes, she led them through the date and the days of the week. Letter by letter, each child spelled out the words as she pointed to them. M-O-N-D-A-Y. Over and over again. The room was so drab and the lesson was so drab that I was very grateful when the teachers finally decided they could abandon the daily routines and lessons and go outside to enjoy some sunshine. On our way out, a little boy came over to me and cupped his hands over my ear. "I saw a monster eat a lady," he whispered. Two more children watched him intently and then inched over to tell me their secrets. "My mother is ugly," said one. "I have a boyfriend. His name is Mark," said a third.

We all came up from the basement to a gloriously sunny day. The parking lot of the church also served as the day care center's playground. It was a large, blacktopped area surrounded by a hurricane fence that ran right along the sidewalk of busy Columbia Road. At the back end were two small, terraced, grassy areas. There were a few benches on one level and that was all.

But out here, I began to see what was special about this center. The care givers were doing something I hadn't seen in most other centers I had visited. They weren't using this outdoor play-time as a break from the kids; they weren't "watching" the children. They were playing with them. They played in a way adults rarely do, with a kind of pleasure that made me wonder who was having more fun, the adults or their charges.

Several little girls were playing jump-rope games, and two of the teachers huffed and puffed, laughing, along. A few of the boys were playing with a large rubber ball, helped by a young man from the church whom they all knew. Several children discovered there were ladybugs up in the grassy areas, and soon they all clambered up to start a collection.

About this time, Joanie decided to take a break to walk down to the drugstore to buy some soda for the other adults. I accompanied her for a chat along the way, and we talked about how she got into this line of work.

"My husband died ten years ago," she said. "I worked in maintenance at the church and worked at the five and dime before that. But I always wanted to get into child care." When an opening came up at the center, she went after it. She took a few required courses in child-related topics. That was eight years ago, and she's been here ever since. At the time we talked, Joanie was fifty-two years old. "It's kind of hard," she said, "but I love it." Part of what's important to Joanie is the community atmosphere of working at Pilgrim. She lives on the street just behind the church; she nodded her greetings to handfuls of people as we walked past the small stores, and she joked with the counter clerks at the drugstore. "I still work here three evenings a week," she told me.

Times were tough all around at Pilgrim Day Care Center, but the teachers were not really complaining. They are paid about the average wage for day care workers in the Boston area. That isn't a lot, but "it's a job," they seemed to say. The Department of Health and Human Services used to sponsor twenty children and four teachers at this center, but funds have been cut back to sponsor only sixteen children and three teachers. The USDA has cut its food subsidies by 25 per cent, but there is still food for everyone. The teachers, like the Pilgrim center itself, are the humble survivors.

It took all the theories of experienced child care professionals, heavy financial backing, and several years of operation to come up with a day care center as good as Children's Village in Cambridge, Massachusetts. The children march into their center in the mornings side by side with career professionals going to their jobs in the contemporary glass and brick building owned by Abt Associates, a research and consulting firm. Driving into the Abt parking lot, set perpendicular to the street and somewhat hidden, makes you feel immediately as though you're entering a special kind of place, off the beaten track of noisy traffic and busy streets. Books from in-house authors are on display next to the reception area. Lovely outdoor areas are visible through the large glass windows. Well into the interior of the building is a large cafeteria that opens onto an outdoor court-yard.

Clark Abt, president of Abt Associates, began the Children's Village day care center in 1972, in large part because he was the father of two preschool-age children. It started as a for-profit venture but soon proved to turn no profit and was changed into a tax-exempt operation.

The center occupies the end of a wing of the building and opens out on two sides to an enormous, inviting, and splendidly equipped playground — a heaven on earth for preschoolers. The center no longer enjoys the grand patronage it did in its early years: Clark Abt's children have gone off to school, and Abt Associates has come on the tougher economic times familiar to the soft-money consulting industry. Children's Village is now simply a renter of space from Abt Associates, more or less like the other groups who occupy the buildings. They do pay a little less than the other renters but, the director told me, their rent was tripled in January of 1983. It's strictly business now. The administrators of the center don't feel in a strong position to lobby for favors; they feel as though they're living under some cloud of "Oh, that's just a day care center" now.

Sixty-five children were enrolled at the Children's Village when I visited. Nineteen adults cared for them. The waiting list is impressive; some parents inquire about places for their children before the children are even born. The director told me of one family whose name came to the top of the list when their child was just a newborn. So eager were they to secure a place that they pressed the director to let them pay three months' tuition (about $2,000) so that their baby could have the spot when he reached the requisite starting age of three months. "This is ridiculous," said the director. "It's totally unethical to me." She wouldn't let them do it.

The teaching staff is carefully chosen and assembled in a delicate balance. There is a team-teaching effort in each class, not the usual formula of head teacher plus assistants found in most centers. Here, the staff is hired with a variety of strengths in mind. "We don't insist on impeccable backgrounds," the director told me. She said that she looks for a combination: someone good at bureaucracy, someone who may have a high school diploma but be great with kids, someone who's expertly trained and strong on child development. The staff is paid an average of $7.25 per hour, very high for the field. (Kinder-Care, for example, was involved in a lengthy arbitration over wages in 1983, at which time its assistant room supervisors were making $3.68 an hour and room supervisors were making $4.03 an hour.) They work only six-hour stretches to avoid burnout.

Families pay mightily for the privilege of sending their youngsters to Children's Village. Infants cost $153 per week. Toddlers (fifteen to twenty-five months), "sprouts" (twenty-five to thirty-six months), and preschoolers (three to five years) pay on a decreasing scale, down to $91 per week for the oldest ones. One mother who was in the office signing up her second child, a newborn, told me that after her child care costs, she cleared $4 a week on her paycheck.

Obviously, most of the children here come from well-to-do families. (Only six children are subsidized by the government's Title XX funds; the center's fund raisers supply another $12,000 in scholarship money.) In addition to the hefty fees, parents are expected to contribute an hour of their time each week to the center, serving as chaperons on field trips or as classroom helpers (which the center encourages). Failing to put in your hour means you're dunned an extra $6. That sum may be a small disincentive to a lawyer billing his time at fifteen times that rate, but the director says nearly all the parents participate anyway. "They want to be involved. They want to know a lot about their kids . . . 99 per cent of them are perfect families. They've read their Berry Brazelton."

Most early childhood educators agree that parental involvement in a child's life away from home is critical. But not all parents or day care workers are as aware of this as the parents and staff at Children's Village. At a conference I attended for educators in 1983, one day care staffer after another told her tales of trying to encourage parental involvement with the center, trying to open lines of communication between parents and centers. "Every day when the father picked up his child, I had

to thrust myself between the child and the door, walk back-
wards down the sidewalk in front of him, just to tell him a few
things, get a few words in about how his child did that day,"
one said. Her tale is not atypical. Researchers studying one uni-
versity-based day care center found that parents spent an average of 7.4 minutes per day in the center. Some 10 per cent of
them did not even enter with their children in the morning.

On the bright June morning when I visited Children's Village,
it seemed that most of the center's children and teachers were
out on the playground. It was a large L-shaped area, so big that
all kinds of activity could be going on in the sandbox in one
corner, unbeknown to others playing under the trees in another
corner or up on the climbing equipment in a third. At one point,
I watched a mother try to extricate herself from a screaming
toddler, an event that usually piques the curiosity of the other
children (perhaps they later exchange pointers on how to entrap
Mom or Dad). She was able to manage her departure, despite
the noise involved, in a place where no one noticed it.

There were tractor-size tires for the children to climb on, two
enormous slides, a big fortlike place for them to hide in and
climb on, and getaways under the trees. The children seemed to
roam on a looser tether here than I had seen in any other center.
One tiny child spent a good twenty minutes feeding small stones
into an opening in one of the huge tires. A couple of the older
ones crawled into a concrete construction cylinder and were
lying almost upside down, knees crossed, chatting away like old-
timers passing the time of day. Several others wandered around
carrying bats or yard tools. The teachers also wandered about,
or stopped to sit or stand in small clusters, chatting among
themselves.

There were so many adults that sometimes they seemed to
outnumber the children. The care givers here, at least on the
playground and during the informal times, seemed to act more
like mothers do with their children than I had seen at other
centers, where they clearly were like teachers with their students. These adults didn't necessarily impose themselves into the
middle of a group of children or organize their playtime for
them, but they kept watch, and when a child needed help or

attention, they were there immediately. I watched one woman gurgling and making funny faces for fifteen minutes to a delighted chubby-cheeked infant in a walker. Another time, a young care giver I was talking with broke off in mid-sentence to run after a little troublemaker who had bothered a couple of children one too many times.

The three- to four-year-olds' room was one of the nicest in the center. Its huge windows looked out onto the sandbox, and the outside door led right to it. There was a gathering area at one end, a few tables and their chairs at another, several nooks and crannies for curling up to look at books or play make-believe. Large shelving units brimmed with collections of magazines, paints, cans, and trays full of all the snippings and trappings of preschool artwork. A funny five-foot-long poster, looking like so many preschoolers had tromped with painted bare feet along it, hung on the wall. The science table was more picked over than in many centers, where it often sat, looking untouched, through a whole season of nature. The art that hung from the ceiling or was taped to the walls here wasn't as beautiful or precise as that I saw in some other centers. The reason, it seemed obvious, was that the children actually did more of it themselves. Here there were butterflies and spiders hanging from the ceiling, string paintings, ladybugs, and an insect and flower poster. At snack time, the children ate from personalized place mats they had made themselves.

Today the young class was continuing its unit on insects. It was spider day. A young, pregnant teacher, the most gregarious of the three in this classroom, gathered all the children into a circle and read a book about spiders. They sang "Itsy Bitsy Spider" and had a lesson on how spiders catch flies. Then the brave ones among them came up one by one to have a conversation with a scary-looking paper spider. It looked like fun. And it clearly reflected the time and organization that had gone into the day's activities. (The staff meets regularly a few times a week to plan their activities and portion out the work, which makes for smooth, engaging, enjoyable mornings such as the one I was seeing.) While the spider lesson was going on, an older woman sat nearby, ready to pick up and help out any child who might lose his attention or cause some small disturbance for the others. The lesson was too interesting today for that to happen.

During the lesson, the third teacher prepared the children's snack. Today it was crackers, milk, and fresh cantaloupe. The children came to the table, sought out their places according to their individualized place mats, and sat down. They sang a little song, "Put your finger on your chin, and now you may begin," and began eating. They passed the milk in its small pitcher and poured it themselves. There was no long wait for the food to appear, as I had seen at many other snack times. There wasn't time to hang around and get into trouble, a little push here, a pinch there. While they were eating, I studied the messages and notes on the wall. They were mostly from the month of May, which was just barely past: "5/11: Julia and Jody have gum up on the shelf for when moms come to pick up"; "5/11: JoEllen will pick Tony up at 11:00"; "5/18: Danny not to sleep more than one hour." (The last one, any parent will recognize, means that Danny has reached the stage where he gets so tired during the day that he still needs his nap, but then he sleeps so hard and long that he'll be up half the night.)

There are infants from three to fifteen months old at Children's Village. Ten of them share a staff of four. As at most centers, the babies here don't keep to any regular schedule, except for feeding. When I went visiting them, not too much was going on. Most were asleep. Those who were awake were eating in their little dining room. Their quarters were attractive — a comfy crawling area, a nice big playground to share. Since there were so many caretakers, these babies were able to get around more than most in day care. They went visiting the older children's rooms sometimes, and even got to go outdoors for an occasional walk, one by one with a caretaker, to the nearby store for errands.

This, like the Austin Community Nursery Schools, was day care the way it should be.

❧ 8 ❧

The Effects of Day Care

MY OBSERVATIONS of day care centers are necessarily unscientific and incomplete. I visited enough centers to feel that I had sampled the broad range, seen the good and the bad. But can their effect and quality be assessed in more than an anecdotal way? The answer is a qualified yes. Scientists and researchers have asked the same questions that parents ask themselves. What is day care doing to my child? Is it helping or hurting? How can good day care be distinguished from merely adequate or bad day care?

Even the leading voices in the field agree that all research on day care suffers from some awkward limitations. Most of the center-based studies have been conducted at high-quality or better-than-average centers (such as ACNS or Children's Village) that do not represent day care at large. Much of the research has been conducted in clinical, testlike surroundings rather than in more casual and representative real-life settings. Control groups may be as closely matched as possible, but of course it's never possible to "control" for the many factors besides day care that make one child different from another. The experimenters' measures of adjustment, achievement, and development are necessarily subjective. The research is conducted almost exclusively in day care centers (rather than family homes or at home with housekeepers or nannies), where less than 10 per cent of children in child care spend their time. The field is so new that longitudinal studies will have to wait until the children grow up. Et cetera.

By its very nature, the kind of research that aspires to assess how one small part of a human being's life affects the rest of his personality and development is less precise and definitive than, say, research into molecular structure or plant hybridization. As every parent knows, certain children are the way they are from their first moments of life; as everyone, parent or not, understands, luck and random occurrence can change the most carefully thought-out plans. How, then, can anyone convincingly say that years in a day care center have had this or that effect on a child's performance in school or satisfaction in life?

So far, most analysts have stuck with a sensible "it depends" when describing the effect of day care. It depends on the personality of the child and on the quality of the child care situation. It depends on how much caretakers talk with the children and on the differences between what the child would be getting from his parents and what he gets from his caretakers. It may be different for boys and girls. It depends statistically on such things as the parents' income, their race and education, and the number of parents living at home. It depends on other less quantifiable things: how much a working mother likes her job, how unhappy she would be if she were at home instead.

Even with all these restrictions and caveats, the volumes of studies have so far led to a conclusion, albeit a careful and uninspired one. According to the researchers, time spent in a good-quality day care center seems to have no significant effect on a child's development, socially, intellectually, emotionally, or physically, compared to the time spent at home.

This evenhanded, apparently moderate statement conceals, however, some highly disputed opinions. It is like the man with one hand in a pot of boiling water and the other in the freezer; he knows he should feel comfortable "on average," but still is in some distress. Some people claim that center care does not seem to disrupt the emotional bond of a child to his or her mother; others insist that the day care phenomenon is simply too new to permit conclusions about the children's emotions, including the effects on them when they become adults. Children in day care centers usually spend more time "interacting" with their peers — but this means negative interaction (fighting) as well as positive. Children who spend their days in day care centers are often described in research findings as being more "aggressive" than children who spend that time at home, although some researchers point out that this may be a temporary phenomenon and may not be undesirable, at that. Intellectual skills, like social skills, often appear accelerated in children from day care centers. But this seems to even out in the first few years at elementary school.

The uncertain and tentative nature of the finding that good-quality day care does not adversely affect a child's development somehow gets lost in most press reports. For example, consider the way that Judy Mann, a columnist for the *Washington Post*, described one of the recent day care studies:

> The National Institute of Education has undertaken two major reviews of the research it is sponsoring and reached a conclusion that ought to warm the heart of working mothers: Their children do as well in school as the children of mothers who stay at home.
>
> In fact, the research is showing that the children of working mothers who are professionals, low-income, or black do better in school than their peers whose mothers stay at home.

In Mann's version, the findings about day care were so unambiguously upbeat and positive that they practically amounted to an endorsement of two-career families. Anyone who knew only as much about the findings as Judy Mann reported — which covers nearly all of her readers — would naturally agree with the reasonable-sounding idea that these studies ought to "warm the heart of working mothers." But what about the studies themselves? Is that actually what they say? Anyone who compares the scientific findings (collected in *Families That Work: Children in a Changing World*, directed by the National Research Council in 1982) with Mann's newspaper summary cannot help but notice the differences.

Technically, the studies support many of Mann's claims, in the sense that specific sentences can be picked out to agree with her assertions. In one of its general conclusions, a chapter called "The Influence of Parents' Work on Children's School Achievement" states that "studies of maternal employment have demonstrated, with very few exceptions, that on achievement, the children of working mothers differ very little from the children of non-working mothers."

But the overall tone of the report is much different from the chipper "warm the hearts" impression left by the newspaper column. Immediately after the sentence just quoted, the author of that chapter, Barbara Heyns of the Center for Applied Social Science Research at New York University, adds: "It behooves any serious scholar reviewing the literature to approach the research with a measure of skepticism." The reason for this skepticism, she states, is the vast sea of unknowns and unknowables that surround research into children's performance. The children are still young, and the studies are not exhaustive; it is hard to control for such variables as divorce and other sorts of stress. "A good deal of the literature that attempts to trace the effects of mothers' working on children lacks a cogent theoretical focus or a realistic image of family life."

After a dozen more pages examining studies and their limitations, Heyns concludes:

> One major difficulty with the literature on maternal employment is the definition of work. At best, the connection between employment status and time spent working is ambiguous. Little attention is paid [in the studies] to the duration of work, its proximity to home, or the time involved. The definitions adopted are arbitrary and lack theoretical specificity; few studies consider the number of hours worked as more than a classification device. No study has dealt adequately with the diversity of employment patterns prevalent among mothers during the course of the family life cycle [that is, mothers who work only a little when their children are very young, and gradually increase as the children go to school]. The possibility that mothers may withdraw from active participation in the la-

bor force as a consequence of the behavior or performance
of their children seems not to have been considered [that
is, the mothers whose children *were* having trouble already
decided to quit]."

After a fair reading of this report, most people would agree
that its main factual finding was the one Judy Mann featured —
that there is no hard proof that a mother's employment affects
the child's performance in school. But no one could read more
than a headline summary of these hedged, qualified conclusions
and see anything in them to warm anyone's heart.

I don't mean to pick on one columnist, and it must be pointed
out that Judy Mann has also written about conflicting reports.
Newspaper reporters and columnists have to write to daily
deadlines, which often makes it impossible for them to read the
research reports thoroughly. The reason I mention Mann's column is that it is so typical of the way research about day care
reaches the public. However thoroughly the researchers may
hedge their conclusions to reflect the uncertainties of experimentation and reporting, somewhere along the road from re-
searcher's report to public opinion, the sense of caution is lost.
The limits of the subject group, the shortcomings of the mea-
surements, the conditions under which the study was done —
all of which were disclosed by the researchers — are usually
overlooked. The qualifications of the findings ("in lower-income
families," "in girls," "in children whose mothers worked full-
time," "in blacks") are skimmed over. Bolder, more general, and
less accurate statements evolve and soon begin to take on a life
of their own.

There is a tremendous market for this kind of simple reassurance. As parents we often look to science for answers to questions that are otherwise impossible to answer, including, "What
will happen to my children if I work?" We seek encouragement
about the path we have chosen: "See, it's better for me to be at
home; I'm really helping my kids become well adjusted." We
look for justifications: "Research proves it! I knew I'd be a much
better mother to my child if I didn't have to be at home with
her all day long." We build our defenses: "As a working mother,

I spend as much time with my child as a mother who doesn't work."

The research isn't really supposed to be used to resolve our insecurities, assuage our guilt, direct our decisions. It can't. We're not "most parents"; we're not "average" families; we don't have children "in general." We come with all the complications of our lives that defy the application of these studies as literal truths. The little boy I watched that day at Li'l Cowpokes Child Care Center was so outgoing, so independent, that he seemed to be thriving and blossoming. He could demand attention and go far to shape the world around him in the form he preferred, even at a large group center. I don't know what his family situation was like, and what he gave up in not being with his parents, but I could guess that for him, this ordinary day care center was fine. He was thriving, despite research that says that "most" children do better in small groups and with more than the attention of one caretaker for every twenty-seven children. But the little girl who spent her morning whimpering and shying away from all contact was shriveling in the same environment. For her, you could point to those same statistics as explanation for her difficulties.

The history of one statistic about day care illustrates the contortions through which "scientific findings" have been put. This piece of information, which almost everyone who has read about the subject has encountered at least once, is usually stated thus: "Research shows that working mothers spend as much time with their children as nonworking mothers."

I first paid attention to this assertion because it seemed so contrary to the lesson of my daily life and because having more time to spend with my children was precisely the reason I left full-time work. Since then, I have seen it turn up in most journalistic accounts of child care, from newspaper stories to essays in *Working Mother* magazine. Judy Mann, for example, told her readers in 1983 that "working mothers, according to the studies, spend almost as much time caring for their children as nonworking mothers." The 1984 Home and School Institute's conference, entitled "Working Parents and Achieving Children," presented an eight-page review of "Research Findings on Working Mothers." Question 4 and its answer read: "Do working mothers spend less time with their children? No: . . . The working mother who is 'time poor' seems to work harder at maintaining some level of activity involving child and spouse, eliminating personal leisure time instead."

Where did this "fact" come from? How did it evolve? Is it true?

The notion apparently had its birth in 1982 with the publication of the National Research Council's oft-cited report, *Families That Work: Children in a Changing World*. In the chapter referred to earlier, "The Influence of Parents' Work on Children's School Achievement," Barbara Heyns wrote, "Studies of time use suggest that working mothers spend almost as much time caring for their children as do nonworking mothers."

To support this contention, Heyns cited the handful of existing studies of how parents use their time, winding up with the then-most-recent study, by some veteran researchers. She said the most recent data from family time budgets, summarized by J. H. Pleck and M. Rustad for the Center for Research on Women at Wellesley College, suggest that "in 1975–76 nonworking wives with at least one child under age 5 spent about 6.5 more hours per week in child care than employed wives. Among wives with children ages 6 to 17, employed wives spent 4.5 fewer hours per week in child care. If one controlled for the number of children as well as their ages, the discrepancy between working and nonworking mothers would decline further."

The first point to note is that the principal study on this subject concluded that there indeed *was* a difference in the amount of time working and nonworking mothers spent with their children. The difference may not seem to be enormous in absolute terms — about an hour a day for those with younger children and forty minutes a day for those with older children — but since the researchers asserted that *non*working mothers spent only a little more than two hours a day caring for their children, the working mothers' total was about 50 per cent less than that of nonworking mothers. In itself, this would hardly seem to support the "almost as much time" conclusion. But as it turns out, even these hourly measures bear little connection to the world in which parents and children actually live.

What about those 6.5- and 4.5-hour differences? How were they calculated? The researchers who conducted the study did not observe mothers as they dealt with their children. Instead, they asked each mother to keep a diary of how she spent her time. Each "act" was coded by researchers into one of ninety-six different categories. These were then aggregated into a smaller number of summary categories, including "basic and other housework," "basic and other child care," "paid work," and "sleep."

The important point to notice here is how strictly child care was defined in the study. You could count minutes or hours in that category only if you were taking care of children and not doing anything else. As one of the researchers explained about the study afterward, "The 'primary child care' measure utilized here . . . is quite restrictive in its definition: [it refers to] activities codable as caring for, playing with, or helping children with homework in respondents' initial, unprobed descriptions of the behavior, and excluding many other adult activities in which children were recorded as present."

To be entirely clear on this point, let me reemphasize what the researchers measured. For the purposes of this study, the only time that counted as time spent with a child was all-out, undisturbed, down-on-the-floor-with-the-blocks time, while every other real-life activity, such as going with a child to the grocery store, doing the laundry, walking the dog, or making dinner, did not count. Most parents know that just the opposite is true. The concentrated playtimes are important and valuable, but the hundred other unplanned moments in the day can be even more so, just as in a marriage or friendship. My husband and I read about history and music and science with our children (time that "counts"), but we also talk with them while in the car, in the yard, or around the stove (time that does not count). It is hard to tell which of these kinds of contacts has been more important to the children's development or in our sense of a bond with them. I would hate to give up either of them. But it is only by totally ruling out the informal moments spent with a child that the researchers were able to come to their conclusion that the nonworking mothers spent 2.16 hours per day "caring" for their children versus 1.2 hours a day for mothers who worked.

The "almost as much time" illusion is only one illustration of the ambiguous nature of research on child care and the distortions in its presentation in the press. In another study, conducted in 1977 by the same Institute for Social Research at the University of Michigan that sponsored the 1975–76 time-use study, respondents didn't keep diaries but instead estimated the amount of time they spent on different activities, for example, "home chores" and "paid work." This time, the results were dramatically different. Joseph Pleck reported that "respondents' estimates of their child care are 310 to 654 per cent higher" than those of merely two years before. The differences were not in the parents' behavior but in the researchers' assumptions — specifically, in their definition of "child care": "The 1977 [study's] language ('taking care of or doing things with your children' when the youngest child was under ten, and simply 'doing things with your children' when the youngest was over ten) undoubtedly included many activities excluded by the more restrictive definitions used with the [1975–76 time-use study]."

Even the more recent measures of "time spent with children" bear scant resemblance to the real world of parents and children. Perhaps the clearest illustration is a study conducted in 1981. A panel survey of "Time Allocation in American Households" reported on the average number of minutes parents spent in "educationally related" child activities. Here the researchers divided the parents' activities with children into "conversing," "teaching," "playing," and "reading." The researchers reported that during the week, nonworking mothers spent seven minutes each day teaching their children, six minutes a day playing with them, thirteen minutes a day conversing, and one minute a day reading to them. Working mothers, by contrast, spent four minutes a day teaching, two minutes a day playing, four minutes conversing, and one minute reading. What's a difference of fifteen minutes a day — especially if it means career fulfillment and a second income?

I don't know whether to laugh or cry about such "research." Thirteen minutes a day in "educational conversation"! What possible connection does this have to the afternoons I spent with my three-year-old, as we went together through our round of activities, one or the other of us talking all the time? How can talking about teddy bears, saying no to sugared cereals in the aisles of grocery stores, and explaining what the telephone repairman is doing up on the pole be any less important or "educational" than counting, singing the alphabet song, reciting the days of the week, or even reading books? To a child, real life, daily life, is educational in its every detail.

My daily life — not theories, but the life I've lived — makes it impossible for me to believe that most of my time with my children can be categorized and evaluated in any of these ridiculous ways. My common sense tells me that while I was working eight hours a day, I had less time to spend with my sons, and now that I'm home for the majority of their day, I have far more. The difference is not a full eight hours a day, but it is certainly a good portion of it. The time I spend devoting full attention exclusively to them is of a different nature from the time we spend together, rushed and hurried, trying to get our day's necessary demands accomplished. But I'm not at all ready to count even these moments out of the grander scheme of raising children.

9

Day Care: The Demand

WE COME NOW to what I think of as the most difficult aspect of day care, the need to reconcile two basically contradictory ideas.

On the one hand, there are the obvious problems of day care, which I have tried to describe in the preceding pages. The greatest reassurance that researchers can offer about day care is that they have no clear evidence that it does children harm. This is modest comfort at best. The caveat that accompanies these findings — "provided that children are in good-quality care" — leaves me chilled. The centers I saw offering "good-quality care" were rare. The more typical centers were mediocre or bad. There were days when I cried for the children I had seen, in anger at the way they were treated and sorrow for the way they would spend their childhoods. It should be clear from what I have said so far that I think most children are better off when their parents can care for them and that parents should try harder to make this possible.

On the other hand, there is reality. We don't have enough places for all the children who now need day care, and their numbers are sure to grow. The trend toward two-career families shows no sign of weakening. As the baby boom generation continues to have its own children, it is predicted that the population of children under six years of age will rise by about 20 per cent, from 19 million in 1980 to 23 million in 1990. While arguments about the effects of day care might alter some individual decisions, more women will inevitably continue to enter the work force, including the mothers of these young children. In 1980, there were 7.5 million children under six years of age with mothers in the work force. By 1990, there will probably be more than 10 million. Therefore, it is irresponsible to talk about a world in which day care does not play an important part. It is also unfair, because it writes off the welfare of the many children who are, and will be, in day care centers. Anyone who cares about children should also care about what goes on inside those centers.

The inescapable importance of day care is the reason I will now discuss subjects that may seem at odds with what has gone before — namely, ways of improving day care. Even for those who believe, as I do, that fewer children should be in day care centers, it is important to consider the reasons that many centers are now inadequate and the specific steps that can be taken to make them better. It might seem neater and more emotionally satisfying to take a hard-line stance — children should be with their parents, so we shouldn't even talk about improving day care — but that kind of absolutist thinking has helped create the present mess. The costs of inadequate day care, let me emphasize once again, are paid not by the adults who come up with tidy political formulations but by those boys and girls who pass much of their childhoods in these centers. In the sections that follow, I will examine the economic and political forces that have made day care what it is today and consider the policies that might make better day care more broadly available.

To understand the economic environment in which day care operates, we have to look at both the demand and the supply sides of the transaction. The growing demand for day care from families in which both parents work is often thought to be a totally uninteresting issue, since its explanation seems so obvious. According to the standard interpretation, there is no mystery about why so many more women are working. They *have to work*, if they hope to make ends meet:

- "Eighty per cent of women have to work," according to Sandra Porter of the National Commission on Working Women. She has said that anyone who shrinks from this fact is "perpetuating a myth of choice."
- Elinor Guggenheimer of the Council for Senior Citizens says that 96 per cent of women work at low salaries or wages as sole earners in the family or for an important second income.
- "Seventy-five per cent of the women who work listed money as a major reason for their working," according to a Gallup Survey for the White House Conference on Families in 1980.

While the stated percentages and proportions may vary, the conclusion is the same: The "choice" between working and not working is like the choice between a Mercedes and a Cadillac, an almost frivolous decision that most people will never be fortunate enough to have to make.

For many women (and men), this description of the "choice" to work is obviously correct. But is it an accurate portrayal of the circumstances in which *most* women make their decision? It seems to me that the available statistics about mothers who work are far more complicated, and their implications far more ambiguous, than we usually are told. The facts and figures about working mothers underscore what common sense should already have told us: that the "need" to work varies enormously from person to person and often depends less on straightforward economic pressures than on more individual definitions of success, family roles and obligations, and material desires. Let us examine some recent statistics, because they may help explain where the popular conception of "having to work" is accurate and where it misses the point.

To begin, slightly more than half of all adult women work. As of 1983, 49 million women, or 53 per cent of all women sixteen years of age and older, were in America's labor force.*

---

* "Labor force participation" rates include not just full-time workers, nor even just full- and part-time workers, but also those who are "unemployed," in the government's technical sense of unemployment, which means that someone has registered with the state labor offices seeking work but hasn't

Of those, 19.5 million working women were mothers of children under eighteen years of age. (Unless otherwise noted, all references in this section to "children" refer to children under the age of eighteen.) They represented 60 per cent of all mothers.

The younger her children, the less likely a woman is to work. Sixty-eight per cent of women with children aged six to seventeen are working, versus 59 per cent of women with children aged three to five and 48 per cent of women with children under three years of age. More than half the women with children under three, then, do not work. But it is women with the youngest children who are heading back into the work force at the highest rate. Between 1947 and 1980, there was a fourfold increase in the percentage of mothers of preschool children in the labor force. In just five years, from 1977 to 1982, the percentage increased by almost 8 per cent, from 40.6 to 48.2 per cent.

Most discussions of working mothers divide women into two clear categories: those who work and those who do not. But these categories are not necessarily as rigidly separated as some statistics would indicate. Jobs can be part-time, full-time, or more than full-time. They can be year-round or seasonal. These — and other variables, like length of commute to work and whether or not parents can stagger work schedules — often determine the real issue here: how much time working parents have to spend with their children.

Many of these distinctions cannot be determined from published statistics, but the single most important one — the number of hours spent on the job — can, at least to some degree. The U.S. Department of Labor regularly gathers and publishes statistics about part-time versus full-time work. Its definition of "part-time" covers a wide variety of situations:

> A person is classified as having worked at part-time jobs
> during the preceding calendar year if he worked at civilian

found it. Many welfare programs require individuals to register as looking for work in order to get benefits. They are thereby included in the "labor force participation" statistics, even if the individuals never hold a job and do not wish to.

jobs which provided less than 35 hours of work per week in a majority of the weeks in which he worked during the year. He is classified as having worked at full-time jobs if he worked 35 hours or more per week during a majority of the weeks which he worked. . . . A year-round full-time worker is one who worked primarily at full-time civilian jobs for 50 weeks or more during the preceding calendar year.

In other words, the Labor Department's "part-time" category includes everyone from the auto worker who was laid off for half the year and took a job on the side, to the young mother who took on a salesclerk's job for a month before Christmas to earn extra money for the family, to the woman who works five hours a day, five days a week, fifty-two weeks a year, as a lawyer or librarian or laundress. Despite the broad reach of the "part-time" category, however, the Labor Department's data point to some conclusions and trends. Just as women with younger children are less likely to work at all than women with older children, among those who do work, the ones with younger children are more likely to have part-time instead of full-time jobs. The proportion of all working mothers who work part-time is 29 per cent. But 34 per cent of those with the youngest children (under age three) work part-time, as do 28 per cent of those with children aged three to five, as opposed to only 27 per cent of those with school-age children. What these figures suggest is that working mothers try to accommodate the higher demands of younger children by shifting into part-time jobs.

So, while the statistics reveal that women are undoubtedly more likely to work than they have ever been before, and while women with the very youngest children are returning to work at a faster rate than anyone else, things are not as clear and simple as they are often made to appear. Instead of rushing into full-time jobs, mothers who reenter the work force are trying to strike some compromise between children and work. More than one-fourth of all working mothers work part-time, and of mothers with very young children, nearly two-thirds either do not work at all or hold only part-time jobs. As their children grow older, to preschool age and then on through their school years (when they're out of the house much of the day), more mothers begin to work, and they work longer hours.

The first thing to be said about women who "have to work," then, is that most women find ways to stay home when their children are little. Remember, about half the women in this country with very young children do not work at all. This suggests that the age of their children is a vital factor in women's decisions about working. It is an economic factor to the extent that child care costs matter, but it is surely a cultural, emotional, and even physical one as well.

The complex set of imperatives behind women's decisions about work — the cultural ones about children, the personal ones about desire, the professional ones about timing — often seem dwarfed by the single economic imperative that families need a working mother's income.

There are two broad categories of women who, according to most analyses, "have to work." One consists of women without husbands and the other of women whose husbands earn too little to support a decent standard of living. To have a "choice" about work, you presumably must have a spouse whose income is sufficient.

The National Commission on Working Women says that 26 per cent of the women in the work force have never married, and another 19 per cent are now widowed, divorced, or separated, for a total of 45 per cent of all working women. These 22 million women with no spouse would seem to have no alternative but to support themselves. From a common-sense point of view, it appears obvious that nearly all of them need to work and have no wide latitude of choice about the matter. Yet the evidence suggests that their situation is more complicated than is usually imagined.

Five million of these single women have a total of 10 million children. Of single mothers with children six to seventeen years of age, 77 per cent are in the work force, compared to 65 per cent of comparable women living with their spouses. Interestingly, the difference between single and married mothers almost disappears for those with younger children. Of single mothers with children under the age of six, 53 per cent are in the work force, compared to 52 per cent of those with husbands present. This significant statistic — 47 per cent of single mothers with young children do not work — suggests that even under the strongest economic pressures, many women are deciding not to work.

The pattern of part-time versus full-time work is also different for single mothers. Single mothers work longer hours than do married mothers. Of the single mothers with school-age children who work, 82 per cent do so full-time, compared with 70 per cent of mothers with husbands present. Of single working mothers with children under six, 77 per cent work full-time, compared to 65 per cent of comparable married mothers.

Unemployment rates for single women with dependent children are two to three times higher than those for other women. In 1983, for instance, single mothers with children six to seventeen years old had a 12 per cent unemployment rate; those with children under six, 22 per cent; and those with children under three, 28 per cent. The comparable rates for mothers with a spouse present were much lower: those with children six to seventeen, 5 per cent unemployment rate; with children under six, 9 per cent; with children under three, 9 per cent.

Although many things seem clear about the plight of the single mother, even the instances of women with no choice but to support themselves illustrate how hard it is to use aggregate statistics to draw a direct connection between economic pressures and personal decisions. Everyone knows that single mothers must work, and in fact two-thirds of them do. But that means one-third of them do not. They are not working full-time, or part-time, or even seeking work. That is, for every two single mothers who are working or seeking work, there is one other member of this category that absolutely "must work" who is not. They are, presumably, making it some other way — although evidence suggests they are not making it very well at all.*

---

* As of 1982, a female-headed household with one child had a median income of $11,170 per year, compared to $27,742 for a married couple with one

The poorest single women are those with the youngest children. There are 2.8 million children under six who live with their single mothers. The median income in those households is between $5,000 and $6,000 per year. The Bureau of the Census lists the poverty level for a family of two at $6,700. This compares to a median income of $23,000 per year for families containing the 15.7 million children under six who live with both parents.

Child support is one source of income, although less than three-fourths of the women legally entitled to child support actually receive it, and the average child-support payment is only $2,100 per year. Welfare is another source. The Department of Health and Human Services reported in its latest study (May 1982) that there were 6.6 million children benefiting from Aid to Families with Dependent Children (AFDC) payments. Of these, about 89 per cent were in homes where the father was absent. A family with two children received an average of $322.18 per month.

The second broad category of women who "have to work" is those women whose husbands do not earn enough money. In examining their choices and decisions, we move onto rocky terrain, because there is no objective way of determining how much money is "enough." (For most people, I suspect, the answer to "how much?" is "a little more.") An income that is thought of as meager in one place — say, $15,000 in New York City or Boston — may seem much more comfortable in Houston or Sacramento. A given amount of money will go a lot farther when a child is six years old than when she is sixteen. My purpose in exploring this issue is precisely to emphasize its subjectivity: although economic pressures frame the choices each family must make, their own values determine the very different directions they may go. To put it another way, it is very hard to

---

child. A woman with two children had a median income of $8,750, compared to a married couple's $27,745. (The Bureau of the Census lists the estimated poverty level in 1983 for a family of three at $7,940.)

tell, simply by looking at a husband's income level, whether or not his wife "has" to work.

I have spoken to many working women over the last several years about the reasons both they and their husbands work and have heard a range of answers. One woman needed extra money for the clothes and toys she bought her children and the family's modest entertainment, a Friday night out for pizza. Another needed it for the mortgage on her family's summer home. One woman needed it for the car she anticipated buying when her son turned sixteen. Another needed it to replace the family income lost through the husband's child-support payments to a previous spouse.

The Bureau of the Census determines official poverty levels for families in different circumstances, but everyone knows how imperfect a guide that is to "minimum" or "essential" needs. Even if factors that are somewhat calculable — like geographical region and age of children — can be entered into the equation, other factors — plans for education, medical expenses, differences in taste, and economic priorities — complicate the definition of a family's "needs." There is no absolute answer. Every family decides for itself the point at which a second income is necessary. The National Commission on Working Women says that $15,000 a year is a family's rock-bottom income level, below which "there is no leeway for family development," which presumably means maintaining a certain standard of living in future years. According to the commission's figures, 21 per cent of all working women have husbands who earn less than $15,000; these women, by its definition, clearly "have" to work. But is the correlation between a husband's income level and a wife's decision to work quite as clear and simple as such analyses would suggest? Not really.

Although the likelihood of a wife's working goes down slightly as her husband's income goes up, the difference is remarkable only at the lowest (below $10,000 per year) and the highest (above $35,000 per year) income levels.* The more interesting figures are in the middle ground — the income levels

---

* At the time these statistics were compiled, households with husbands making more than $35,000 represented less than one-fifth of all households.

TABLE I

Percentage of Working Wives, According to Husband's Income

Income in Dollars	1982	1983
1 – 9,999	62	62
10,000 – 14,999	68	69
15,000 – 19,999	70	72
20,000 – 24,999	67	68
25,000 – 29,999	65	68
30,000 – 34,999	63	66
35,000 – 49,999	58	61
50,000 – 74,999	54	56
Above 75,000	43	52

between $10,000 and $35,000 per year, where most American families fall. There the statistics show very little variation. As Table I indicates, wives are almost as likely to work when their husbands make up to $35,000 per year as they are when husbands earn $10,000, $20,000, or $25,000 per year.

Furthermore, these statistics show how very difficult it is to conclude that mothers at *any* income level feel they "have to work." Of the wives whose husbands earn $15,000 a year — the level the National Commission on Working Women defines as the floor for decent family life — about 70 per cent work. The remaining 30 per cent, of course, do not. This means that for every seven working women whose husbands earn less than $15,000, there are another three women who don't work, even though their husbands' earnings are in the same bracket.

If the husband's income level does so little to predict the likelihood of the wife working, at least through the working- and middle-class income ranges, is there another, more powerful, explanatory factor? Yes, there is: the presence and age of her children. Women with preschool-age children work much less overall, regardless of their husband's income level; and unlike any other group of women, those with preschool-age children

TABLE II

Percentage of Mothers Who Work, According to
Age of Children and Husband's Income

Income in Dollars	Children's Ages		
	6–17	3–5	Under 3
Under 3,000	67	62	45
3,000 – 4,999	57	60	33
5,000 – 6,999	59	61	43
7,000 – 9,999	66	58	48
10,000 – 12,999	69	59	50
13,000 – 14,999	70	67	54
15,000 – 19,999	70	63	55
20,000 – 24,999	67	58	44
25,000 – 34,999	64	53	43
35,000 – 49,999	57	42	34
Above 50,000	49	37	28

are much less likely to work when their husband's income crosses a threshold of about $20,000 per year. The figures are shown in Table II.

What the statistics seem to show, then, is a different conception of "have to" than is usually discussed. Except for the upper and lower ends of the income distribution, wives are neither more nor less likely to "have to" work as their husband's income rises or falls. What they do feel they "have to" do, by this evidence, is stop work when their children are little. Fewer than half of the mothers whose husbands earn less than $15,000 are at work when they have children under the age of three. Mothers whose husbands earn between $25,000 and $35,000 are exactly as likely to stay out of the work force when their children are young as those whose husbands earn between $5,000 and $7,000. As their children grow older and, especially, as they are away for much of the day at school, mothers from different income groups return to the work force at surprisingly similar rates.

Another way to examine this question is to ask what difference it makes to a family's economic standing to have the mother work. For two-parent families, the median income in 1982 was $27,500 per year. In those families where only the husband worked, it was $25,000; in those where both husband and wife worked, it was $30,000. This does not mean that wives are earning only the $5,000 differential between the two groups. Working wives contribute about 25 per cent (if they're working part-time) to 40 per cent (if they're working full-time) of the total family income of two-paycheck families, so those families would presumably fall behind economically if the wives did not work.

The issue of "falling behind" and "staying even" is an important one, because a mother's decision to go back to work is often portrayed as a means to avoid falling behind in the race with inflation. This was, for example, the theme of a recent analysis in *American Demographics* magazine. The magazine published a chart showing the change in median income between 1975 and 1979 for families in a variety of categories. Part of the chart is reproduced on the next page.

The conclusion the magazine drew from these data was that wives had poured into the work force as the only hope for keeping families even with inflation. It said:

> Now look at the enormous variation in income by household type revealed [by the table]. At the upper rungs of the income ladder in 1979 were married-couple families with wives employed full-time. Their median income of $26,196 contrasts sharply with the overall median family income of $19,611. . . .
>
> In other words, it took the addition of more than 3.2 million employed wives to increase unadjusted median family income $5,942 between 1975 and 1979, a sum whose value was almost entirely eroded by inflation. *Had wives not gone off to work, American families, in the aggregate, would have suffered substantial declines in real income* [emphasis added].

This is certainly fuel for the have-to-work argument, but is it true? Look at Table III again, and follow the line for "wife not in paid labor force" — in other words, families in which the wife did not work either in 1975 or 1979. Between 1975 and 1979,

TABLE III

Family Types and Median Income, 1975 and 1979

Total Number of Families
(in thousands)

	1975	1979	Increase or Decrease
Total Families	56,245	58,426	3.9%
Wife in Paid Labor Force	20,833	23,763	14.1%
Wife Employed	19,334	22,537	16.6%
Full-time	13,512	15,881	17.5%
Part-time	5,821	6,657	14.4%
Wife Unemployed	1,499	1,226	−18.2%
Wife Not in Paid Labor Force	26,486	24,416	−7.8%
Male Householder, No Wife Present	1,444	1,706	18.1%

Median Family Income
(in thousands of dollars)

	1975	1979	Increase
Total Families	13,719	19,661	43%
Wife in Paid Labor Force	17,237	24,957	49%
Wife Employed	17,584	25,291	44%
Full-time	18,262	26,196	43%
Part-time	16,223	23,055	42%
Wife Unemployed	13,260	18,569	40%
Wife Not in Paid Labor Force	12,752	17,750	39%
Male Householder, No Wife Present	12,995	16,867	30%

the median income of these families increased from $12,752 to $17,750, or by 39.2 per cent. Similarly, the median income of families with "wife unemployed"* increased by 40 per cent during the same period. What was happening to prices during those years? Between 1975 and 1979, the consumer price index rose by about 36 per cent. Therefore, families in which wives did not work stayed even with inflation. Indeed, both of these categories, "wife unemployed" and "wife not in labor force," kept very slightly ahead of inflation. (The only group that suffered a serious loss to inflation, according to the table, was "male householder, no wife present.") While individual families may well have needed two incomes to cope with reverses in their lives, that simply is not provable in the aggregate. On the whole, the statistics show that families that changed from one breadwinner to two moved briskly ahead, not only of the inflation rate but also of other families in which one parent stayed home. If a family moved from "wife not in paid labor force" in 1975 to "wife in paid labor force" in 1979, its median income rose from $12,752 to $24,957 — a 95 per cent increase, or more than twice as much as would be needed to "keep up" with inflation.

On balance, then, what we can say is that the popular impression that mothers are streaming back to the work force is not untrue but is oversimplified. Every day, mothers make compromises in order to spend more time at home. The compromises are greatest when the children are very young: a sizable proportion of those mothers work only part-time, do not work at all, or live on less income than they might otherwise have.

The familiar argument that mothers have to work is, similarly, not untrue but misleading. More single mothers work than married mothers, although many still do not work. Women married to men whose earnings place them in the bottom fifth of the income distribution are more likely to work than women married to men in the upper fifth — but only slightly more than those in the middle. It seems that although economics certainly plays an important role in women's decisions to work, money is by no means the only or always the most important factor.

* "Wife unemployed" is considered to be part of "paid labor force."

Many families decide that the costs of one income, which are mainly financial, are easier to bear than the emotional costs of trying to earn two.

Statistics tell us plainly that the need for day care for the children of working parents will always be there and will increase. But what statistics only hint at, and only upon close scrutiny, is how complex are the forces behind women's decisions about work—and, thus, the demand for day care.

❧ 10 ❧

Day Care: The Supply

WHAT ABOUT THE SUPPLY of day care? Why does nearly everyone seem to feel that not enough is available and that too much of what is available is mediocre or worse? Here we find another complex mixture of economic and cultural forces, which together have produced what economists call a "market failure," a situation in which supply and demand reach balance at a point that most people find unsatisfactory.

To understand the economics of day care centers, we have to step back and consider the range of child care possibilities that working parents confront. Most children, of course, are not in day care centers. They are in family homes or with their own parents, who may be working split shifts in order to care for their children themselves. In principle, parents simply need to decide which type of care they prefer — large groups, family homes, babysitters, themselves — and arrange it. But any parent who has looked for child care knows it doesn't work that way at all. The unifying theme in most parents' accounts of their search for child care is the random nature by which they hope to locate good care for their children. A few information/referral/resource centers are springing up around the country now, making the first systematic inroads into the intricate underground networks by which parents locate day care for their children. But primarily, parents find that they must ask neighbors, ask friends, strike out on their own with the Yellow Pages, place ads, answer ads. It can be tiring, depressing, frustrating, time consuming, and even harrowing. For the parent trying to do it while holding a job at the same time, each of the above adjectives can be preceded by "very."

"Luck" is the byword for finding good child care. Most parents today who have found a great child care situation feel as if they've been blessed. Almost every mother I've ever talked to about a happy situation makes the same kind of comment: "I'm really lucky. I found this terrific woman who watches a small group of children in her home." Or, "I'm so fortunate. I never would have been able to work if I hadn't lucked into this wonderful day care center."

Within the maze plenty of care is available, although not always the best, for children from middle- and upper-income families. Parents who lose their in-home caretakers may have to scramble for replacements at the last minute; they may have to have their children taxied across town for after-school care; or they may have to hire a Monday–Friday patchwork of after-school babysitters. These parents will probably exhaust their communications networks and themselves before they come up with even a partially satisfactory solution. The search will be frustrating and awkward and inconvenient. But finally they will find something, because they can pay for something. Whatever problems they may have with day care, they will find some kind of supply to meet their demand.

If this is the prospect for the middle- and upper-income families, consider how much more daunting the obstacles are for poor families. Their need to work is more urgent, their search for child care is at least as frustrating — yet they have no certainty that they will eventually find a solution, because they don't have the money to pay for it. Through the 1960s and 1970s, government programs subsidized the supply of day care for poor families. (Ironically, some of these programs provided the best group care, as at the Austin Community Nursery Schools.) But in the early 1980s much of that subsidy was eliminated.

The major source of direct funding for child care from the

federal government is the Title XX Social Service Block Grant, which provides subsidies for lower-income families on a sliding scale according to the family's income. (The program's name is pronounced "Title Twenty," and for clarity's sake I will refer to it that way from this point on.) For low-income families who are not in a position to take advantage of the tax breaks for child care costs, this is the only relief the government offers. The funding for Title Twenty was reduced by 21 per cent during the Reagan administration's cutbacks in domestic spending in 1981.* The other major supplement is the Child Care Food Program, a Department of Agriculture program that funds meals or provides food for children in day care centers and family homes. That funding was cut by 30 per cent in 1981.

It is difficult to assess the impact of these cuts, but in 1983, the Children's Defense Fund compiled a report to that end. Among its findings was that most states have had to reduce the number of children receiving Title Twenty help since 1981. These included:

> New York: 8,400–12,000 fewer children
> Illinois: 10,000 fewer children
> Virginia: 4,000 fewer children
> Pennsylvania: 2,000 fewer children
> New Hampshire: 1,000 fewer children

Almost invariably, directors I talked with in the day care centers I visited told me they had lost spots for Title Twenty children during the last few years. Four here, three there, five there. Children's Village in Cambridge, Massachusetts, lost four of its ten Title Twenty spots and its CETA-sponsored staffers as well. Pilgrim Day Care in Dorchester, Massachusetts, lost four or five

*To put this reduction into perspective, recall the budgetary situation when Ronald Reagan took office. He had committed himself to increase military spending, cut tax rates, and balance the federal budget. Accomplishing all three goals simultaneously might have been possible if the president had been able to reduce other categories of federal spending drastically enough. This proved impossible, since the largest amount of nondefense spending is for politically popular programs, such as Social Security and Medicare. Therefore, the president's first round of reductions, in 1981, was substantial in one area only: the so-called means-tested programs, those directed at the poor. Nearly all of the child care subsidies fell into this category, and were cut.

children and one care giver and food subsidies. They say they "make do."

Although the stories I heard from my randomly chosen centers were touching, they were not as dramatic as the stories uncovered by the Children's Defense Fund and reported in testimony before the Select Committee on Children, Youth, and Families in the House of Representatives on April 4, 1984. For example:

> In Wilmington, Delaware, the Salvation Army opened a center to serve the children of working poor families. Recently, it faced the prospect of closing because of dwindling enrollment. About two-thirds of its children used to be subsidized by Title Twenty; now only about one-third receive subsidies.
>
> A Grand Rapids, Michigan, day care center used to serve fifty-five children, all of whom received public subsidies. Now the center serves thirty-one children, none of whom receives a subsidy.

Where are children like these going? In most cases, the parents are doing the best, or the only thing, they can. Many make do with cheap family homes, which are often overcrowded, poorly supervised, sometimes squalid and dangerous, and certainly unregulated. Many parents enlist older siblings, keeping them home from school on a rotating basis, to care for the youngest children. One single mother I met told me she regularly bounced grocery checks in order to keep up her child care payments. Some parents simply lock the door behind them as they leave for work and hope and pray their children will be all right.

The situation is essentially the same for needy school-age children. Title Twenty funds for after-school programs have been cut as well. The Children's Defense Fund estimates that 6 to 7 million children thirteen years and under "may go without care for long parts of the day while their parents work." This is more than one child of every six in the nation. The Children's Defense Fund concluded: "There is no reason to believe that the many children who lost Title Twenty child care have been picked up by other programs." There is simply not enough care available for low-income children.

Beyond the question of the absolute numbers of places in day care centers, there is the question of quality: Why is so much of today's day care so bad? What could be done to make it better?

A surprising amount is already known about the factors that make for good and bad child care. Research conducted over the last fifteen years has put us in a position to draw up guidelines for the proper operation of day care centers. Much of this information came from the National Day Care Study, sponsored by the Administration for Children, Youth and Families in the then Department of Health, Education, and Welfare. The study was conducted in 1979 to examine cost and quality issues in federally subsidized day care programs. Raymond Collins, director of the Office of Program Development and Office of Developmental Services in the Administration for Children, Youth and Families, has underscored the importance of this study: "The [National Day Care Study] results demonstrated, for the first time in a scientifically conclusive way, that certain regulatable program characteristics were associated with behaviors of children and care givers and with children's gains in the cognitive, language and socioemotional domains." In other words, better regulations could create day care centers where children were happier and learned more.

Specifically, the study provided facts, figures, and suggestions about the nuts and bolts of improving day care. According to the study, positive classroom dynamics, improvements in children's behavior, and higher scores on the Preschool Inventory (PSI) and the revised Peabody Picture Vocabulary Test (PPVT) were found to correlate with three key characteristics: smaller numbers of children in the day care group, better staff-child ratios in the classes, and care givers who have had education or training in subjects related to child care.

Most of these points seem sensible, even obvious. But the efforts to implement such findings — to translate them into regulations and standards by which day care centers must operate —have been repeatedly frustrated, at least on the national scale.

Traditionally, state and local governments have borne almost all the responsibility for regulating day care centers. But when the federal government expanded its funding of child care in the

1960s, it also became involved in establishing standards and requirements for the centers that were to receive aid. In 1968, Congress authorized a set of regulations, known as the Federal Interagency Day Care Requirements (FIDCR). In 1975, they were revised and made part of the Title Twenty grants of the Social Security Act. That same year, the Department of Health, Education, and Welfare began a three-year evaluation of the requirements. These findings led to further revisions in 1980, which drew particularly heavily on the results of the 1979 National Day Care Study. These new requirements took effect in October 1980, but within two months, Congress imposed a moratorium on the standards because of fears about the cost involved in implementing them. Further delays followed and then, in 1981, as part of the Reagan administration's cutbacks in Title Twenty funds, federal regulations were virtually eliminated, and supervision of the federally funded centers was once more passed back to state and local governments.

State and local regulations vary enormously, and on the whole they fall well below the recommendations of the 1979 National Day Care Study and the now defunct 1980 regulations for federally funded centers. The most recent compilation of state and local standards is the Multiyear Comparative Licensing Study, begun in 1976 by the Administration for Children, Youth and Families. It now contains an updated six-volume appendix, the *Profiles of State Day Care Licensing Requirements*, which lists state-by-state requirements as of March 1981. From this list, two studies have been conducted that have compared the states' regulations, one by one, to the 1980 federal regulations — one study for the zero- to two-year-old age group and another for the four-year-old age group.

On the crucial question of staff-child ratios, the states were much more lax than the federal government. Emily Schrag, author of the study for the zero- to two-year-olds, reports that the 1980 federal regulations recommended one staffer for each three children under two years old and one staffer for each four children who are two years old or above. It further recommended that group size for zero- to two-year-olds be capped at six.

Schrag described the emphasis with which HEW issued its regulations:

> The Department has applied the staffing requirements suggested by many child development experts for children under two years old. . . . The Department agrees with commenters who stressed the special needs of children under three years old in day care centers. We believe it is critical to ensure that these young children receive the close attention and nurturing necessary for their healthy development and to ensure that there are enough caregivers present to protect their physical safety. The Department recognizes that these ratios, particularly those for infants, will be costly, but in balancing these costs with the needs of this group, we believe the strict ratios are justified.

In contrast, Schrag described what the state regulations as of March 1981 required:

- Only one state required a one to three staff-child ratio for infants under two years of age, and even that state permitted a one to ten staff-child ratio once the children reached two years nine months.
- Twenty-one states required a ratio of no more than four or five children under two per care giver.
- Eight states presented a mixed picture, requiring, for example, a one to five ratio for children up to one year or not walking, and a one to eight ratio for toddlers between one year and two and a half years of age.
- Several states had no stated regulations for staff-child ratios for children under two, and the remaining states and territories permitted ratios of six, seven, eight, and occasionally ten infants or toddlers to one care giver.
- Only sixteen states had any regulations governing group size — which, according to the National Day Care Study, not only proved to be an even more powerful determinant of program quality than staff-child ratios but seemed not particularly costly to improve. One state mandated a maximum group size of six, although it required only one staffer for those six children. Two states required a group size of twelve or fewer; the

other thirteen states that had any regulations for group size at all permitted groups of six, seven, eight, ten, twenty, and thirty-five children.

Raymond Collins of the Administration for Children, Youth and Families conducted a similar investigation of comparative regulations for four-year-olds. He found, similarly, that "it would appear that states have paid little heed to the child care research. Neither the findings that point toward improved child outcomes nor those that highlight favorable cost-quality trade-offs have been acted upon by most states."

Collins found that all but two states had some requirements for staff-child ratios. (The two exceptions were Connecticut and Mississippi.) The rest ranged from a required ratio of one to five to one to twenty. Only four states required ratios under one to ten. The majority had ratios between one to ten and one to fifteen. As for group size, thirty-three states had no requirements at all. Of those that did, the maximum allowable group size ranged from a low of ten in one state to a high of forty-five in another, with half the states specifying twenty children per group.

When the federal requirements for federally subsidized day care centers were abolished at the start of the Reagan administration in 1981, the states also relaxed their enforcement. The Children's Defense Fund has reported that since the end of federal supervision, "thirty-three states have lowered their child care standards for Title Twenty programs." As programs started running out of money because of the federal budget cuts, they had one logical step to take: they tried to build up their revenues, by taking in more children, and cut back on their expenses, by hiring fewer care givers. The Children's Defense Fund has said, "States that were already facing budget constraints generally seized this chance to increase the number of children they allow per child care worker."

Even the often-lax state standards give an exaggerated picture of the degree of supervision that actually occurs. Weak as they are, the standards are often not enforced. Many states found that one way to keep afloat after the 1981 Title Twenty cutbacks was to eliminate the licensing and monitoring staff of their programs. In 1980–1981, Arizona conducted four monitoring visits per center per year. The rate dropped to two the following year and to only one (a state health inspection) the next. Idaho cut its regional licensing staff from twelve to five in the same period.

In the state of Texas, the Department of Human Services Licensing Branch regulates all child care facilities. It is responsible for reviewing facility applications, conducting on-site inspections, and issuing licenses and registrations. In 1979, there were 14,000 child care facilities in Texas; by 1982, there were 22,000. During those same years, when the potential regulatory workload was increasing by more than 50 per cent, the Licensing Branch staff steadily declined from 375 people in 1979 to 243. The state estimate for 1985 is more than 34,000 facilities. To supervise them, Texas has asked for 346 staff members, or fewer than it had in 1979.

One of the other responsibilities of the Licensing Branch is investigating and acting on "critical incidents," including complaints and child abuse, brought to its attention. Table IV illustrates the increase in "critical incidents" that accompanied the rapid expansion of child care facilities and the decrease in staff between 1979 and 1982.

In a written report, the licensing branch said that the growth in workload and reduction in staff have "seriously eroded the department's capability to provide preventive protection to the over 500,000 children in out-of-home care in Texas. The $16 M [million] requested for the 84–85 biennium will *only* enable us to keep up with the projected growth in workload and rising costs due to inflation. Staff workloads will be at the '81 levels of operation they were when we began this biennium."

Controls over group size and staff-child ratios are important, not because they can guarantee good-quality day care — they are only a prerequisite — but because they reduce the likelihood of truly abysmal situations. The most important source of good day care is good teachers and care givers, and here there is room for at least modest amounts of hope. Movements are under way

TABLE IV

Increases and Decreases in Child Care Facilities, Staff, and Complaints

	1979	1982	Increase or Decrease
Facilities	14,003	22,230	58%
Licensing Branch Staff	375	243	−35%
Complaints	2,168	4,113	90%
Child Abuse in Day Care Facilities	79	313	296%
Revocations or Denials	71	178	149%
Appeals	14	32	114%
Injunctions	9	29	229%

across the nation to certify care givers, not simply on the basis of academic credentials, which often have little bearing on the ability to work with children, but on tests related to the skills that make for day-by-day success in the center.

The Child Development Associate Credential (CDA), for example, is a national, competency-based credential. According to Millie Almy, professor at the University of California, Berkeley, "It is awarded after one or two years of individualized, flexible, field-based training, when the trainee can demonstrate the accomplishment of a set of competencies deemed necessary to promote the development of young children in a group setting." Applicants for the CDA need not meet any general education requirements, take a certain number of credit hours, or go through any work-training programs. What is asked of them is that they show their mastery of specific skills, or "competencies," that matter in day care work. As of April 1983, twenty-six states and the District of Columbia required that at least one category of staff at a center hold the CDA. Seven more states were including CDA requirements in drafts of day care regulations.

That is the hopeful part. The rest of the day care staffing story is a complicated and troublesome one that reflects the sharply divided, two-tier nature of the day care industry.

The problems are serious, though not at their worst, among the upper ranks of the profession — the trained, qualified, experienced day care professionals. These are the people who hold adequately paying though very far from lucrative jobs. The 1982 median income for child care workers was $10,155, with the majority having no medical or pension benefits. Since child care, like teaching, nursing, clerical work, and librarianship, has historically been a woman's job, the pay has always been low. Change for the better will come, but slowly. The profession will survive largely because of the dedication and commitment and love of job that the best and most creative people put into it.

The more severe part of the problem lies in the bulging bottom ranks. Anyone who looks there will discover a deep, swirling eddy of untrained and inexperienced staff, who live in a world of low pay, high turnover, and low incentive.

In the state of Texas, for example, the state requirements for day care staff workers are hardly rigorous, but many of the workers I saw barely met even those qualifications. According to the law, staff members must be eighteen years old or hold a high school diploma or be a student enrolled in a child care–related program, be able to read and write, and not have been convicted within the preceding ten years of a felony or a misdemeanor classified as an offense against person or family, a violation of the Texas Controlled Substances Act, or of public indecency.

Most low-level day care workers are women, usually in their teens or twenties. Typically, one of them will say that she went into day care because she left high school, needed a job, and couldn't find anything better than work at the center for minimum wage ($3.35 an hour, $134 for a forty-hour week, less than $7,000 for the full year). The *Child Care Employee News* reports that when wage increases are distributed, they are often inequitable: "Percentage increases always benefit the higher paid staff in absolute dollars. This widens the gap between aides, teachers, and administrators and creates tremendous tension."

The typical employee, then, arrives with little training, works in tough conditions, and quickly burns out. Then she looks for greener pastures or simply moves on. Yes, there are exceptions, but they are simply that—exceptions.

It is impossible to overemphasize the importance of low staff pay. If day care centers are bad, as many are, and if the workers often seem to resent being in the centers even more than the children do, can that be so surprising, considering the rewards they are given? In some professions — teaching and the ministry are the most familiar examples — relatively low wages were traditionally offset by relatively high prestige. (Teachers' wages started going up as their prestige started going down, but that is a different story.) Day care workers receive no such hidden compensation. Their low social prestige confirms the message delivered by their low wages: in the eyes of the world, their work is not worth much, and neither are they.

Attitude may not matter in some jobs. You can fry a burger, fell a tree, or probably even fly a plane (though I'd rather take a different flight) if you have a lousy attitude. But caring for children is different. There, attitude is everything. In dealing with small children, one's emotions, spirit, energy, and personality matter more than anything else. To do the job right, a day care worker has to perform like a soprano hitting a note exactly. Her best product is the tone and tenor of her interaction with children.

Money by itself cannot insure a good staff. But too little money can almost certainly insure a bad one. Without enough money, it is hard to attract good people to a center and, perhaps more important, it is impossible to keep them. The best day care workers will always be different from, say, corporate lawyers. They will always have to place a higher premium on a sense of service than on financial reward. But can we expect them to build a career on minimum wage? Or to think that their personal service is valued and respected when we put so very low a price on it?

The answer to improving day care, then, is much less complicated than we might have feared. All we need to do is impose more and better regulations and hire more and better day care workers, each of whom we will pay a better wage. Those things done, we can insure every child who needs care a spot in a high-quality institution.

In theory, it should be neither complicated nor difficult to do these things. But in practice, it is all but impossible, because each of the steps that could improve day care has a common trait: they all mean that someone has to spend more money. This, however, is something that no interested party — not parents, not business, not government — seems willing to do.

11

Paying for Day Care

IN MANY AREAS of public policy, we have passed the point where we can be confident that spending more money will, by itself, relieve many of our problems. We cannot be sure that a larger defense budget will lead to greater military strength nor that raising school taxes will make our children do better in school. Day care is not yet at that point. To be more precise, while money will not automatically cure what is wrong with day care, every proposal for improving it involves higher costs. Who will pick up the tab? Whether it is parents, state governments, the federal government, businesses, community groups, or private donors, the sums required are staggering. The financial challenge is most substantial where care of poor children is involved. Even now, the supply of child care does not meet the demand from low-income families, and the gap is expected to widen.

Mustering the financial resources to deal with child care is especially difficult because prevailing attitudes are in such a state of flux. There are national guidelines on unemployment compensation and medical care for the poor but not on helping parents who need to work to care for newborn infants or sick children. National parental leave policies are nonexistent, and public funds committed to day care are less than they were before 1981.

Some of the most destructive attitudes about child care arise from those who rely on it most: us, the parents. As a rule, parents think that day care should be cheap or, in any case, cheaper than it is. We complain aloud or at least grumble to ourselves about how much we have to pay our children's caretakers, even teen-age babysitters. By most measures of other professional services, the costs are not that high. Why do they seem so high to so many parents? More precisely, why does market resistance keep them from rising above the national median of $2,200 to $3,200 per year for a three- to five-year-old child in a group center, even though it is practically impossible to hire an adequate number of adequately trained staff members for that price? I think there are two reasons.

The first is the healthy and generous assumption that child care, like other kinds of loving services, can't really be priced or bought. Grandparents and relatives have done it in the past, usually for free, and they continue to do it now. Their services are often invaluable and irreplaceable. Many families consider it vulgar, even sacrilegious, to name a sum that approximates the value of these services. How can $4.25 an hour convey the love and attention given a grandchild, a niece, or a nephew?

But the reluctance to pay for day care also stems from a second, bad tradition. Whenever jobs have been primarily held by women, those jobs have been poorly paid. In the nineteenth century, "women's work" included service as domestics and positions in factories and mills, all of them ill paid. As Carol Hymowitz and Michaele Weissman, in their history of women's experience in America, have written:

> Women's unskilled work never provided them with a living wage. The piece-rate system, combined with the sex division of jobs, made women the cheapest pool of workers in the labor force. Studies of working women in the late nineteenth and early twentieth centuries show women received one-half to one-third the wages of working men. A female tobacco stripper in 1900 earned about $5 a week to a male cigar-roller's $10. A seamstress in the needle trade earned $6 or $7 compared to a cutter's $16. Discrepancies in wages paid to men and women were

not simply the result of differences in jobs. Even when men and women did the same work, women were paid considerably less. Employers often justified unequal pay by claiming that women were only working for "pin money."

When women moved into white-collar jobs and, more slowly, into the professions, substandard salaries moved with them. What happened to women economically in the office was typical of what happened to women breaking into other new professions. Hymowitz and Weissman have written, "Before the invention of the typewriter and the telephone the office had been a male domain. Male clerks handled correspondence, kept the books, and received visitors. When women were hired in offices, clerical work was restructured, and its status declined. Women were offered and accepted lower pay than that given men."

Even when women did exactly the same white-collar jobs as men — switchboard operators and librarians, for example — they were chronically paid less. Nurses and elementary school teachers are the two most familiar examples of jobs dominated by women, and they are traditionally underpaid. Child care workers are emerging as another illustration of the way women may be trapped when their occupations are classified as "women's work."

There is an additional twist for day care workers. Their salaries and wages come not out of school board appropriations or hospital budgets but directly and (in most cases) exclusively from parents' pockets. In most families, I suspect, that is subconsciously translated as "mother's pockets" — which are the least deep pockets. Single mothers have no choice but to pay costs themselves, and married mothers often feel that child care fees should come out of the wages they earn. If a husband is earning $25,000 and a wife $15,000, the cost of day care will usually be compared to the wife's $15,000 — not to the husband's salary or to the total of the two parents' earnings or to the other satisfactions the parents take from their jobs. When combined with the assumption that the labor involved in caring for children is unskilled and should be cheap, the ceiling on parents' conception of "reasonable" day care fees is lowered even further. And so we have the double bind of the market for day care: the same fees that seem exorbitant to most parents leave conscientious day care operators unable to make ends meet.

How much does the day care industry itself alleviate or add to the economic problems? The answer requires looking at the very different financial arrangements under which different kinds of centers operate. Day care centers are run as either proprietary (for profit) or nonprofit institutions. Traditionally, most have been nonprofit, but the trend is now the other way. In 1977, 59 per cent of centers were run for no profit versus 41 per cent for profit. Today, the National Association for Child Care Management, the national trade association for proprietary child care centers, says the split is about fifty-fifty, and the proprietary share is increasing.

There is a natural division, even an antagonism, between nonprofit and for-profit centers. The former have no obvious goals other than to serve children, even if they sometimes serve them poorly. The goal of the latter is to turn a profit while serving children. Important as the distinction between nonprofit and for-profit centers may be, however, the real dividing line in day care is between the large, multicenter, for-profit chains (for example, Kinder-Care) and all the rest of the day care industry, which ranges from nonprofit centers to the smaller proprietary facilities. The large chains do not yet dominate the industry; they now make up only about 15 per cent of the for-profit centers. But they are rapidly expanding, and they increasingly set the tone for what is expected of the day care industry. They are also significant because their development illustrates a special case of "market failure": what the chains need in order to maximize profits may well be incompatible with what children need in order to thrive.

The heart of this issue — just how these large chains blend the profit-making motive with caring for children — seems somehow to have been left out of the endless debates about day care. Even Bettye Caldwell, the president of the National Association for the Education of Young Children, has written in defense of the for-profit centers, as part of her defense of day care in general. In 1982, she wrote in the *Child Care Information Ex-*

change, "There is a popular notion that somehow it is wrong for day care centers to make a profit off of the children they serve. No one objects to authors of children's books, pediatricians, toymakers making profits. Essentially all people ought to make a profit off of the service they provide. To single out day care as an exception makes no sense at all. We should all be able to make a decent living from what we are doing."

Caldwell is right, of course, that care givers and administrators should receive fair compensation for the services they provide — just as pediatricians or authors themselves do. (Although she didn't say so, she might well have added that the world would be fairer and day care would be better if the chasm between pediatricians' earnings and day care workers' earnings were narrowed.) All day care staff members, be they the teachers in the rooms or the administrators who serve to provide a smooth-running system, should of course be paid. By and large, they should be paid much better wages than they currently receive. But in defending day care for profit, as part of a united front against any criticism of day care, Caldwell blurs the distinction between two very different concepts of payment and profit-making.

There is nothing at all wrong with day care centers operating like smart businesses and even trying to make a profit. The prospect of profit interests people in starting day care centers, thereby making more care available than otherwise would be, and it entices people to try harder to attract new customers, as in any other commercial venture. But a threshold seems to be crossed when we move from the local child care center, doing its best to be successful and hoping that its price and service will attract a growing clientele, to the national chain, which views each local installation as a profit center, interchangeable with any other economic asset. In the first case, much of the profit finds its way back into the center, either because the owner herself works there (and therefore receives a higher wage) or because she knows that her long-term prospects depend on keeping the center up. In the second case, the profits that come out of National Franchise Day Care #103 may eventually be used to pay dividends to shareholders, or finance diversification into an unrelated business, or increase executive salaries.

In general, corporations should be free to use their profits as they see fit. If they couldn't pay dividends, people wouldn't invest; if they couldn't diversify, they might eventually go under. This is as true for the publishers of children's books and manufacturers of children's toys as it is for steel companies or computer makers. But certain kinds of "industries" — health, education, and child care — do not always lend themselves to for-profit operation. Through much of our history, they have been insulated from pure market force either through legislation (the creation of public schools) or by custom (the operation of community hospitals and church-related schools). Partly this has been for reasons of fairness: every child deserves an education, regardless of his or her parents' income. Partly it has arisen from the notion that certain values transcend the market: no one should be denied urgent medical care merely because of poverty. To look closely at the for-profit child care chains is to see that here, as in medical care, the more closely the operation resembles other businesses, the more it neglects its clients' real needs.*

What makes caring for children different from, say, manufacturing petrochemicals or serving hamburgers in a national chain? In other industries, the market can adjust to a wide range of quality in the product being sold. If the hamburgers are somewhat inferior, the customers are still not going to starve or die of food poisoning; if they are sufficiently dissatisfied, they can go to another restaurant or eat at home. If a petrochemical purchaser is more concerned with price than quality, he will make do with an inferior grade. The flexibility of the market serves producer and supplier well by offering different degrees of quality at different prices. Significantly, there is a limit to how low the degree of quality is allowed to go. The government forbids either the hamburger stand or the petrochemical plant to compete by scrimping on health and safety measures. The

* For the parallel development of for-profit hospitals, see Paul Starr's *The Social Transformation of American Medicine* (New York: Basic Books, 1982).

hamburger stand is not allowed to sell tainted meat for half price, and the petrochemical plant can't cut costs by refusing to stock safety gear for its workers. These standards must be imposed on the market by an outside force, because the market cannot produce them on its own. (Why should any company be the first to buy safety gear unless it is required?)

Consider the similarities to the market for day care. When profits from the local Kiddie-Care franchise are sent off to be used for dividends or diversification, by definition they reduce the quality of care in that center below what it could be if the profits were reinvested there. So far the story is no different from that of McDonald's. But here, the market for quality is not quite as flexible as it is for polypropylene or Quarter-Pounders. The children themselves are utterly powerless to "choose" an appropriate level of care. Their parents rarely have — or take — the time to make informed, discriminating choices about levels of care. (How many centers are usually available to choose from? How many hours can parents spend inspecting them?) Because the social prestige accorded child care is so low, most parents feel they're overcharged no matter what they're paying. As a result, many day care centers exist in an atmosphere of permanent crisis, under conflicting pressures from parents who think they're spending too much and staff members who feel they're earning too little. The one variable in this equation that is easiest to change, the one quickest way to reconcile the competing pressures, is to cut back on quality, that intangible combination of staff, facilities, and program that makes such a difference in each child's happiness.

Other things being equal, the for-profit day care chains will cut back more heavily on quality than other day care facilities, because they're exporting more money away from the centers. If nonprofit centers take in a hundred dollars per child per week, they are free to use all of it for salaries, renovations, upkeep, materials, and supplies — that is, for the welfare and improvement of the center. When most small, for-profit centers receive a hundred dollars, most of it will also go back into the facility itself, since these are typically small businesses whose owners live nearby and regard the center as their most important business investment. But when a local franchise of a national chain receives a hundred dollars, some of the money must be sent back to headquarters, to provide dividends and profits and pay corporate salaries that grossly exceed what local day care owners take from their businesses. Yes, it is true that corporate investments originally made those day care centers possible. But at a certain point, we have to ask whether the "care" they provide may be worse than no care at all — or, to put it more reasonably, whether children would not be better off with either a broader network of nonprofit centers or commercial centers operating under much, much more stringent quality standards. If those standards were imposed, some of the national chains might decide that this market no longer offered attractive opportunities for them.

Sharon Kagan and Theresa Glennon, in their review of the controversies surrounding for-profit child care, have written: "Proprietary operators maintain that efficient managerial skills make their centers profitable without any reduction in the quality of care provided." Being part of a large company, they can theoretically partake of quantity purchases at much lower prices and use their leverage to find locations in prime market areas where land and rent are cheap. They concentrate on areas where licensing and zoning requirements are lenient (for example, in those states that permit more children per staff member or set no limits at all) and in areas where employment rates are high, as are numbers of preschool-age children. Kagan and Glennon point out the high concentration of for-profit centers in the South and Southwest, which fit this description well.

There are several different ways to measure the quality of care in these centers. Despite all the well-recognized limits on using money spent on a government program as an accurate measure of value received, it is truer in day care than in most other areas that the more money spent per child on care (staff, goods, etc.), the better the care. On average, nonprofit federally funded centers spent $2,190 per child in 1978. For profit-making, nonfederally funded centers, the figure was $1,230 per child per year, or about 45 per cent less.

Perhaps more important than the overall amount of money

spent is its composition. In economic terms, as well as in impact upon the child, the most significant item in the budget is pay for staff members. Nonprofit centers, according to the Kagan and Glennon study, spend about 73 per cent of their budgets on pay. But the for-profit centers, with lower budgets to begin with, spend only about 63 per cent on pay.

More dollars spent on staff means two things: a better staff-child ratio, a measure that all studies of child care agree is critical to quality, and higher staff wages, with the common-sense result that the higher the wage, the more highly trained, experienced, and stable the staff. Can it be a surprise that turnover rates at nonprofit centers were lower, at 13–15 per cent per year, than at for-profit centers, at 17–20 percent? *

From the child's point of view, what matters most about a day care center is not its program of activities or its menu for lunch but how attentive and dedicated the care givers are and whether they stay around long enough to give him some sense of constancy. Too few day care centers of any sort excel by this measure, but more of them are found among the nonprofit centers than the for-profit chains.

The for-profit centers maintain, in their defense, that their record of compliance with state regulations is stronger than that of nonprofit centers. But Kagan and Glennon have reported on a study conducted by the Women's Research Action Project in 1974. It found that "cost-cutting methods used by the proprietary centers that were owned by chains went beyond efficiency into areas that seriously affected the quality of care provided to the children at those centers. The report stated that while all centers met licensing requirements, *none exceeded minimum standards* [emphasis added]." Kagan and Glennon mention a

---

* Precise turnover rates are difficult to determine and may well be considerably higher than these figures, which were collected about a decade ago. The *Child Care Employee News* (Fall 1984) reports that their own studies and studies by local groups around the country have found turnover rates between 15 and 30 per cent per year. A Bureau of Labor Statistics report finds that "workers in day care centers, nursery school, Head Start and other child care professions except family day care left work at a 41.7% rate in a 12 month period in 1980–81."

1977 study that compared current levels of staffing with those that would have been required by the Federal Interagency Day Care Requirements in 1968. It found that for-profit centers would have to increase their labor expenditures substantially, by 25 to 51 per cent, in order to meet minimum federal requirements, while nonprofit centers would have to increase their spending by 4 to 20 per cent.

Kagan and Glennon said of for-profit chains:

> Centers were clean and bright, but unimaginative. Ratios were 1 staff person for every 10 children, as required by law, but the staff received no paid breaks and in the afternoon may have had little energy left to be divided among ten children. Low-paid and vulnerable to sudden layoffs when enrollment declined, the staff often suffered from low morale, which in turn led to a serious discontinuity in staffing, even from month to month. The [Women's Research Action Project] report further indicated that instead of using income to improve quality, funds not required for operations were generally funneled into other investment.

If money is not being used "to improve quality," where is it going? Is there enough of it to make a difference?

Perhaps the most accurate way to gauge the economic success of large day care chains is to ask those who have an unsentimental view of its prospects — the stock analysts who rate day care companies as investment opportunities. From their perspective, the business looks very good indeed.

The big for-profit chains have expanded more than any other kind of child care facility in recent years. Kinder-Care, for example, is described by Standard and Poor's Corporation as the "largest professional operator of private day care centers in the U.S." There is every indication that Kinder-Care and the rest of the large, for-profit day care industry are in good health. The company is still opening new centers — 825 centers serving approximately 85,000 children were operating in 1983, up from 759 in 1982, with more than a hundred under development. Revenues rose 10 per cent during the 1983 fiscal year, to a record $128 million. Net earnings were up 68 per cent to $11 million, and earnings per share after a 4-for-3 stock split rose from 49 cents to 69 cents.

Because the chains hope to cater to the growing group of middle-class children whose parents want to put them in day care, companies like Kinder-Care, with their convenient locations, convenient hours, large number of programs from infant care to after-school care, and recognizable names, are bound to grow even more. Nevertheless, they are diversifying beyond child care into other activities. Kinder-Care now owns and operates ten walk-in immediate-care medical facilities for minor medical emergencies. It has also started Kinder Life Insurance Company, and a licensing and merchandising division that includes photography, a line of children's clothing, night-lights, preschool learning kits and educational books.

I am not a stockbroker or a scientist, so I view these developments solely with a parent's eye. To me, there are certain aspects of large-chain proprietary day care centers that are as revealing as anything the scientific studies have found. If a for-profit center can expand into operating emergency care medical centers or life insurance programs, shouldn't it first provide adequate play equipment for toddlers and milk for their lunches? I have seen Kinder-Care centers that skimped on those basics in order to save a dollar here and there. If a for-profit company can pay its shareholders dividends that increased by 41 per cent in 1983, shouldn't it first pay its day care workers enough so that it could attract and keep a more qualified staff, rather than one that turns over three directors a year and has a toddler staff so lazy they shoo the children away from them on the playground?

If the child development experts place prime importance on the question of staff pay, so does Kinder-Care, but in the opposite way. Kinder-Care holds a notoriously hard line on its overall pay policies. In lengthy and bitter negotiations in 1982 and 1983, Kinder-Care bargained over staff pay scales with sixty-five striking union members of the Ontario Public Service Employees Union, who were teachers at the Kinder-Care-owned Mini-Skool day care chain in Toronto, Ontario. The *Child Care*

Employee News, a quarterly newsletter for child care workers, reported that at the time of the strike, assistant room supervisors were making $3.68 an hour, room supervisors were making $4.03, and cooks were making $4.28. (The general Ontario minimum wage is $3.50 per hour.) According to the Ontario Public Service Employees Union, most day care workers in the Toronto area were earning between $9.28 and $10.26 per hour. Said Christine N. Hoeldke, a day care worker in another privately run center in the area, "They're really at the bottom. I don't know of anyone else [in day care] who works for less than $5 an hour." The union demanded a 50 per cent increase in wages. After seven months, they settled for a 15 per cent increase for the first year and an additional 10 per cent for the second year.

Combining the profit-making motive with serving children is a tricky affair. A blanket statement saying it can't be done is decidedly unfair. But when services that matter to children and profits that matter to investors are competing for the same dollars, the temptations are great. Quite simply, the best economic interests of the chains do not depend on the quality of service they offer the children but on the strength of the dividend they offer their shareholders. Other kinds of day care centers, for-profit and nonprofit alike, may not be perfect. But their weaknesses and faults are random, not built in. They do not stem from this one driving economic factor — the need to generate large-scale profits — that has a constant and pernicious effect on the quality of care the children receive.

Some child care advocates, who are generally loath to hear any criticism of day care, maintain that there is a danger in criticizing the proprietary chains too loudly. With so little government support now for nonprofit centers, they say, for-profit centers offer the best alternative for parents and the most likely prospect for the continued expansion of day care in a desperate market. There is something to what they say, but not enough to justify an argument in favor of large-chain proprietary day care. On the contrary, the failings of the chains should be used as evidence of just how critically we now need government involvement (in the form of subsidies and regulation) and industry involvement (in the form of subsidies for its employees' child care costs). The strongest and most thriving centers should not be those in which the costs of providing decent care are in direct conflict with the company's legitimate desire to earn a profit, but those that are designed to serve the best interests of the children. Given the simple economic fact of day care — that most parents cannot or will not themselves pay the cost of supporting the best-quality care — designing and running those centers means necessary economic help from the government, acting on behalf of its young and future citizens, and businesses, acting on behalf of its workers.

Business would seem to have a direct interest because of the growing realization that employees' responsibilities to their children compete directly with their responsibilities to their jobs. Government, of course, has a responsibility to watch out for the general welfare of its people. How are business and government meeting these responsibilities?

The private sector *is* beginning to respond to the growing needs of its workers who have children. Many businesses have initiated programs to ease the tensions between work and family, but it has been a time of trial and error. There are no precedents to follow, so a little bit of just about everything has been tried. Some companies offer information and referral services to help parents locate, quickly and easily, child care services that will have what they're looking for. Some offer counseling for parents who are not sure what they should be looking for. Companies can often provide such services easily, since they can simply hire outside consultants to give expert advice. Some offer a variety of time-related liberties, such as flexible working hours, maternity and paternity leaves, leaves for general family purposes, and sick-child leaves. These are more inconvenient for the businesses and offering them requires a greater commitment than simply offering advice.

Other companies offer various kinds of financial assistance. One is the voucher system. A company provides a voucher or chit worth a certain amount of money (often based on a sliding scale according to family income), which can be applied toward child care costs in a family's center of choice. The parents present the voucher to the day care center, which redeems it for cash from the corporation, or the parents tell their companies where they would like the payments sent. In effect, the company subsidizes or shares the cost of its employees' child care.

The better-paid employees in some companies can benefit from another kind of financial assistance, the salary reduction plan. Under such a plan, an employee's child care costs are deducted directly from his income. Instead of earning $30,000 per year, for example, the employee's stated salary might be reduced to $26,000, plus $4,000 in child care benefits, which can be used to pay for day care at a center or with a housekeeper or nanny at home. The employee is paid with two checks, one representing child care costs and the other the balance. This system represents a big tax savings for upper-bracket earners since the child care check is not taxed. By exactly the same reasoning, it represents a subsidy from the rest of the tax-paying public to this generally more affluent group.

One innovation popular among parents is the "cafeteria benefits" plan. Rather than determining what benefits — health coverage, vacation plans, etc. — its employees should have, a company can give them the option to choose among the benefits themselves. Since not all parents are looking for the same kind of help, these smorgasbord benefit packages are often appealing. For example, a wife may want to forgo health insurance benefits from her company if her husband receives more attractive family coverage from his. She may opt instead for a child care voucher.

In a few cases, parents have another option: the on-site day care centers that have occasionally been established by a company or a consortium of companies, labor unions, universities, local governments, or hospitals. These facilities are rare because they reflect a deep commitment and cannot be quickly or lightly arranged. Many businesses naturally resist such entanglements, feeling that child care is simply not their concern. They may want to keep out of employees' private lives, or they may not want to complicate what they regard as a natural separation between work and family. In 1980, the *New York Times* published an article that illustrates how such centers *can* work well for everyone.

> In Morristown, the Pumpkin Shell Learning Center was organized in 1972 by Betty Ruhalter, then a member of the women's auxiliary of the Community Medical Center, which is now the Mount Kimball division of Morristown Memorial. She sought to draw younger personnel to the hospital and to answer community requests for day care.
>
> "The idea took some selling," Mrs. Ruhalter recalled. "Board members were hostile at first. They didn't think they should be in the day-care business."
>
> Eventually, they agreed to supply a vacant nurses' residence rent-free and to pay for remodeling, utilities and insurance. The auxiliary raised funds for equipment and continued to finance improvements. Parents paid $43 a week for their children, who bring their own lunch.
>
> "We utilize the hospital's natural resources," said Janet Dilanni, Pumpkin Shell's director, adding that children entertained patients on holidays and planned to "adopt grandparents" from the hospital's extended-care facility.

Nancy Jennings is the director of the Pumpkin Shell Learning Center now, twelve years after its founding. A private, nonprofit operation, the center is still affiliated with Morristown Memorial Hospital and receives funding from them. The rest comes from parents, who pay $57.50 per week for full-time care. There are sixty-five children at Pumpkin Shell now, about 35 per cent of whose parents work at the hospital. It still plays a role in attracting nurses to the hospital, reports the director, but probably not a tremendous one. It still maintains its social ties to the hospital, too; children go over there for holiday parties and the kindergarten class visits the older patients every month for a "lesson."

Like families, businesses are each a little different. What a company's employees want, and what the company can realistically offer, vary from place to place. On-site day care may work well for big companies or institutions, but it has not caught on everywhere. Only about five hundred and fifty companies, most of them hospitals, have on-site or nearby facilities. Similarly, flextime may work well for businesses in which the product itself is all that matters, not where or when it is produced. It will not work for offices that rely on classic nine-to-five workdays, where clients or customers expect people to be present, or for factories where a team effort is necessary.

The biggest changes are coming, naturally, in high-growth industries (which are less bound by tradition), in those with labor shortages (which must do their best to please employees), and in those least affected by inflation (which feel less strapped than other industries). Hospitals, which need nurses, are among the leaders in providing on-site day care facilities. But their generosity knows certain bounds: some hospital day care centers are restricted to serving only the children of nurses, not the children of orderlies, dieticians, and other hospital staff who are in less demand. Banks, insurance companies, and the federal government are also sponsors of day care centers. But not all of these have sliding-scale fees, which means that many of the lowest-paid employees, who are most likely to be in a pinch when it comes to child care, can't afford to send their children to their own on-site centers. Similarly, a salary reduction scheme may be worth several thousand dollars to the high-paid attorney who can deduct the cost of a housekeeper or babysitter from taxable income, but it is worth far less to that firm's secretary, whose few thousand dollars paid in child care fees would be taxed at a much lower level anyway.

A few businesses, some of them exceptional models in the area of family relations, seem to be acting out of what might be called the goodness of their hearts, or at least are demonstrating a definite commitment to certain social values. Family-owned companies can and have initiated programs simply because someone at the top told them to. This was the case with the Abt company's day care center, which was described in Chapter 7. The companies that offer these varieties of help to employees and families have mostly found it well worth their while to do so. When relieved of some of the stress of balancing work and family, their employees have become better, more reliable, more productive workers. From the company's point of view, the benefits include aid in recruitment, positive attitude of employees toward work and employer, good publicity, improvement in community relations, and lower absenteeism and job turnover.

But unless you happen to be lucky enough already to work for a company or business with such practices, you may be stuck a long time waiting for something to change. Individual workers are rarely in a position to push for such institutional policies. It's tough to lobby for time off for sick children or assistance in paying for child care if you're in a job without a lot of rank and know there is a long line of people who would be happy to step in should you find yourself too discontent. Those in the best positions to lobby — the women and men with young children of their own who have climbed high enough up the ladder that they would be missed — are often the least likely to need most of these benefits. They can afford their private child care arrangements (often housekeepers and nannies); they can slip out early to take a child to the doctor; they can work at home with a sick child. And often, many of the things they would personally lobby for, such as salary reductions for child care, are not what the majority of other parents need.

Furthermore, many working women on the rise feel strongly that their children can't play a more obvious role in their business lives than occupying a picture frame on the corporate desk. When even admitting you have children (and therefore have some competition, however thoroughly repressed, for the company's claim on your time) can be a drawback in the boardroom, who is going to spend time lobbying for on-site child care? An item in *Working Mother* magazine, a barometer of attitudes among professional women who are mothers, put it this way:

> Most women get the message that they mustn't look as
> if they're putting their child ahead of their job. Says Marcie
> Schorr Hirsch, director of career counseling at Brandeis
> University in Waltham, Massachusetts, and private consul-
> tant to career women, "My clients tell me stories like this:
> The babysitter calls from home, and your child is sick. You
> leave the office. But you get the distinct frosty feeling that

this is not a good reason for you to go. The question really isn't taking personal time. If someone calls a male employee and says, 'Your mother slipped on the ice and broke her hip. Please come to the hospital,' he doesn't get that frosty feeling. It's the stereotype of the woman's putting her children before her job that's hurting the working mother."

This feeling is not exclusive to women. A survey by Catalyst, Inc., a national advocacy organization for women's work and careers, found that of one hundred and nineteen Fortune 500 companies that offered men parental leaves, only eight reported any men taking advantage of them. "In spite of the official policy in place, the corporate culture may give off a clear signal that parental leave is not an option for men serious about their careers," says Phyllis Silverman, the Catalyst director of career and family programs.

When dealing with its own working-parent employees, the federal government has applied several procedures similar to those of private business. But in its policies for the general public, it has been much less innovative.

Although day care has been operating in this country since the nineteenth century, it has always operated under the assumption that parents should arrange and pay for the care of their own children. At certain times of crisis, the government has made limited responses: during the depression, the Work Projects Administration sponsored day nurseries for children of its workers; during World War II, the Lanham Act provided funds for day care centers and nursery schools for children whose mothers were called in to work for the war effort. (Once the crisis was over, however, women lost their wartime jobs and children lost their day care. Things didn't ever quite return to "normal," though, as the number of working mothers began its steady ascent.) In the 1960s, the Head Start programs were begun for disadvantaged children.

The lack of any comprehensive national child care policy is both a cause and a symptom of the government's inaction. Attempts to establish one have come close but have never reached fruition. In 1971, after months of bipartisan effort, the Comprehensive Child Development Act made its way through Congress. Had it become law, it would have provided child care subsidies for welfare recipients, new child care facilities, larger income tax deductions for child care, and a variety of programs for preschool children designed to improve their health, nutrition, and education. The bill passed both the House and the Senate but was vetoed by President Nixon, at least partly in response to the outcries from the most conservative right-wing activists.

This veto affected child care policy for more than a decade; it was arguably the most important event in the politics of child care since the publication of *The Feminine Mystique* in 1963. Nixon did not merely decline to sign the bill but called it "the most radical piece of legislation to emerge from the 92nd Congress." He likened it to siding with "communal approaches to childrearing," echoing the right-wing arguments about "Sovietizing" American children. In the aftermath of his veto, even moderates shied away from further support of child care legislation. Periodically during the 1970s, weaker versions of the bill came and went, without any result.

Today, two federal government programs provide about 80 per cent of federal child care benefits to working parents. One is the Child and Dependent Care Tax Credit, and the other is the Title Twenty Social Services Act, the post-1980 cutbacks in which have already been discussed.

The Title Twenty funds are administered by the states, and eligibility requirements and payment schedules vary enormously from one state to another. "For example," writes W. Gary Winget, a fellow at the Bush Center, Yale University, "in 1979 one state provided no Title Twenty child care benefit, and expenditures in other states ranged from 5 per cent to 50 per cent of the [state's] Title Twenty funds." In Delaware in 1983, the upper limit of eligibility for a family of four was an income of $12,421. The Department of Commerce estimated the poverty threshold for a family of four in 1983 at $10,180. The state reimbursement was $48 per week for a day care center (the average weekly cost for center care for a three- to five-year-old child is roughly $40 to $60) and $27.50 per week for a family home.

In 1978, Title Twenty child care benefits amounted to $596 million. In 1981, they reached $707 million. After the 1981 budget cuts by the Reagan administration, total combined federal and state spending for Title Twenty child care dropped by 14 per cent to $623 million.

Title Twenty requires that families remain below a certain income level to be eligible, which can act as a disincentive to a family's having a second income or as a deterrent to working for raises that would lift the family out of poverty but also out of eligibility. "On the one hand," comments the Civil Rights Commission on the Catch-22 aspects of the situation, "the mother can only go to work if the family has child care that it can afford; on the other hand, the family can only maintain eligibility for Title Twenty child care if she earns less than $5,000" (assuming a husband's income is $8,500).

Two smaller programs, the Title IV-A Child Care Disregard of Aid to Families with Dependent Children (AFDC) and the Department of Agriculture's Child Care Food Program, make up the rest of the direct payment child care subsidy package offered by the federal government.

Ten states have shifted child care support funds from Title Twenty to Title IV-A, otherwise known as the Child Care Disregard Payment, to try to make up for the reductions in Title Twenty money. But this program is less advantageous to poor families than the Title Twenty program. Title Twenty offers poor families a voucher, which they can use to pay for child care services; Title IV-A offers after-the-fact reimbursement for child care expenses, which is far better than nothing but requires poor families to put up cash, in hopes of later repayment, for services they can't really afford. It also places a ceiling of $160 per month on reimbursable expenses, which forces many families to use lower-quality care than is required in centers that receive Title Twenty funds. And because of the way the Child Care Disregard Payment is calculated into their AFDC grant, families can end up with less money than if they had received Title

Twenty funds. The crucial factor in this calculation is the "$30 and ⅓ Disregard." In general, welfare programs reduce the amount of their benefits as the recipients earn more money on their own. The "$30 and ⅓" provision allows a family receiving AFDC to keep the first $30 of its outside earnings each month with no reduction in AFDC payments, plus one-third of all monthly earnings above $30. Since the Child Care Disregard Payment is deducted from a family's earned income before the "$30 and ⅓ Disregard" provision is applied, the size of the "$30 and ⅓ Disregard" is lowered. In other words, the family gets to keep one-third of a smaller sum than if the calculations were made the other way.

The Child Care Food Program, directed by the Department of Agriculture, provides food or money to nonprofit child care centers or family homes and to centers receiving Title Twenty funds for reduced-price or free meals. In 1981, these funds were cut by 30 per cent, or $130 million per year. In addition, the CETA act, which helped fund staff in child care centers, was eliminated in 1981.

Apart from subsidizing child care directly through Title Twenty and related programs, the government offers indirect support through the Child Care and Dependent Tax Credit, which taxpayers may claim on IRS form 1040. As is the case with most tax deductions and credits, the child care credit mainly benefits middle- and upper-income families. Under this provision, parents who are working or going to school can subtract a portion of the cost of child care from their taxes. If a family's income is $10,000 or less, the credit equals 30 per cent of the expense. The formula used for calculating the tax credit gradually changes, giving a lower credit to families making more than $10,000. The credit is reduced by 1 per cent for each $2,000 of income, up to $28,000. For families with an income above $28,000, the credit equals 20 per cent of expenses up to $2,000 for one child and $4,000 for more than one child.

Although the formula would appear to favor lower-income families, they often cannot afford to spend enough on day care to take full advantage of the credit, while professional-class families easily can. The Congressional Budget Office estimates that only 7 per cent of the benefit from this credit plan goes to families with adjusted gross incomes below $10,000 a year.

In an analysis of the current federal child care aid systems, W. Gary Winget has suggested that "the most effective, reasonable, and economical approach for making child care affordable for all working families" would be a combination of maintaining the current Title Twenty programs but adjusting the tax credit system even further to aid low-income families by raising their credit percentages from 30 per cent to a maximum of 90 per cent.

Naturally, there are alternatives beyond the outlines suggested by Winget. All of them must be tempered by the knowledge that the government needs to reduce its financial obligations, not expand them, and that "middle class" benefit programs, such as Social Security and Medicare, have proven to be the most expensive and most difficult to contain. There are ways, however, of beginning to improve care for the children of working parents without making the federal deficit any worse, and perhaps even to contribute to its solution.

One possibility would be to eliminate the salary reduction plan, in which employers pay some day care costs directly, reducing the employees' taxable income accordingly. This benefit for upper-income parents results in lost tax revenues, which must be made up by heavier taxes on everyone else. If those taxes currently being lost were paid by the families at the upper income levels, then families at the lower income levels could deduct a higher proportion of their child care costs from their tax payments. This could be done without overall loss to the federal budget.

Another possibility is to look to a country like Sweden, which has a successful child care policy, for ideas. Although social and political conditions differ dramatically between the two countries, Sweden has experimented with child care in ways that might inform our decisions here. At first glance, the Swedish policy might seem to favor one group at the expense of others. Under Swedish family law and the Swedish health insurance system, it is assumed that parents of young children need extra time and money more urgently than other people. All families are granted nine months' maternity or paternity leave for each birth, with partial compensation and the right to return to the job. The government also provides generous housing allowances for families with children, time off for sick children (up to sixty days per year), and the right to shorten the workday to six hours until the youngest child is eight years old. The official rationale is that over the course of people's lives, it all evens out. The same families who receive extra help when their children are young provide that help to others, through their taxes, during the other stages of their lives. The United States isn't Sweden, and we have chosen not to have a tax structure that supports such extensive social aid. Even if we believed in it in the abstract, this would hardly be the best time to adopt it, when politicians are searching for ways to reduce government spending. But one part of the Swedish policy may be applicable: the concept that certain people need help more than others. The most costly American social programs are those, such as the retirement and medical programs, that apply to everyone, regardless of need. It seems inevitable that spending for these programs will be reduced somehow, either by giving everyone a little less or by focusing their benefits on the people who need them most. The Swedes illustrate one way to draw such distinctions. Their policy reflects a view that raising children is costly, time-consuming, and important, and that there are times in children's lives, for example when they are sick or infants, when only a parent will do.

Short of paying outright subsidies, as in Sweden, there are other areas in which the interests of children and child care might be linked with other programs already in existence. A link between Social Security and day care is one possibility. Social Security now accounts for about a third of all federal spending. Everyone over sixty-two who has paid into the system or has had a spouse who paid into the system is eligible to receive funds. Funding Social Security payments is already a major budgetary dilemma and will grow worse. People are retiring earlier and living longer, so the balance between years spent paying in and years spent drawing out has been skewed. Further, the population is gradually aging, so there are fewer workers supporting more retirees. Now, because of changes made in the 1970s, the benefit schedule is such that most recipients, including the wealthy, receive a windfall. A retiree who has earned the average wage all his life and spends the average number of years in retirement can expect to receive Social Security benefits worth two to three times as much as all the contributions he made during his working days, plus all his employers' matching contributions and all the interest those contributions might have earned.

Whatever the ultimate solution to the funding imbalance in the Social Security program, there is a natural connection between policies for retirement and for child care. We have a resource — the able elderly in our society — and we have a need — the very young children of working parents with inadequate or nonexistent day care. I am not trying to offer a detailed design for a program that would match the resource with the need, but I do mean to suggest a principle that should be considered in planning the future of Social Security and day care: that the more able and healthy Social Security recipients be given an opportunity to "earn" some of their Social Security dollars by part-time service in day care centers.

This proposal obviously will not work for everyone. But it could work well for many. Plenty of elderly people are fully capable of being involved in community affairs, volunteer work, and leisure activities and are eager to do so. They still lead active lives. Many are clearly experienced with children, having raised their own families, and would bring tremendous assets to the system of child care from their own lives and perspectives. They would also gain, in most cases, a real sense of involvement and satisfaction.

Staffing centers with senior citizens is an idea that has been tried and proven successful in some centers around the country already. The work by older people should not be the more physically taxing positions on day care staffs, but every head teacher needs assistants; every nursery needs more hands to rock babies and give feedings; every center needs more adults to read stories, tend minor emergencies, and administer the personal attentions that are routine events in children's daily lives.

This suggestion will not solve all the problems of Social Security financing, nor will it solve all the shortages of competent staff in day care. But it will go a step toward both ends.

Another issue we will someday have to begin debating again is resumption of the draft or a broader form of nonmilitary national service. I believe there are good reasons for supporting a national service obligation of some eighteen months for every man and woman at about eighteen years of age. It would inspire a sense of service to the country, break down the class barriers, and give the more disadvantaged youth a chance, as the armed forces traditionally have done, to begin a trade or develop working experience.

It is natural to think of day care as part of these discussions. Making day care work a part of national service would have many benefits. For young people, it would offer training and experience in a profession. For a day care center, it would mean having competent, entry-level staff who were committed to a term of service that exceeds the current temporary status of most beginning day care staffers. For day care as an institution, it could also go a long way toward raising the dignity of the work of caring for children by making it part of a national commitment to caring well for all our people.

Young people could offer a kind of help that senior citizens could not — the more rough and tumble, hardy kind of play that toddlers require, and the organized activities on playgrounds or at swimming pools that school-age children who are cared for in after-school programs require. It would offer these older children a chance to have a kind of big brother or big sister contact. Because it would give many more young people who were themselves approaching childbearing years realistic experience with young children, it would inevitably open their eyes at least a little wider to the difficulties and the worthiness of caring for children.

12

The Politics of Day Care

IN THE LAST SEVERAL CHAPTERS, I have tried to concentrate on the facts about child care: why people need it, how much they pay for it, what it means to children, how it might be improved. In the following section, I will deal with child care as an *idea*, that is, as a cause, a symbol, a subject for political and ideological debate.

Child care is important as a symbol, because it represents the point where two worlds touch: the world of family and the world of work. Family is an increasingly important symbol to the political right, which feels that traditional family values have come under heavy assault. Work is especially important to the feminist movement, which has opened up possibilities for women's advancement mainly in the arena of away-from-home work. The idea of child care, then, is of great significance to each of these groups, but for opposite reasons. The step that seems, to one side, most important for women's advancement — freedom to leave the home and enter the workplace — seems to the other to be most threatening to family structure. The political symbolism has become so powerful that it often obscures important differences of detail. There is no readily apparent logical connection, for example, between one's views on day care and one's views on abortion, the Equal Rights Amendment, gay rights, or prayer in schools. But the symbolic connection among them now seems so obvious that if you state your opinions on one issue you are thought to have spoken your mind on all of them. Once I was talking with a day care advocate — about day care and nothing else. When it was clear that our views differed, she said to me, "Oh, and I can guess how you must feel about ERA and reproductive rights, too." Even if I had persuaded her of the truth — which was that my opinions resembled hers on most of those other issues — it would not have made any difference. It was as if I had cheered a touchdown by the opposing team.

Sometimes passionately held convictions help elevate our public decisions. Where would we be if no one had been passionate about slavery or civil rights? But passion about the idea of child care has, I believe, made things worse for everyone. Not only have the convictions of the profamily and the feminist extremes pushed them away from reasonable compromises — the conservatives resist reforms in day care that could improve the lives of millions of children; the feminists tolerate mediocre day care because they don't like to hear criticism of day care as an institution — but they have also thwarted the evolution of a political outlook that would take the welfare of children, in the day care center or at home, as its first premise and deduce its specific prescriptions accordingly.

As with abortion, the death penalty, and other contentious social issues, the debate about day care has become emotional and polarized. You're either for it or against it, and there is not much middle ground. Often the area of disagreement extends even to what day care is. Some people who "don't believe in day care" really mean that they wouldn't consign their children to large, impersonal day care centers, but they happily do send them to family homes or nursery schools. Meanwhile, some people who say that "day care is fine for children" are thinking about several hours a day in a family home, while others have in mind the ten-hour-a-day group day care centers. Nearly everyone forgets to count babysitting or care by a relative as "child care," and certainly it is not considered "day care."

My purpose in this section of the book is to examine the way the *idea* of child care has affected the politics of, first, the con-

servative movement and, second, the feminists. I do not mean
to pair these groups as mirror images whose positions conve-
niently cancel each other out. But I do think there is one important similarity in their positions, which is the subordination of
children's interests to some other political goal. What our political recommendations might look like if the order were reversed,
and children put first, is the subject of the final part of this
discussion.

In the political arena day care, in the sense of organized care
for large groups of children, is more often discussed than any
other form of child care. Partly this is because of the centers'
growing popularity. Partly it is because they present a manage-
able subject for political debate: day care centers focus the discussion. To their supporters, they seem to be a more democratic
way of making similar care available to all children, and to their
opponents they seem to be a threatening incursion of the state
into family life.

The most familiar conservative criticism of day care is that it
amounts to a near-totalitarian separation of child from parent
and should in no way be encouraged. For example, in December
1983, the Select Committee on Children, Youth, and Families
of the House of Representatives issued a report about child care.
Among other things, it examined the ways in which the federal
government could become more deeply involved in day care,
such as concentrating its support on the neediest recipients, expanding its overall level of support, and encouraging private
firms to provide more day care for their employees. In short, the
report recommended that the federal government do more to
encourage day care. But four Republican members* filed a dis-
sent, which made clear that they considered support for day care
to be unacceptable, as a matter of first principles.

"Let's look for a moment at the real subject of our discussion,
the children," the dissenting statement said. "When we talk
about the comparative costs of care for infants, toddlers, and
pre-school children, we ought never to forget that we are talking
about children who will be taken from their mothers and cared

*Representatives Thomas J. Bliley, Jr., of Virginia, Dan Coats of Indiana,
Frank R. Wolf of Virginia, and Barbara F. Vucanovich of Nevada.

for primarily by strangers from the first months of their lives." Before the government even dreamed of supporting day care, the dissenters said, it must answer the ultimate question: "How does day care affect our children?" This is certainly a good question, but it will not be answered with confidence any time soon — and in the meantime, millions of children are in child care, and millions more go without any supervision at home.

Often, conservative opponents of day care say that they recognize that some mothers have to work, and they even sound broad-minded about it. The Reverend Jerry Falwell, leader of the Moral Majority, has said, "My pastoral advice is if the wife must work, the husband should make the extra effort to compensate in any way possible for her absence. . . . I think families can raise children successfully if the husband and wife find it necessary to work. It is my belief the husband is as much responsible for rearing children as the wife." Similarly, Paul Weyrich, executive director of the conservative Committee for Survival of a Free Congress, has said: "Where there's a single parent, or where the father simply cannot earn sufficient funds to support the family in a reasonable style, then a mother often has to work for the benefit of her family."

Yet the logical progression seems to come to a halt at this point. If Falwell and Weyrich really believe that mothers must sometimes work, does it not follow that someone must look after their children? If day care is therefore necessary, shouldn't the conservatives join in supporting improvements in the institutions where these children will spend so many hours? Apparently not, if that means further expansion of federal power. Rochelle Beck of the Children's Defense Fund points out that the Moral Majority is one of the "'profamily' interest groups [whose] effective lobbying and fundraising efforts go on to oppose federal funds for child care services."

The conservative spokesmen are not actually against improvements in day care, but they oppose all the steps — especially further regulation and subsidy — that would make improvement possible. They support the kind of laissez-faire, catch-as-catch-can child care system we have today, whereby some combination of luck and money is the only answer to finding good care. For example, Weyrich has said: "If a mother has to work, she should try to see to it that her children are cared for by another family, or by other family members. What is detrimental is when so many kids are left in day care operations with strangers . . . a child learns to hide the things he's worried about from some day care attendant."

Can Weyrich have imagined what it is like to "try to see to it" that a friend or relative handle all the day care? He is right about the drawbacks of large day care centers but is content to wish the problem away, since this fits the convenience of his overall political views.

In 1977, Phyllis Schlafly, leader of the anti-ERA movement, touched on day care in her book, *The Power of the Positive Woman*. Her statement still stands as a fair reflection of the "profamily" conservative attitude today, despite its acknowledgment that some parents "have to work." She wrote:

> The energies and dedication of the Positive Woman are needed as never before to fend off the attacks on the moral, the social and economic integrity of the family.
>
> Take, for example, the tremendous drive to set up childcare centers — taxpayer-financed, government-managed, "universally" available for "all socioeconomic groups" regardless of means. This adds up to an attempt to make it public policy to remove babies from the family unit and place them in an institutional environment.

The dangers of such institutional influence are so obvious to Schlafly and others on the right that they need not even be mentioned. With babies in centralized, state-run institutions, the all-pervasive tyranny of big government will be that much closer at hand.

Chester Finn, a professor of education and public policy at Vanderbilt University who espouses the conservative position on day care, also sees the need for day care as evidence of a weakened family unit: "Certainly one major drift of 'progressive' opinion in recent years has been toward a loose and accepting definition of the family, combined with firm and insistent demands on the larger society to assume responsibility for the well-being of children." To him, these demands are most insistent and irritating when they come from needy families, and especially when they involve day care. "Government can transfer resources, thereby easing some of the direct economic hardship of the underclass family, and it can supply certain social services — all the while risking increased dependency — but it cannot substitute for parents."

Obviously the government cannot "substitute" for parents; but there are certain families in which parents cannot or will not care adequately for their children. To what extent will those parents' sins be visited upon their children? By defining those parents as morally unworthy — which in some cases they may be — the conservatives have successfully excluded the innocent *children* of those families from the universe of those deserving public help. This position leads easily to a dismissal of subsidized day care as a national need. But nothing in this argument acknowledges that, in any conceivable version of future American society, many children are sure to remain in day care centers. What is to become of them? Are they not as deserving of profamily love and concern as anyone else?

Connaught Marshner, director of Family Policy for the conservative think tank, the Free Congress Research and Education Foundation, says that government involvement in child care would only mean mass, low-quality, center-based care and that private arrangements are better. This is simply wrong. The grim history of day care reveals that government has been more responsible in setting standards for higher-quality care than private enterprise. And it shows that the current every-man-for-himself strategy of arranging for child care means that luck and money determine the quality of the day care experience of a child. Continuing it will only perpetuate the uneven delivery of services we now have.

As is so often the case in political life, the inflexibilities and excesses of one extreme are fully matched by the other. While the conservatives of the world oppose day care in principle as an extension of big government, many on the left support it for equally doctrinaire reasons, with equally faint attention to the welfare of the children involved.

For leaders of the women's movement, which has done so much to remove barriers to occupational success for women, it is natural that day care be seen in a special light. It cannot be thought of simply as an attractive idea that might open new possibilities for certain people. It is more than that: it is indispensable, the key to everything else. Unless the children can safely and happily be left in someone else's care, what is to become of all the potential advances in the outside world?

The feminists accurately described the Catch-22 situation for mothers: women compromise their chances of getting and keeping good jobs because they can't afford the excellent day care that would be necessary if they were to give full priority to their careers, and they can't get the excellent day care they need for their children because they don't have lucrative enough jobs to pay for it. The feminists are not deluding themselves with dreams about the fathers quitting work to tend the children while their wives move up. They are too realistic for that and, by their logic, it might be unnecessary, if professional caretakers can do the job just as well. Day care has to be the answer. The idea does not seem outrageous on its face; children have, after all, gone to nursery schools and kindergartens for years. The only people who seem to be objecting are those who feel threatened by the idea of women succeeding in the workplace at all.

Can it be surprising that criticism of day care has become such a taboo for the women's movement? People may be willing to entertain private, among-friends complaints about the defects or costs of certain centers or certain approaches, as long as everyone understands that they all believe in day care as an institution. But when the criticism is conducted in public, where the gains made by the women's movement still seem so fragile, can it be anything but a hostile act? It is but a short step from criticizing day care to suggesting that there might be fundamental conflicts between parenthood and career.

So it is that feminist leaders, including many perceptive analysts of society's secret rules and messages, tend to defend day care with a blind, unperceptive passion. They have little patience for hearing anything Bad about something that is so basically Good.

Many liberals and feminists end up sounding as doctrinaire and defensive about day care as, for example, Bettye Caldwell, president of the National Association for the Education of Young Children, a professional organization for preschool educators, who has recently denounced several skeptical reports about day care. No doubt Caldwell, who represents those who work in centers, is sincerely concerned about the conditions that make large group day care difficult for many children, but she has reserved her public fury for something else — the *reports* about bad conditions, which she says give day care a bad name. She has said that one of the day care profession's major challenges is to improve its public image; from there it is a short step, which she and many others have taken, to viewing any report of day care's real problems as a victory for the other side.

Caldwell said, in remarks to the 1983 Junior League Parenting Conference in Washington, D.C., "It's just devastating to read some of the things that are written by supposedly responsible journalists." She was particularly outraged by an article published in 1983 by the *Texas Monthly*. The author, Dominique Browning, described what she saw when she visited day care centers in and around Houston. Caldwell cited the "incredible story" that Browning told in her article as an example:

> Whenever an adult enters the center, every child thinks, for a split second, that that person is Mommy. Each child wants to see Mommy so badly that he anticipates her arrival at any moment and he assumes that anyone coming in from the outside is Mommy. A short, fat man wearing a baseball cap came in one afternoon to sell Mrs. Royer a new kind of cleaning fluid, and as he sprayed the stuff in his mouth to demonstrate how safe it was, five or six little heads bobbed up and greeted him with a cheery "Mommy!"

Caldwell told the Junior League that she had been to a lot of day care centers in her time and had never seen anything like that. "Either they hid those children when I came by or that's a gross distortion of the reality that's out there," she remarked.

The problems Browning and others have described are real;

Bettye Caldwell may not have seen day care centers like those Browning described, but I have, and I did not have to look very hard. There are two possible explanations for the attitude Caldwell expressed: either she is unaware of what day care centers are really like, which is almost impossible to imagine, or she is well aware but finds it harmful for the day care cause to have people dwell on the "negatives." Meanwhile, tens of thousands of children are sent off to such centers each day.

Ellen Goodman, a columnist for the *Boston Globe*, has taken a similar tell-me-no-bad-news line. In 1983, for example, she took offense at the American Medical Association's warning that day care centers were becoming dangerous sources of infections and disease. She wrote, "Sometimes the State of Day Care is like a distant third-world country. It only gets into the paper when something goes wrong there. . . . Following the course of this story . . . I noted how much attention we focus on the relatively minor problems germinating in the lives of those who do have access to day care. By comparison, we easily overlook the problems of those who don't have access."

Yes, the "problems of those who don't have access" are serious. But is that a reason to write off (as Goodman clearly intended to) reports about the shortcomings of day care as it actually exists? Has she spent enough time in the centers to see what these "relatively minor problems" look like? Like Goodman, many feminists seem to think that acknowledging day care's defects is too grave a political risk even to be contemplated. In fact, they end up defeating their own purposes, because pretending that problems with day care do not exist, when so many people know from their own experience that they do, gravely weakens the case for making more and better care available.

Liberals in general have found it hard to confess the limitations of their social programs, even though warts and imperfections are inevitable in even the best-run organizations. For this reluctance they have paid a steep political price in credibility. There is a lot of very bad day care out there, but the institution of outside-the-home child care must be strong enough to withstand scrutiny and criticism, or it will not improve and flourish.

13

The Profamily Movement

THE POLITICAL DISCUSSION of parenthood is not confined to day care, even though that is the subject of some of its most publicized disagreements. It also extends to a consideration of women's general place in society. Should women be free to advance, professionally and socially, as men have? Or do they have a "natural" place at home?

The conservative profamily movement, which has been so prominent in the fights against both day care and abortion, rests on the belief that there are preordained roles for the two genders. According to its tenets, there is an "ideal" division of labor and authority within the family, which should not be tampered with by government order or social experimentation. In the "ideal" family (I emphasize the word because it plays such a large part in profamily literature), the husband is the breadwinner and the decision maker. Next to him is his wife, his helpmeet but not quite his equal, who is the maker of the home and the caretaker of the children. It is assumed that the children do best when cared for by the mother at home. And it is assumed that the woman can find all her fulfillment in life by taking care of her home and children.

The political right offers a clear, thorough, and complete explanation of the woman's place at home. It is good (traditional, Christian, given) to be there; every woman has a responsibility (to her husband and her children) to be there; she enjoys security (her right to support by her husband) in her position; she should find all her satisfactions there (from raising her children); it is important that she be there (to her family, she is irreplaceable).

One of the most prominent proponents of these views is Phyllis Schlafly, whom the *Conservative Digest* calls the first lady of the profamily movement. What Schlafly would have for all other women is her version of a perfect life — that is, a life much like her own.

I met Phyllis Schlafly one late June afternoon in the Capitol Hill office of the national profamily organization she started, the Eagle Forum. She had been motherly when she answered her phone when I first called her at her home in Alton, Illinois, solicitous in making arrangements for a meeting that would suit my schedule. From what I'd read in *Ms.* magazine and elsewhere, I had been expecting to find when I met her in person a harpy, a harridan, or at least an excessively brisk woman. What I met instead was an attractive, professional-looking woman — calm as an executive, warm as my best friend's mother. She was gracious when she ushered me into her office, more like a hostess having me in for coffee than like the relentless driving force behind the anti-ERA movement across America. "Hello, Debbie. Sorry to keep you waiting. Tell me about your book. Have you got a copy of *Sweetheart*?"

I had read her biography, *Sweetheart of the Silent Majority*, and I had read many of her monthly newsletters, *The Phyllis Schlafly Report*. (By the way, it wasn't easy to locate these publications. I first started looking when we lived in Austin and met up with an attitude I soon learned was widespread. At the time, I didn't know the names of Schlafly's books, or indeed if she had even written any. I called a bookstore in Austin that specialized in women's books and asked if they carried any or knew about any. "I don't know if she's written anything and we certainly wouldn't carry it if she did," the woman on the phone snapped. I finally ordered everything through the Eagle Forum.) From talking with her, I soon knew many things about Phyllis Schlafly's personal life: that she worked her way through college toiling in a munitions factory; that she taught all six of her children to read; that her children were all doing well. From reading, I had learned much more: that she wrote and published her own numerous books; that she lived in financial security with her wealthy husband; that she had waged several unsuccessful campaigns for political office; that her husband was much older than she was; that she had had a "governess" for her children for at least one summer.

In between the lines of her conversation and writing are the facts — few in number but critical in scope — that are the prerequisites to the "perfect" life she has led: she has an education, she has money, she has a supportive and loyal husband, she is healthy herself and has healthy children. These are some of the factors that have undoubtedly paved the way to her accomplishing as much as she has during her years but have also undoubtedly contributed to her seeming lack of compassion and understanding that life does not always run so smoothly for everyone else.

The problem with the conservative blueprint for women's lives is that for most women, life just doesn't work the way Schlafly thinks it should. Half the women getting married now can expect to be divorced; by 1990, one child of every four under ten years old — almost 9 million children — will have lived with only one parent at some point in his or her life. More than one-quarter of the women who are legally entitled to child support payments do not receive them. In hard economic times, husbands will lose jobs, and women can still expect to earn only about 60 per cent of what men earn. These facts are widely publicized now, but we can pretty well guess that during the days when divorce was rare and when women kept their counsel, discontent and trouble also existed — only secretly.

Schlafly, however, seems to have turned a blind eye to statistics like these, turned a judgmental ear to the stories of troubled women. She complacently advises women to stay home, resting assured that "since God ordained that women have babies, our laws properly and realistically establish that men must provide financial support for their wives and children." Where, oh where, has she been?

Connaught Marshner is a generation younger than Schlafly but, like her, a mother and a real and visible power in the conservative movement. Marshner, like many women who are in the middle of raising young families, speaks her conservative opinions with more realism than Schlafly does.

I met Connaught Marshner one December morning in her office at the Free Congress building on the quickly renovating fringe of Capitol Hill. She is an attractive, kind-looking woman in her mid-thirties, with dark, shoulder-length hair pinned back from her face. She has a company phone in her car so she can conduct business on her long commutes to Virginia, where she lives with her husband, who is a professor at a small college, and her two elementary-school-age sons. On her desk sits a photo of one of her sons bathing her infant daughter who, she tells me at a difficult moment in our talk about families and work, recently died from heart disease. Unlike Schlafly, Marshner has been roughed up by life. Her family's good health and continued prosperity have not been givens for her.

Marshner agrees with the right's version of the "ideal" family, in which the mother stays home with the children. But, she explains, "ideal" comes with two large qualifications: "if" a family can afford for the mother to stay home and "if" she can be fulfilled at home. High mortgage interest rates and the expectations with which women are now raised mean that many will work.

This part of the conservative platform — that it is all right for women to work — sounds like the declarations I have heard from any number of liberals and feminists. The difference lies in the emphasis. For Marshner and many of the more up-to-date (post-Schlafly) conservatives, the fact of working mothers is just that — a fact. It is not a goal or an opportunity or a promising development, all of which it usually is to feminists, who believe that women's most important battle for equality must be waged in the workplace. Getting women to work is not Marshner's cause. For her, women work because they are called upon to, either for economic reasons or for community needs. Women, being "other-oriented" by nature, as Marshner puts it, respond to a call from others to work, rather than to inner drives.

A mother who works or who is divorced or single, according to Marshner, can still raise a "traditional" family. The idea of "tradition" rests much less on the structure of the family or the detailed division of family labor than on a sense of mission about moral standards. The family must live by, and the children must be inculcated with, "a system of moral norms which, once well-defined, are taken to be without exception."

In some general sense, it's hard to quibble with Marshner's morality. It sounds like an effort to raise good, honest, generous children — something all of us, conservative or liberal, strive to do. But Marshner's definitions of a "traditional" morality are more specific than this and include prominently her staunch belief that, when push comes to shove, the father is the figure of authority, the final decision maker in the family. "The husband is the head of the household," she says. "He *should* have responsibility for making final decisions. That *should* be the case."

Somewhere between Schlafly and Marshner the conservative pendulum rests. Much of the right still ignores the basic truth about women at home: that they are in a state of financial dependency. This is not necessarily evil — it is the situation in my family's household, by my husband's and my own choice — but it requires something more than Schlafly's pacifying assertions that women needn't worry about these things.

Every woman needs to make sure she can take care of herself and the children if circumstances should change, and to this need the conservatives seem blind. Without being fatalistic but simply facing facts, this means making financial provisions for such unforeseen but common occurrences as divorce or illness or death, and at least thinking of contingency plans as an alternative to intolerable situations at home, such as infidelity or physical abuse.

For their self-protection, women need some form of insurance, a cushion to fall back on. It may be education, which would equip them to earn a living (even if they had preferred not to while the children were little and their husbands were still alive or in the household); it may be extra money, from an insurance policy or pension; it may be a network of extended family or friends, which can help absorb the shock. But in whatever form, the insurance is necessary: otherwise women cannot be sure they can function independently if they need to.

This planning need not imply, as Schlafly suggests, that women who make such preparations are spurning their families. She has characterized the provoking call of the feminists thus: "Come, leave your home, your husband, and children and join all those unhappy females in a new sisterhood of togetherness." It does not imply any less love, trust, or confidence in a marriage or family situation. It means simply a wise precaution against life's sometimes unpleasant surprises. Behind every statistic of divorce, widowhood, or poverty is the story of a woman whose life did not turn out the way she planned.

The right ignores not only the need for these provisions for the unexpected but also plans for the inevitable. The responsibility of caring for children, consuming as it may be, has limits even while it is going on and will someday be over. What are women to do then?

Women as individuals have always spoken and acted on the need to reach out, to stretch themselves, to fulfill their own ambitions, just as men have. In the last twenty years, women have spoken and acted as a gender, a united group, more than ever before. But women's basic human desire to accomplish something in their lives, besides the valuable work of raising children, and to do so with no less pride or dignity or seriousness than they displayed in child rearing, is pooh-poohed by Schlafly. She implies that it's all a matter of bad attitude — "whether you wake up in the morning with a chip on your shoulder or whether you have a positive mental attitude." Once you stop moping around the house and letting yourself get Big Ideas about meeting challenges in the outside world, then your troubles will disappear. Stop feeling sorry for yourself, Schlafly scolds: "If you think diapers and dishes are a never-ending repetitive routine, just remember that most of the jobs outside the home are just as repetitive, tiresome, and boring." Similarly:

> If young women think that there are greater career satisfactions in being elected to important positions, traveling to exciting faraway places, having executive authority over

large numbers of people . . . than there are in having a baby, they are wrong. None of those measures of career success can compare with the thrill, the satisfaction, and the fun of having and caring for babies, and watching them respond and grow under a mother's loving care. More babies multiply a woman's joy. . . . If you complain about servitude to a husband, servitude to a boss will be more intolerable. Everyone in the world has a boss of some kind. It is easier for most women to achieve a harmonious working relationship with a husband than with a foreman, supervisor, or office manager.

Rita Kramer, author of *In Defense of the Family*, suggests that some feminists "attempt to substitute one form of tyranny [child rearing] with another [working at a job]." But she's wrong to write off the real needs some women feel about their non-child-related pursuits. She suggests that most women who are at work don't really want to be there and have just been forced there by conformist pressures: "This speaks . . . to the situation of the woman who is ambivalent — whose natural desire to be with her baby may give way to the social pressure to 'be somebody' in a society that is increasingly telling women that what counts is achievement, however trivial, outside the home, just so it is outside the home and apart from child rearing."

Social pressures certainly do play a large part in many women's decisions to work. But I doubt that most women who work see the situation quite as neatly as Kramer suggests. She underestimates the depth of feeling and the scope of the ambivalence that many women have about their desire to broaden themselves beyond child rearing.

With little understanding of how tearing an issue this is for many women, members of the right blithely offer an array of milquetoast alternatives for keeping busy outside the home. Their encouragement is confined, and their enthusiasm is constrained, to suggestions that are reminiscent of the club movement of the 1860s for middle-class "women of leisure." Carol Hymowitz and Michaele Weissman have described the situation of late-nineteenth-century women who, thanks to new technology that helped with the housework, found themselves with time on their hands. Many joined "clubs":

> First there were the local groups. These tended to be garden clubs and ladies' associations which devoted themselves to what was known as "self culture." Members sat through interminable lectures on Japanese flower arrangements and other arcane subjects. . . . For most women the clubs remained a pastime rather than a vehicle for self-realization. The clubs provided middle-class women with an avenue of escape from boredom at home.

Schlafly's suggestions are uncomfortably similar to this movement of an earlier century:

> The biggest problem for wives in their middle years is boredom and idleness. It can even be a fatal disease. . . . Women in their middle years are particularly susceptible to this disease. The duties of motherhood are suddenly lifted. The duties of being a wife have been reduced by the private enterprise system to a few hours a day. This gives her entirely too many idle hours to stew about the minor physical and psychological problems of menopause. . . .
>
> Every community is crying for the kind of volunteer work that women can best give: welfare, hospital, educational, cultural, civic, and political. All these avenues provide opportunities for women to perform useful services to the community — and in so doing to become happier, more interesting, and more fulfilled. . . .
>
> A good cause can provide an outlet for her continuing maternal urge in the years between the time when her children go off to school and when she is discovered by her grandchildren.

Volunteerism certainly meets a basic human need. It can be deeply satisfying to help others when they cannot help themselves; it can be fulfilling to perform services and accomplish tasks, even if it isn't for pay. Weekly duty as a hospital volunteer, attending meetings for community service clubs, participating in museum benefits, doing library work — all these have their place, and most of us do some of them at different points in our lives. The shortcoming of the conservatives' viewpoint is not their recognition of the merits of volunteerism; it is their simplistic notion that it can and should be enough for all women. Not everyone can find a life of fulfillment in volunteer work, just as not everyone can find fulfillment in a boardroom, a courtroom, a hospital, a university, or at home.

To read the right's hymns of praise to The Family, one might guess that the welfare of children was the first and last item on its list of concerns. One could assume that it believes the reason mothers and fathers should take their assigned places in the family hierarchy is so the children can thereby benefit. Mothers should stick to their places at home because the children need them there.* Fathers should keep bringing home the bacon to the patiently waiting dependents because then the children will have a secure environment and learn the "natural" roles of men and women.

The details of the right's position, however, amount not to a constant focus on children's welfare but to a seeming disinterest in children and their needs. There is an abstract, peculiar sense of what children are like. I can't claim, especially after meeting them, that conservatives don't love their children as much as anyone else does. It is a part of the human spirit to care so deeply about children. After much immersion in their literature, though, it seems to me that the conservatives' view of children is remote, studied, and at odds with the practical realities of daily life.

Once again, Phyllis Schlafly is a remarkable example. As she tells it, she was able to write books while her children played

---

* While I agree with the right that young children do best at home with a parent, there are two major differences between my position on this and theirs. First, I think fathers are just as capable of — and indeed should be just as responsible for — being at home with children as mothers are. And second, unlike Phyllis Schlafly, who maintains that even nursery school is bad for kids, I think part-time nursery school for preschool-age children is good for the children and necessary for most mothers. In my interview with her, Phyllis Schlafly said to me, upon hearing that my own two boys had been in morning nursery school since they were two years old, "Keeping children at home until a late age is very advantageous. Not only do I not believe in child care centers, I don't believe in nursery school or kindergartens, either."

contentedly about her feet. "I was able to compose and write with children right around me," she explains and adds, "My husband can't do that."

Having spent the last three years in such an effort myself, with my children ranging from as young as one year to as old as seven years during that time, I know the difficulties of writing with children around. I can do it only when my children are away — sleeping, at school, at friends' houses. Surely Schlafly has forgotten. Could her children really have colored or built with blocks around her feet for sustained periods without interrupting with questions, requests for glasses of water, trips to the bathroom, or fights? Or perhaps she closed her study door and the children just knew not to enter. (I have read articles by mothers who boasted that this was their secret to working at home and "caring" for their children at the same time.) That could possibly work, occasionally, for a ten-year-old, but it certainly won't—and shouldn't—work with a child of three.

Phyllis Schlafly's reminiscences of children greatly resemble Marabel Morgan's. Morgan is the author of *The Total Woman*, a book that made her notorious for recommending, among other things, that women lift the spirits of their tired breadwinners by greeting them at the front door clad only in Saran Wrap. Children flit in and out of her book in the role of beribboned Shirley Temples.

Morgan says she counseled one mother to "draw out the venom inside a person" as a tactic for dealing with a recalcitrant child. She writes, "Her daughter was practicing for piano recital, and she kept whining nervously, 'I just can't play that number.' Instead of saying, 'I know you're going to do fine,' the mother asked, 'Do you feel you might not do well in the recital, honey?' The girl cried, 'Oh, Mom, you do understand. I want to be just like you when I grow up. We have the best family!'"

And she relates the story of the successful disciplining of a three-year-old: "When a close friend spanked his three-year-old for hitting the baby, he did it in a loving way. Afterward the child hugged him and said, 'Thank you for saying no, Daddy!'"

Well, I have been around a lot of children for a lot of years now, and I have never, ever, seen a child behave like that.

It would be nice if every family ended up with the handsome, bright, well-behaved, and thoughtful children that the conservatives seem to believe are the inevitable products of mother-raising. If we knew there was a such a correlation, parents would, I think, feel much less anguish in their decisions; we would all stay home to raise perfect children. But what I have seen in my experience with children is a lot more complicated than this.

I think Schlafly does everyone a grave disservice when she implies that a perfect life with a perfect mother will automatically produce a perfect child. "A mother can see the results of her own handiwork in the good citizen she has produced and trained," she writes, putting the burden of responsibility for how the child turns out on the mother's shoulders. She congratulates mothers on successes they aren't responsible for — and implicitly charges them with failures they can't control.

Of course, children are not their own creations, and much of the way they end up does reflect their parents' efforts. But parents — even full-time parents — exercise only a limited control over their children and the way they will turn out. The false congratulations that Schlafly issues are vestigial remains of a child-rearing philosophy that led so many mothers of the previous generation to lose perspective on their own lives and live vicariously through their children, both in important things like how well Susie did in school and in trivial things like how many hits Billy had in the Little League game.

Bearing and raising a child is far more complex and far less controlled and programmable than Schlafly would have us think. There is not much room for bad luck in her world. What if a child is born ill or impaired in some way? Is a mother to feel any less pride? Does it mean you have failed if you have nothing to show off to your friends and neighbors? What if you raise a plumber or a short-order cook instead of a lawyer or a business executive? What if you raise a radical instead of a conservative? Just as you can't control the sex of your child, the skills she is born with, or the beauty he inherits, you can affect but not determine your child's future, his personality, her "success." You can choose to have a child, but you can't choose the child you get. You can do your best while raising your child, but you can't claim or bear responsibility for the life your child leads. Yet this is the burden, and the reward, that Schlafly seems to assign to mothers who spend all their energies raising children.

With its narrow definition of family roles and of women's possibilities, then, the right disserves children's interests in several ways. It preaches complacency about the financial and occupational preparations that can protect women and children if their family's luck turns bad. It discourages women from meeting challenges in the world outside the home, thereby reducing the spiritual resources that can enrich their years with their children and help them set a more promising example for their daughters. In addition, many conservatives have succumbed to the usual temptation of the comfortable to forget about (or condemn) those on whom fortune has not smiled. As a result, the movement is indifferent to measures that can improve conditions for children who are not from "ideal" families and need to rely heavily on day care.

No one on the right sees a conflict between children's interests and the movement's tenets; they think they are identical. I disagree, but the effects I have described, harmful as I think they are, might nonetheless be described as incidental, unintended consequences of a movement that is really focused on other things.

In the case of the women's movement, with which I am in much more sympathy than I am with the political right, the conflict has a different source. Nothing about it is incidental or indirect. The movement's most basic goal is at odds with the idea that parents, especially mothers, should be personally responsible for raising their children. That conflict is the subject of the next chapter.

❧ 14 ❧

The Women's Movement and Motherhood

THE HISTORY of the latest phase of the women's movement began with the publication of Betty Friedan's *The Feminine Mystique* in 1963. From then to now, despite differences in policies and personalities, one idea has been constant: the central arena in which women should achieve and demonstrate their success is the workplace. Consequently, the natural thrust of the women's movement has been to get women out of the house and into the working world.

Home was depicted by Friedan as a domestic penal institution for women, one that trivialized their efforts, dragged down their spirits, closed off their minds:

> They baked their own bread, sewed their own and their children's clothes, kept their new washing machines and dryers running all day. They changed the sheets on the beds twice a week instead of once, took the rug-hooking class in adult education. . . . Their only dream was to be perfect wives and mothers; their highest ambition to have five children and a beautiful house; their only fight to get and keep their husbands. They had no thought of the unfeminine problems of the world outside the home; they wanted the men to make the major decisions.

Friedan's message — that women were desperately unhappy in this kind of life and needed to get out — should not have been astonishing or startling. But the response to it was. Many women as individuals had felt all the symptoms she described, but they saw themselves as oddities in a sea of happy suburbanites. Friedan's book gave women a focus, a sense of union, drawing them together in a communion of spirit. In the first year of its publication, *The Feminine Mystique* sold an amazing three hundred thousand copies. And whether it was intended to be so or not, *The Feminine Mystique* became a manifesto for getting women into the mainstream of life, which was translated as going to work.

While the women's movement has carefully proclaimed that its intention is to give women, all women, the opportunity to choose how they will lead their lives — as professionals, as wage earners, or as housewives — the focus of their efforts is obviously the workplace. The home was where women had been forever. It was seen, at least in the immediate aftermath of *The Feminine Mystique*, as part of the problem. It is where women have had to cope with problems in personal ways, behind closed front doors. None of these traits make the home a likely setting for challenging or critical breakthroughs. Those are to be found in the workplace, where women are relative newcomers, where there is hope for change. The workplace is where issues can be hit head-on, where lawsuits and showdowns can produce change. Discrimination in jobs, equal pay, right to advancement — all can be addressed. The workplace is still where the most important battles are being waged, where the crises are — and where the fun and the money are. For the most part, the advancement of women has been defined by the women's movement as advancement in the job market. The workplace is the arena, and women as workers — not women as homemakers — are the players.

On a personal level, the workplace seems to offer an answer for just about all the problems and complications of women's lives. You can tick off each problem and think of the quick-fix solution that will come from going to work. Dependent on your spouse? Get an income, become self-sufficient. No power to back up your opinion? Get equal power with a paycheck — money talks. Bored? Get out of the house and in with interesting people. Feeling unappreciated, uncompensated? Get a job with a paycheck. Lonely? Get out of the house and into an office. Everyone taking you for granted? Find recognition with an official-sounding job.

Only one thing is missing, of course, and that is a conception of how all this affects the children. Leaders of the women's movement never quite say that jobs should come before children. Those from the mainstream of the movement take great care to say that children *are* important and to point out that many of their guiding lights are young mothers themselves. Still, the momentum of their efforts has carried them in a certain direction. Busily, bravely fighting battles that need to be fought in politics and the workplace, they naturally prize that kind of achievement more than any other. Understanding as they might theoretically be of women who choose not to work, at some level they have to see each such choice as a step backward for the cause. Therefore, the feminist position on child care has taken the form that has been familiar for at least the last decade: robust endorsement of day care as a necessary ingredient in answering women's problems and bitter denial that there can be anything inherently wrong with outside-the-home day care or any deep conflicts between parenthood and career.

There is more to mothers' lives than day care, of course, and the women's movement can rightly claim to have been the housewife's principal advocate on precisely those practical issues of financial security and protection against mistreatment and bad luck that the right wing neglects. Their efforts in three areas — insurance, pensions, and Social Security — deserve a moment's examination to illustrate what the women's movement has accomplished for women in general, including mothers at home.

In insurance and pensions, the women's groups have objected to rates, terms, and conditions that are set on the basis of sex. The results, they claim, are largely unfavorable for women. For example, women often pay more than men for the same health insurance coverage. And, with their intermittent work patterns (taking time out to raise children), women don't fit the rules and provisions of retirement systems. Pregnancy and childbirth are often excluded from coverage or qualify only for very inadequate coverage. Women often receive smaller monthly retirement payments than men because the actuarial tables predict that they will be collecting over a longer period of years.

Groups like the Women's Equity Action League, the National Organization for Women, and the Association for Business and Professional Women have pointed out some special problems concerning nonworking women, such as disability insurance and pension options. Women who are not employed outside the home are rarely able to obtain disability insurance, and it is rarely available to women who work part-time. This, says Representative Barbara A. Mikulski (D., Maryland), is "because the insurance companies cannot decide [that is, will not be troubled to decide] what constitutes a real disability for a housewife."

There are similar inequities in joint and survivors' pension options. Under a typical pension plan, a working spouse (usually the husband) may elect to take a smaller monthly pension than the full benefit that is due him in exchange for a guarantee that if he dies, his spouse will get her widow's benefits. For example, "If your husband is entitled to $300 a month at age sixty-five and you are three years younger, a typical survivor's plan would reduce his pension checks to $240 a month, but pay you half ($120) a month in widow's benefits if he dies." But the husband is not obligated to accept this arrangement. He may elect to waive the option in favor of taking full benefits while he lives. In that case, in the event that his wife outlives him, she is not eligible for *any* widow's benefits for the rest of her life. Under current law, a husband may make this decision, which can impoverish his wife, without saying a word to her about it. It is his decision alone; she need not provide any written consent. *The Chronicle of Higher Education* reports that only 30 per cent of the men eligible for it currently choose the survivors' benefit option, meaning that all the rest of the wives run the risk of being left no widows' benefits from their husbands' pension plans. Many will learn this unpleasant truth only when their husbands die and the pension checks suddenly stop. The women's groups have advocated a perfectly reasonable change: a requirement that both parties give written consent before the option is waived.

For Social Security, the feminist groups have advocated reform aimed at improving the fairness and adequacy of provisions for *all* women. In 1982, they point out, the average man received $430 per month in benefits, and the average woman received $308. (Retired female workers averaged $335 per month, compared to $438 for retired male workers.) These inequities arise, the feminists say, from historically low wages for working women and an undervalued estimation of homemakers' contributions to a family's income.

In the current Social Security system, a woman can at age sixty-five draw on benefits based on either the money she earned during her working life or the money she receives in "wives' benefits," amounting to one-half her spouse's benefit. Many women who are eligible to choose either category find it more lucrative to choose the wives' benefit. If a woman is widowed, she receives the full pension due her deceased spouse. However, many younger widows fall into the "widows' gap," which stretches from the time their youngest child turns sixteen and loses his or her eligibility for benefits until the widows themselves turn sixty. Furthermore, if a woman chooses to take her benefits at age sixty, instead of waiting until she is sixty-five, she forfeits 28.5 per cent of her monthly benefit for the rest of her life. If a woman is divorced and not remarried, she is entitled, like a married woman, to half her ex-spouse's benefit, provided they were married for at least ten years (recently reduced from twenty years). However, she may not claim her benefit until her ex-spouse stops working and becomes eligible for his benefits.

The women's groups have articulated certain concerns about these arrangements that particularly affect homemakers. For instance, when Social Security calculates a woman's personal account (which she can draw on instead of taking "wives' benefits"), any period longer than five years spent out of the job market, caring for children for example, counts into the formula for her benefits as zero dollars earned, thus reducing her benefits accordingly. This is so even though the wife's work at home may have been essential in enabling her husband to earn his income. Moreover, homemakers are not eligible for Social Security disability benefits unless they have been working for five of the ten years previous to the disability. So, if a woman is injured on her job after having raised a family and then worked four years, she is not eligible for disability.

Feminists call for Social Security reforms for both working women and homemakers, to disengage them from a lifetime of economic dependency. In an effort to "recognize a woman's contribution to marriage as an economic partnership" where the roles of both homemaker and paid worker are acknowledged, the Women's Equity Action League supports a system of "earnings sharing." Under earnings sharing, a husband and wife would, for Social Security purposes, each be credited with half the family's total earnings during the marriage, whether both of them were working or not, plus individual earnings gained before or after the marriage. Later, each would receive pensions based on his or her own personal account, eliminating the need for wives' benefits. For the homemaker, earnings sharing could thus also provide disability benefits and survivor protection to those who have never worked for pay.

This proposed system applies the same set of rules to men and women, but Phyllis Schlafly and other conservatives point out that it is the one-income couple with the homemaking wife whose benefits will drop. For example, if a man was entitled to $350 per month and his wife to half that, or $175, under the current system their combined benefits would be $525. Under earnings sharing, the same couple (provided the wife had never earned any income) would be entitled to a total of $350, or $175 for each. The feminists want to eliminate wives' and widows' benefits, Schlafly says in her newsletter. "The feminists want women to be able to receive Social Security benefits *only*: (a) if they are in the labor force paying their own taxes, or (b) if a husband pays double taxes for the privilege of having his wife in the home."

Judith Finn, writing for the conservative Free Congress Research and Education Foundation, sees elimination of the wife's benefit as a challenge to the traditional family: "If we want to give the two-income family a higher rate of return than the single workers with the same earning records . . . there is no logical reason why the homemaker and the traditional family should bear the cost of that increase in benefits through elimination of the wife's benefit. . . . The most important reason for retaining the wife's benefit is that it would continue to allow married women to choose homemaking as their primary career."

In addition to carrying the ball for nonworking women with pension- and insurance-reform proposals, the left also claims to be defending women at home by laying bare the complicated domestic politics of housework.

Out of the feminists' early concern over the traps of housewifedom came a serious questioning of the way women at home were living. Feminists warned that life at home could lead to a host of serious problems: boredom, frustration, narrowmindedness, depression, withdrawal from society, vicarious living, dependence. It is a credit to the women's movement that women at home are now forewarned of these real and important hazards, and they can try harder to avoid or manage them. One issue in particular has been singled out as the major culprit. It means problems for all women but takes on a special dimension for women who are at home all the time: housework.

Housework, of course, knows no political boundaries; it's there for conservatives and liberals alike to face. For the right, housework has not posed a philosophical problem. It is simply part of the agenda of the housewife. For the left, however, it's not been so clear an issue. Housework has long been a feminist cause, although the movement could often not decide whether it was work to be extolled or denigrated. As Barbara Ehrenreich wrote in 1979, "The old feminist ambivalence about housework began to jell into hostile extremes; either housework was trivial and degrading, something to be foisted off on hired help or reluctant husbands as quickly as possible, *or* it was on an economic par with every other human endeavor."

The women's movement has finally sorted this out, at least officially. Letty Cottin Pogrebin, a writer and editor for *Ms.* and the author of *Family Politics*, describes what every woman knows about the work she does in her home:

> Holidays and every day, that cherished thing known as Family Life is purchased with a woman's time and labor. Warm family memories rest on a network of chores she accomplished, responsibilities she remembered, get-to-gethers she organized, messes she cleared away, rooms she made welcoming, food she cooked to please. The rest of the family adds the conversation, games, laughter, stories — the seeds of family closeness. . . . Housework maintains an orderly setting in which family life can flourish.

Pointing out the virtues of homemaking and the necessities of housework, Pogrebin decries its trivialization: "The point is, the housewife is culturally extolled but economically valueless. She's just a 'housewife.' She doesn't 'work.'" Her work is "revered and priceless" when done "for love" but becomes "nearly worthless when done for money" by someone in her place. It is worthless even though, as has often been pointed out, house-wives perform services in cooking, cleaning, chauffeuring, child care, shopping, nursing, etc., etc., that would pay on the open market somewhere in the range of $20,000 per year — if anyone were paying.

But no matter on which side of the fray feminists were aligned, the effect of the controversy has been to awaken women and their families to the notion that women shouldn't be un-thinkingly and automatically responsible for all the work of a family and house that needs to be done. Housework is not an insignificant amount of work, and it should not simply be as-signed to the woman of the house because of her gender any more than auto repairs or yard work should be the domain of the man.

The problems of housework take on different dimensions for the women at home full-time than they do for women who work at jobs outside their homes. It isn't fair in this situation to talk of divvying up housework fifty-fifty; part of the job of being home is being responsible for more of the housework. But even though more housework naturally goes into the job description of a full-time parent than a working parent, that's not to say that everyone in the family shouldn't be responsible for something. For full-time parents, the important lesson to learn from the examination of housework is that they can do less of it. And the point of worrying about it is the inherent danger of housework becoming a priority at the expense of all other endeavors.

While the women's movement may claim to have defended housewives' and mothers' interests on issues such as housework and Social Security reform, things are not all smooth between the women's movement and women at home. It's probably not bad intentions, but only history and momentum that have brought the women's movement to an impasse with women who are staying home. The "liberation" of womankind has come to mean reaching out — out of the home — for equality and opportunity in the workplace. It has not included, at least in spirit, an embrace of women at home.

The organized voices of the women's movement are quick to knock down all such accusations, pointing out that the media are to blame for unfairly depicting their position as being anti-homemaker. "Infuriating," says Letty Cottin Pogrebin. It's a case of misunderstood intentions toward homemakers and their homes, suggests Catharine Stimpson, a professor at Barnard:

> The media, politicians, and other establishment forces have been the ones that have most powerfully projected The Feminist as a howling creature who delights in destruction. She is a home-wrecker, the contemporary equivalent of the scarlet adultress. . . . Behind such lurid twisted accusations is the rational feminist call, not asking women to "leave home," but to see outside work as either an option or a necessity.

The feminists have evidence for some of their assertions. Liberal women's groups include strong contingents of housewives; many of their leaders are mothers themselves; they have pushed for legislative reforms that directly and positively affect homemakers. "The housewife's issues are our issues," says Pogrebin, citing child care, health care, drug addiction, divorce reform and custody, domestic violence, and displaced homemakers. But none of this addresses the question of spirit and tone. The deepest tensions between the women's movement and nonworking mothers are based on the attitudes each side perceives in the other.

On the one hand, working mothers often feel that nonworking mothers are trying to drown them in guilt. The "nonworkers" sneer at them for being irresponsible toward their home and family and charge them with being selfish for putting their jobs ahead of their children's welfare.

Jean Curtis, author of *A Guide for Working Mothers*, cites some of the feelings that working mothers she interviewed related to her:

> As a working mother I would often get a reaction from other women like, "Oh, you work, and what do you do with your children?" The obvious implication was, "Oh, those poor children." I remember one time saying, flatly, "I neglect them."
>
> The other reaction I would get, when we had a dinner party, was that my guests were surprised I could put on a good table, that I could cook well, that the house was pretty and I was charming. They would say, "I never thought of you as domestic!" The implication seemed clear: If you're a career woman, you're obviously a lousy mother and a lousy homemaker. . . .

On the other hand, nonworking mothers often feel the working mothers look down on them, condescend, patronize, make them feel like second-class citizens or weak sisters who just can't keep up.

The comments are familiar: the "And what do you do?" queries that every at-home mother squirms over at introductions; the "What's an educated young woman like you doing at home?" questions; the "If I were at home, I'd go completely bananas" comments, heavy with implication and judgment.

The working/nonworking mother issue often follows standard liberal versus conservative divisions, although not strictly. For the conservatives, this is almost an open-and-shut question. Because of the right's unshakable belief that a woman's place is in the home and her duty is to serve the husband and nurture the children, and because of its undoubting acceptance that these challenges should be enough for any woman, the conclusion that mothers should not work is easily drawn. Women who work for economic reasons are a footnote to their doctrine.

For the left, it's not quite so simple to work out the connections between political belief and personal action. At least theoretically, there is no *inherent* incompatibility between women reaching out for equality and women staying at home. But, as any woman under the age of forty knows, there is an *imposed* incompatibility. It is because, I think, feminists have not yet had the time or made the effort to understand and explore what life at home can be like for women today. The women's movement, it seems to me, is still operating from outdated, leftover stereotypes of the sort it generally condemns.

The feminists may officially say that "choice" is at the top of their agenda for women. But there are too many hints and innuendos that suggest that this talk comes fairly cheap. As much as I would like to believe it, I have — throughout my years at home and well before that — gotten the message from feminists that there was only one "right" choice that I, as a progressive woman and young mother, could make. Why do I feel that? Because of signals like the following:

• I was listening to Gloria Steinem promote her new book, *Outrageous Acts and Everyday Rebellions,* on a radio talk show in the middle of 1984. During the phone-in portion of the show, a caller asked, "What do you *really* think of women who stay home?" The host of the show, a droll, forthright character named Joel E. Spivak, pointed out that in every single show with a prominent feminist, at least one caller would ask some version of this question. Steinem's answer, of course, was that the feminist movement was all about giving women the choice to lead their lives as they want to. She even managed to say that staying home was just as valid and reputable a choice as working. And yet, only minutes before, when she may have forgotten that homemakers were listening, I heard her direct and unflattering references to the "narrow and stifled" lives of women at home.

Why do Gloria Steinem and the feminist movement continue to get these questions, asking what they *really* think of women at home? It is clearly because the company line — that women should be free to choose anything they want, even to stay at home — is so easy for feminists to say but so hard for them to say sincerely. Whenever I hear Steinem say this, I think of some ambitious older parents I know and their pathetic assertions that they're just as proud of their son the high school dropout as of their daughter the corporate treasurer. Perhaps the parents are blindly proud, as only parents can be, but how can Steinem pretend to give respect to people who represent everything her movement has struggled to change? I feel that I'm hearing something closer to the truth when I catch the off-guard comments, when people aren't defending the company line.

• Among the nastier letters I received in response to an article I wrote in the *Washington Monthly* magazine in 1982 was one from Carol Tucker Foreman, a high official in the Department of Agriculture during the Carter administration. The article was about the changes I went through in the first year and a half that I was home full-time with my children — both the adjustments to leaving behind a career (at least temporarily) and the perspective on practicing full-time parenting. In her letter, Foreman wrote:

> Articles that appear to condemn working motherhood find their way into the pockets of those in business, in Congress, and in this administration who would like to limit choice and keep us all barefoot and pregnant and in the kitchen. Some of us don't want that. Others can't afford it. My 75-year-old mother, who worked all of her life first because she had to and then because she wanted to . . . would probably say in response . . . "Choose your own way, but don't spit in the soup we all have to drink."

• One afternoon last spring, I spent over an hour interviewing one of the most visible spokeswomen of the National Women's Political Caucus about women's political issues. We talked about domestic relations, about homemakers' rights, and about my children and my book. On the way out, she asked me, in a sister-to-sister tone, "Well, when *are* you going to go back to work?"

• Caroline Bird, author of several books touted as "bellwethers on the scene of social change," writes in *The Two-Paycheck Marriage* that "there is chilling evidence that homemaking can actually stunt [a woman's] mental and emotional growth. The housewife who complains that her life is making her stupid and 'rusting her brains' may be speaking the literal truth." Bird's evidence comes from a study in the 1960s that compared some "intellectual measures" of women at their high school graduations and four years later. One group had gone on to college; the other group had married and become housewives. Indeed, writes Bird, the housewives "actually regressed." Even worse, Bird says, the difference couldn't be explained simply by the apparently reasonable assumption that the ones who became mothers were less intelligent to begin with: "Those who were bright and well off deteriorated proportionately as much as those who were less privileged at the outset."

• Letty Cottin Pogrebin, in *Family Politics*, addresses the question "Who will raise the children?" and lists, as one option, the full-time parent. But, she writes, "not only is this arrangement growing less common and more economically impractical, it also may be psychologically problematic in terms of isolation of the stay-home parent and understimulation of the child. In any event, it is workable only if voluntarily chosen by an adult positively inclined to domesticity and children."

An article in *Ms.* magazine typifies the limited extent to which the women's movement tries to understand women at home. A full-time mother wrote to *Ms.* complaining that she felt "ignored and patronized by the Women's Movement in general and by *Ms.* in particular." *Ms.* replied with a straight face, "We were confused and somewhat dismayed. . . . We'd published articles on pregnancy, childbirth, a homemaker's diary. . . ." *Ms.* decided that to help clear the air, they'd interview her on the record. They sent Jane Lazarre, author of *The Mother Knot*, a very compelling book about her deep and divided feelings about being a mother, out to spend a morning with Jane Broderick, the author of the challenging letter to *Ms.*, and four of her eight children in their Long Island home. Broderick laid out her positions on feminist issues: birth control, gender-free raising of children, housework, and so on. Although Lazarre felt a certain closeness to Broderick, despite the difference in their life-styles, the closest Lazarre came to finding the key to Broderick's spirit was to focus on two things: her strong Catholicism, which has a lot to do with becoming a mother of eight children but very little to do with feminism, and her explanation that to find her "sense of autonomy" in motherhood, "sometimes it is necessary for me to hide. And I do just that. I really have to sit very still. Just be alone with myself. And become whole again."

All mothers can recognize that sitting very still is Broderick's important gimmick for maintaining sanity. But they also understand that it reveals little about her key to sustaining herself, as a person and individual, in her life as a mother of eight children. Lazarre seemed content with the surface view and did not search for or even find by accident any real insights into full-time motherhood in her morning's interview.

To be fair, an occasional insight slips into the feminist literature. For example, in a mother's diary of her day with small children, published in *Ms.* in 1976, Phyllis Rosser wrote several pages of minute-by-minute and blow-by-blow accounts: "9:50: Stopped to feed the cat because she was making so much noise. 10:28: Sat down again. Sam asked me to watch her turn somersaults. 5:10: Took Sam to the toy store to buy birthday presents for Tim while the boys stayed home with Bill."

Her days were not that interesting to read about, but the final insights she gleaned from examining her own diary were, and they offer an important message to full-time mothers of small children: "I was beginning to understand why raising children was so much harder than working in an office. I was allowing my children to dominate my life with trivia, and that left no time to do the things I wanted to do with them, like painting and hiking. It also kept me from having any blocks of time for projects of my own."

Betty Friedan has come closest to taking the scorn out of the word "housewife," much of which she introduced there in the first place with *The Feminine Mystique*. In her sequel to that book, *The Second Stage*, she writes: "It would seem to me that in the second stage we should move for some very simple aids that make it possible for mothers (or fathers) who want to stay home and take care of their own children to do so, with some economic compensation that might make the difference."

The women's movement has addressed many issues of concern to women at home. But the heart of the matter — how women can lead rich and independent lives at home — is left hanging. The women's movement offers a woman in the workplace a great sense of having asked the difficult questions about her life: why am I working? what can I expect there? where will it take me? It has not done the same for a woman at home. It has not asked the questions that matter to her: why stay at home? how can I find satisfaction there? how does life at home fit with important things in my family's life or the fabric of the larger community?

What, then, am I recommending? For people who are troubled by the blind spots and omissions in the standard political formulas, is there a better alternative? I think there is. It is possible at least to outline a political approach to children and parenthood that emphasizes the things that make a difference in children's lives.

Its first principle is a recognition that, whenever possible, parents should care for their children themselves. It will not always be possible, and many children will get along fine in any case, and other variables may make a greater difference in some children's lives, and all children need time away from their parents and vice versa — all those things are true. Still, other conditions being equal, children are more likely to thrive when they spend most of their day with a parent rather than a hired caretaker. One of our political goals, therefore, should be to create the circumstances that allow more parents to care for their young children themselves.

Simply stating that as a goal is important in itself. "Motherhood" is supposed to be one of the bedrock political values, but it really isn't, not in the sense that politicians talk very often about helping parents care for their children. I have heard many more speeches about inflation, taxes, the deficit, and nuclear war than I have ever heard about parenthood. If genuine concern for the parental role does gain political viability, however, many practical steps should follow: for example, encouraging businesses to change their policies on maternity leave, paternity leave, part-time work, flextime, and job sharing.

The second principle is an insistence that the balance between parenthood and career be worked out by both parents, father as well as mother. In part this is a practical economic problem. Because most women earn less money than most men, when it comes time to select a nonworking spouse, the choice is obvious. How can the family afford to lose its main breadwinner? One of the reasons to push ahead with the feminist campaign for fairer pay is that then it would be more feasible for more fathers to take a few years off to care for the children.

Unfortunately, this issue transcends economics. Too many men view the parenthood/career balance as their wife's problem, of no concern to them. For the sake of the children, and the mothers, *and* the fathers, we need to remind men, day after day until it takes, that this is their problem too. They are as responsible as their wives for finding a way to reconcile their professional ambitions with the welfare of their children.

Third, we must recognize that if spouses — for the time being, mainly mothers — are to stay out of the work force for a while, they need certain practical protections. Here, many of the steps toward reform have already been proposed by the feminists. The items on their agenda, such as pension reform, enforcement of child support orders, and so on, will help permit parents to care for their children without making themselves too vulnerable to fate.

Fourth, we must have day care — more of it, and more of high quality. For reasons I have already discussed at length, day care is a permanent feature of American life. Millions of children will spend billions of hours in these institutions. Those hours can be relatively productive, or they can be actively damaging, depending on how the day care centers are run. For reasons I have also discussed, day care centers are less well suited to normal free-market operation than are most other businesses. If we are serious about improving day care, we must raise the regulatory standards imposed on the centers and put more money into their operation. Increased federal spending, at a time when government programs of all kinds are being scrutinized, is for now an unlikely prospect. If the care of our children is important enough, however, we can find ways to improve day care without simply adding to the federal deficit, perhaps by enlisting businesses in the effort to subsidize care, perhaps by using our human talents more creatively.

Finally, we should insist on a principle missing from all the political manifestoes about women and families I have seen. Parents who stay home with their children should feel just as great an obligation to use their talents and energies as wisely as any young doctor or teacher of either sex. The women's movement and the profamily forces seem to agree that a woman who ends up at home with the children ("by choice" according to the feminists, "by natural order" according to the right) has stepped off of life's main road. She's spending these years at home and there's not much more to say about her. But the parts of the feminist agenda most often directed at the careerists — that they should strive to bring out the best in themselves, that they should be responsible for themselves, that they should be independent and strong — should also be issued, as challenges, to women at home.

15

At Home and Beyond

THE FIRST STEP toward helping women at home to feel challenged was *The Feminine Mystique*, which told some terrible truths about what life at home could be like. The potential for boredom, frustration, and stagnation is a real, inherent hazard of life there. But after this, the help from the women's movement virtually stops. There is no moral support for being at home; there is no encouragement beyond the warning; there is no guidance on how to avert the hazards; there is no suggestion of hope. Full-time mothers are women who, in the nearsighted view of current popular opinion, do very little beyond caring for their children except cleaning, watching the soaps, drinking coffee with friends, and conniving for a new station wagon or freezer.

But what do women at home really do and how do they do it? How do educated women keep from "going crazy," as so many working women say they would do? How do ambitious women "stand it," as so many working women claim they couldn't? How do thoughtful women remain thoughtful, as so many working women maintain is impossible? What are the secrets? Is it simply that full-time mothers (and some fathers) are just different from the rest?

In the years that I have been at home, I have watched other full-time mothers very closely. I have watched, and I have been there myself. I would never deny that the potential of what Betty Friedan warned about is present. The necessities of life with small children can lead you to the brink and leave you there to plunge or turn away. The high ideal of raising your child yourself can on many days degenerate into a struggle simply to maintain sanity, as you stay behind a closed door with infants and toddlers, alone for long hours with them and their infinite, relentless demands. Much of that is necessary. That part is not fun, and it is very, very hard. But it is not all there is to a parent's life.

What I have seen in many full-time mothers gives me great pride in women. It has made me see that they can come through the very difficult task of raising children riding only on a deep belief that what they are doing is worthy and important. It has made me see how they can manage to do not only this but, with imagination, tenacity, and a great dose of humor, "lead examined lives," as one mother described it to me, as well.

Their secret I will now share with you. There is a point, not so far down the road past the numbing days of round-the-clock feedings and constant diaper changing, when you have a chance to gain a toehold on your own life. Maybe it will be as soon as when the first-born starts napping regularly; maybe it will be as late as the day the last-born trots off to nursery school. But then, just when things are getting a bit comfortable, is the critical moment. It's the time to assess your life as you see it taking form. Instead of sitting back, plumping up the pillows and reaching for the chocolates, you must determine how motherhood fits into the life you want to lead and turn in that direction.

But here, alas, comes the hard part. There is no magic formula for "satisfied motherhood." The possibilities for what you do as a mother — for yourself, for your spirit, for your growth — are there for everyone. But there are as many ways to realize it as there are different mothers. And for everyone it is different. There is no single model to follow because, like most things, it depends on many personal circumstances in life: what you can do or like to do, how many children you have, how much money you have, how much support from a spouse you have, what you dream of doing. The only common thread is that everyone has the possibility of doing something.

I know the stories of a few women who have seemed to handle their years of motherhood particularly well. We cannot copy them, but we can use their ingredients to write recipes for ourselves. Following are two such stories.

When I spoke with her in 1983, Chris Campbell was thirty-five years old, the mother of two children, Caitlin and Morgan. She was a veteran of five years as a public defender for the County of Los Angeles, a job she quit shortly before Caitlin was born five years before. Chris now lives in Carmel Valley, California, a small town about a hundred miles south of San Francisco, with her husband, Bud, who teaches third grade at a private school a few miles from their home, and their children.

Chris had gone to college at Berkeley in the late 1960s, had been active in feminist politics, and had gone on to earn a law degree from the University of California. As a lawyer, Chris had worked long days and often evenings and weekends. She had a close relationship with many of her colleagues and was in the courtroom frequently.

Chris had decided before she had children that she wanted to stay home with them. It wasn't a hard decision for her to make. She knew that being a lawyer and working long hours would not mesh with her idea of the way she wanted to be a mother. "It never even came close to a hard decision. I never imagined I could ever go back to work," she said.

Financially, it might have made more sense for Bud to stay home with the children and for Chris to work. He was the teacher who already had experience working with children; she was the lawyer with the greater earning potential. "It was never the situation where we'd sit down with a cup of coffee and say 'who is it going to be?'" said Chris. "I was much more suited in certain temperamental ways." Many of the traits that she used successfully as a lawyer have also served her well as a full-time mother: perseverance, patience, imagination, a sense of humor. "I know how I want my children to be and how I want them to feel about themselves. I'm able to help them do that. You must be willing to if you want to help mold your children. When I'm a good mother, interpreting events for them so they get that sense of themselves—who would be better than me?"

Neither of them saw the change as a dramatic shift in the way they worked as a couple. "We always knew Bud was the sort of person to be involved with our kids anyway. He loves children. And we never had a high standard of living. We have simple tastes — we do things that don't cost very much — movies, camping. We never got used to being high rollers; we didn't have a lot to give up."

Chris's complete shift from full-time lawyering to full-time mothering didn't come easily. At first, in the week she was home before Caitlin was born, there was the shock of going from an "absolutely intense environment to absolute quiet overnight." She left an exciting office where she worked with many colleagues of similar backgrounds, interests, and tastes. When she got home, she said, "I was desperate." That first week, she went out to the store to talk to the clerk about choosing shelf paper —just to have someone to talk to.

Then Caitlin was born and there was an even bigger transition. "As public defender, I controlled my own cases, made my own decisions. I liked to be in charge of things. Suddenly Caitlin was in charge. It was a big frustration." Nothing from her former life applied anymore: what she expected of herself, the goals she set. She had to learn to think of progress as the baby's happiness and her own happiness.

Chris's second child, Morgan, was born eighteen months after his sister. For almost five years, Chris was at home with children, exclusively. She described to me what those years of total-immersion motherhood meant to her and how they fit into the rest of her life: "I'm not going to be here [home] for twenty years, but I want to be involved with the children's activities while I can. I want to have it all, see it, change it, be there. Children are such a small part of life. I don't want to waste a minute of it. I'll have fifteen years of full-time lawyering once they're gone. That's an eternity."

When Morgan turned three, life for Chris again changed dramatically. "It was clear that Morgan was ready for nursery school. All his friends in his playgroup were going, Caitlin was going." Bud's salary was slightly more than $20,000 a year — an amount that had trouble withstanding occasional emergencies and caused them to put off things that they shouldn't put off. They both knew that the only way they could afford the tuition for Morgan's half-day program was for Chris to bring in some income.

Chris came up with a unique system of working that suits her life with the children. She sat down with a friend who was a lawyer and came up with the idea of being a consultant freelance lawyer. She and her friend looked through the Yellow Pages and got the names of likely lawyers. Chris called, presented her history, and asked if they needed extra help. "I made it clear I wanted to work fifteen hours a week, max, on cases or projects that could be confined to school hours. To my surprise, no one said, 'Are you kidding?'" Her business started out slowly, but grew steadily. "Now I have more work than I can handle."

There are trade-offs and compromises, to be sure, in Chris's professional life. She earns much less money than she could; she's relinquished security, prestige, benefits. But she has, in return, gained the two things that are most important to her: the chance to spend her own time on the professional endeavor she most enjoys and the freedom to do it on her own terms.

"It wasn't ever the glamour of the job that appealed to me," Chris said. "It was doing the things a lawyer did and having the chance to be brave and noble on behalf of someone else. It is nice to have those things in my life again."

Sherry Jacks had been a teacher in Austin, Texas, for twelve years when her daughter Meredith was born in 1981. She had taught English in junior high and high school for eight years, then branched out into "humanities" for the last four. She was the kind of teacher all parents hope their children have the good fortune to get — one who saw her work as a calling, not just a job. Sherry regularly worked fourteen-hour days and weekends, too. When she began teaching humanities and found that the basic text didn't meet her standards, she went on to develop her own course, digging up materials from her own collections and travels. She was honored formally for her efforts and skills by being named outstanding teacher at her school in 1980, and among the top three in the whole city. And she was honored informally. When it was time for Sherry to leave to have her baby, all the students begged her not to go.

But for Sherry the best part of working was that she got as much out of teaching as she put into it. "I really loved it," she said. "It was fun to take something that didn't interest the kids at all and try to make it real to them. And I liked the kids. I liked the relationships I had with them."

When she became pregnant, Sherry decided to take a year's leave of absence. "I knew I wasn't going back," she said, "but I hated to close the door totally." After a year, she had to make a decision: return or resign. She resigned. Having done her job so thoroughly for so long made it an easy decision. "I loved it, it was wonderful, I enjoyed it all," she said about school. But after twelve years, "I felt 'full.' I had done it all. I didn't regret anything. I had taken teaching to the hilt. I didn't look back."

Like Chris, Sherry had very definite, solid reasons for wanting to be home. "Having a child is such a blessing, such an opportunity, a miracle," she said. "I didn't want to miss it. I didn't want somebody else raising my child. I wanted to be there for the humdrum, the crawling around on the floor. I wanted her to go to sleep in my arms." With the perspective of a slightly older first-time mother (Sherry was thirty-five when Meredith was born), she added, "I knew the time would fly by."

Sherry's decision had fewer financial repercussions than Chris's did. Sherry's husband, Tommy, is a lawyer, practicing in a small firm he started with a friend. Tommy was as enthusiastic as Sherry was about her staying home with Meredith.

The one reservation Sherry had about staying home, she expressed in nearly the same words that Chris did: "I had been totally in control of my life for thirteen years. With teaching, you're in charge of your day. It's like working for yourself. I knew a baby would be totally demanding. Nothing else in my life had ever been so constant. I would be totally at the mercy of a little person. She had needs and I had to meet them."

Sherry had been thinking about this when she was pregnant with Meredith. It was her high "self-preservation instinct," she said, that led her to pursue something she had been thinking about vaguely for a long time: taking courses at the University of Texas in art history. She had several reasons for doing this: she loved art history; she knew it would be a practical asset to her humanities teaching when she would probably return to that one distant day; she guessed it would offer a balance to her mothering.

Sherry began studying part-time at the university when Meredith was eight months old. "I hired a student to babysit for six hours a week for Meredith," she said. By that time, "it was wonderful. I so liked having that much control. I was able to walk out the door two days a week for three hours and not give Meredith a thought. That time was totally mine. I had no guilt. I was able to be with her the rest of the time." A few times a year, when she was busier than normal with finals, Sherry would drive Meredith a hundred miles north to Waco, Texas, where all of Meredith's grandparents lived. Meredith would spend a few days with each of her grandmothers while — fully appreciative of just how lucky she was to have doting grandmothers nearby ready to relieve her — Sherry studied.

For Sherry, this arrangement, which she's kept in pretty much the same fashion ever since, has been just about perfect. "A lot of the reason school works," she said, "is that I love what I'm doing. For me, it satisfies all those things that teaching used to do."

In telling these stories, I do not mean to suggest that Chris Campbell and Sherry Jacks are typical in any sort of scientific, demographically representative way. Chris has certain advantages: a husband with a flexible schedule, experience in her profession, a low-key life in a rural area that was made for children. Sherry has other advantages: nearby grandmothers, enough money to hire babysitters, a university a mile away. But in another sense, what they have tried to do *is* typical of what many other mothers in many different circumstances have done. Sherry and Chris share certain traits that may well be full-time parents' secret keys to being happy and satisfied at home.

First, they each are sure in their minds of what they are doing at home. They did not stop working just because someone else thought they should. They decided to spend more time with their children because each of them wanted to be a certain kind of mother, one who could be involved closely with even the smallest moments of her children's lives. Each also has a sense of how these few years fit into the larger scheme of life. They understand they will be close to home for several years, but they have many years left after that in which to move out toward a different balance between children and work.

Second, and probably more important, each of these mothers has worked out a realistic plan for being involved in something *besides* raising children, even during the years they spend at home. The details of their plans are different, of course, from every other mother's; as it happened, these two were able to continue some version of the activities they'd had in their pre-children careers. It is important to notice that their plans are realistic and modest. They call for part-time work and part-time school. These mothers do not try to do everything at once, but they keep doing something, thereby continuing to grow and to meet challenges while still being able to give their children all the attention they deserve. Had they tried to do more — if Chris had tried to practice law full-time, if Sherry had enrolled for a full-time graduate course — they would probably have felt frustrated, cheating both themselves and their children. Sherry remarked that keeping the balance takes keen attention. "I can't choose to take classes and do exercise class and do church work. Last year, I was chairman of the board of Sunday school, and it nearly killed me. . . . I know my limits. If I did any more than I'm doing now, I know what would suffer: Meredith. People make those demands on you, you have to meet them, and Meredith would be the one who'd pay for it." Had they tried to do less, they would have felt untrue to the talents and ambitions they had developed through the years. "I'm happy being a mother because I take time for myself," said Sherry. "With art history, I've thought, I've used my brain, I've had a good time. And then I'm ready to play. I don't resent Meredith at all." Neither Chris nor Sherry is secretly trying to be Superwoman; each is trying to meet her responsibilities to society and to herself without shortchanging her responsibilities to her children.

Not everyone can be a part-time lawyer or go to graduate school. But nearly every parent can find ways to remain challenged. If it is important, as I believe it is, for parents to take their children's needs seriously, and to make temporary sacrifices in their own ambitions for their children's sake, it is also important for women to accept the finest part of the feminist challenge, to make their lives matter.

❧ 16 ❧

Being Parents

THE MOST IMPORTANT MESSAGE I carry, after being a mother for almost eight years and after watching and listening especially closely to other parents and their children while writing this book, is simply this: parents are the most important factor in their children's lives. Whether they are with their children two hours a day or twelve, parents are special to children. They make the biggest difference during their childhoods. They make the most impact on the rest of their lives. I say this not with pride but with a humbling sense of the responsibility that being a parent brings.

The bond between parents and children is incredibly strong. The love between them is special; it grows for so many years without judgment, without limit. Parents simply love their children beyond all bounds, often as much for their weaknesses and their faults as for their strengths and gifts. I love that Tommy fights to control his temper as much as I love that he is brave and trusting. I love that Tad won't be dissuaded from his stubborn and unreasonable positions as much as I love that he is generous. Of course I don't love the temper or the stubbornness, but I appreciate how these fit their personalities, and I appreciate how Tommy is fighting to prevail over his temper and how Tad will learn to give in one day.

Parents will do things for their children that no one else would dream of. You could ask a parent if he would cut off an arm for a child and without hesitation, even thinking, he would answer yes, and truly mean it. You could ask a parent about the rage she feels when someone does her child harm. It is not a normal rage that knows normal bounds. There is a depth of feeling, of commitment, of love, that lies beyond the rules of order of the rest of the universe.

Parents may carry these larger-than-life feelings about their children deep in their hearts, but most are never called upon to do extreme things for their children. Mostly we help them conduct their daily lives, help them with manners, with schoolwork, with habits, with their sense of right and wrong, of justice and morals. We help them in ways they can understand, through discipline, play, chores, explanations and talking, and through example. Most of us, as parents, are forever interpreting our actions with our children in some larger scheme. "The kids set the table every evening; it helps them appreciate that someone has to make all these nice things in their lives happen." Or, "We can get a dog if the kids will feed him and walk him every day; they need to learn about the responsibilities that come with ownership." Or, "You can learn to shake hands and say 'How do you do?' when you meet someone; there are certain signs of respect that all people should show one another."

Most of the things we do with our children, like the things we say to them, can seem ordinary, small, mundane. But as I have lived with children and watched children in the company of both parents and caretakers, it has seemed to me that there remains a difference in the way that parents and caretakers approach even the small events of children's lives. At the playground, for instance, where I have spent countless hours in the last seven years, I have closely watched the dynamics of what goes on. I have watched mothers go up a high and dangerous slide behind their toddlers and slide down with them, both getting grubby. I have watched nannies and sitters and their charges on the same playgrounds. Their children will putter on the smaller slides and be pulled quickly away from the high ones, for fear of danger if they venture near. I have yet to see a nanny or babysitter follow her charge up the slide and down.

Similarly, I've watched groups of toddlers in the sandbox. Usually, children with mothers present are left a little longer — to get a little dirtier, to reach the point of sand-throwing fracas — than the children accompanied by their caretakers. They're plucked from the edge of small disaster, be it getting too grimy or engaging in fisticuffs, before they've had the fun, or learned the lessons, of this stage of life.

At homes, I've seen and heard young children, maybe four or five years old, talking back to caretakers in ways I've never heard a child speak to his or her parents — at least not without provoking reaction. The difference is not so much in the words as in the tone. "No, Maria! I don't mean those shoes. Bring me my pink ones!" And there is never a "We don't speak that way, young lady!" or "How do you ask for your pink shoes politely, dear?" or "Think again about how you should ask that question, Amanda," from the hired caretaker.

There's something else that's very special about families: their constancy and their staying power. Parents are the constant presence in a child's life. They are there well before and long after the usually frequent changes of the guard of caretakers. Housekeepers come and go; nannies put in twelve-month stints; day care center staffs will turn over regularly. But parents will always be there.

My observations bring me to a conclusion — perhaps not too radical and perhaps one that is quite obvious, but one I feel with strong conviction: parents, as the unique and special people in their children's lives, need to spend as much time as possible with their children. By this, I do not mean that parents should spend twenty-four hours a day with children. But I mean most of the time. It seems to me that a good babysitter for a few hours a day, a few days a week, is reasonable even for infants. I think that playgroups and nursery schools are wonderful for toddlers and preschoolers. I believe in kindergarten. I believe in school. But I also believe that children do best when they have parents available after school most days, if only to see for a few moments before they head out to play.

I think this message is different in spirit from the way we often tend to think about raising kids now. As adults, we are busy with our own lives, and we go to our greatest lengths sometimes to "arrange" things for the children. We arrange babysitters, after-school activities, summer programs, Saturday sports, music lessons, special tutors, amusements, and entertainments. Even parents of the youngest babies are picking up on the cues and signing infants up for tumbling classes, hiring teachers to give them "lessons" with flash cards. There are classes, programs, projects for children of all ages.

Don't get me wrong. I do the same for my children, although perhaps a bit less of it than I used to. I think much of it is good — good for the children, who benefit from exposure to a broad and expansive world, and good for their mothers and fathers, who through these activities meet other parents, gain some free time, or learn things themselves. But at some point, all these arrangements seem to take priority over what we should be doing: striving to give our children more of ourselves and more of our time. We're all busy; none of us ever has enough time to do all the things we need to do. We all need time for ourselves. But for this short period in our own and our children's lives, we need those precious moments with our children, and they need them even more. I think perhaps we forget, in our rush and efforts to get more and better child care, that we should also aim for more and better time to be with our children.

Doing well by our kids doesn't have to mean buying them things, signing them up for camps, going on the greatest vacations, although all these things are nice. It means, most of all, giving them the sense that they are the most important thing we have, that we want to spend our time with them more than with anyone else in the world. Children, even young ones, are shrewd and perceptive; they can tell what we're doing. A baby will not know, if a parent is gone, what that parent is doing or why. She will simply know the parent is gone. But a preschooler, even a toddler perhaps, will begin to pick up the clues.

We need to think hard about how our work as mothers and fathers fits into our own lives, as well. The feminists are wise to have taught us that all women need challenges, fulfillment, and satisfaction in life. All of us, men and women, have this deep inside us. But does this ambition have to be restricted to the world of paid work? At its best, work can offer a kind of spiritual satisfaction — a special feeling of achievement, a special wholeness, a sense that it is worthwhile, important, irresistible. This is the lesson about work from which women at home should draw. These are the elements of endeavor that women at home should look for — and they are elements that, despite what the women's movement may choose not to say or explore, are indeed compatible with the major commitment of spending one's time at home raising children.

The boardroom or the corner office, where men have traditionally gone to search for challenge and reward and where many women are now following, are not the only places to find these rewards. There is at least as great a prospect of finding them at home.

There is an honor and legitimacy about being home raising children that parents — mostly mothers — *know* exists. I am not talking about hollow words like "raising children is such a hard job" or polite comments about the "patience and stamina it takes to raise kids" that are spoken to fill space, without much understanding or concern. I'm talking about a sense that a parent has that for each child there is a life to help shape and that there is no one else who can do as good a job as she — or he — can. The honor and legitimacy of staying home to raise children will become clearer to everyone when more people show that they consider the responsibility too great to pass off to someone else. The moments of our lives are scarce and precious. When we show ourselves willing to invest them in our children's welfare, the effect can be immense.

Notes

Notes

page   **1. At Work**

21. "Kathryn Schrotenboer is": Christine Doudna, "The New Madonnas," *Savvy* 3, no. 6 (June 1982): 33–38.
22. "Another mother": ibid.

2. At Home

25. "At luncheons": Evan Connell, *Mrs. Bridge* (San Francisco: North Point Press, 1981; originally published by Viking Press, 1959), pp. 35–36.
26. "Women like Brenda Ray": Anita Creamer, "Staying at Home with the Children," *Dallas Times Herald*, July 11, 1983.
26. "Nobody can say": Lois Blinkhorn, "Mother of 2: 'I Was Tired All the Time,'" *Milwaukee Journal*, March 28, 1982.
26. "Every evening": Eleanor Berman, "Stop the Merry-Go-Round, I Want to Get Off," *Working Mother*, December 1981, p. 73.

3. Dads

48. "Even when Bob": David Owen, "Bringing Up Baby," *The New Republic*, October 1, 1985, pp. 38–39.

4. Child Care: An Overview

52. Figures from: Martin O'Connell and Carolyn C. Rogers, "Child Care Arrangements of Working Mothers: June 1982," Current Population Reports, Special Studies, Series P-23, no. 129, U.S. Department of Commerce, Bureau of the Census, November 1983, p. 22.
54. "Take, for example": John Sansing, "How to Find Good Child Care," *Washingtonian* 19, no. 5 (February 1984), p. 83.

56. "series of moves": Judy Mann, "Dropping Out," *Washington Post*, September 9, 1983.
56. "For about 17 years": Virginia Inman, "Day-Care Laws Limit Private-Home Centers That Parents Like Best," *Wall Street Journal*, October 26, 1982.
58. "money the state": ibid., p. 23.
63. Figures from: O'Connell and Rogers, "Child Care Arrangements," pp. 11–13, 22–23.

6. Kinder-Care

86. "truly impressive": Myron Magnet, "What Mass-Produced Child Care Is Producing," *Fortune* 108, no. 11 (November 28, 1983), p. 158.

7. More Days, More Centers

117. Statistics on parents' time in centers: Edward F. Zigler and Pauline Turner, "Parents and Day Care Workers: A Failed Partnership?" in Edward F. Zigler and Edmund W. Gordon, eds., *Day Care: Scientific and Social Policy Issues* (Boston: Auburn House Publishing Co., 1982), p. 178.

8. The Effects of Day Care

122. For references on the effects of day care see especially: Sheila B. Kamerman and Cheryl D. Hayes, *Families That Work: Children in a Changing World* (Washington, D.C.: National Academy Press, 1982), and Edward F. Zigler and Edmund W. Gordon, eds., *Day Care: Scientific and Social Policy Issues* (Boston: Auburn House Publishing Co., 1982).
122. "The National Institute of Education": Judy Mann, "Learning," *Washington Post*, March 30, 1983.
123. All Heyns's quotes from: Barbara Heyns, "The Influence of Parents' Work on Children's School Achievement," in Zigler and Gordon, eds., *Day Care*, pp. 238, 239, 251.
124. For conflicting reports see: Judy Mann, "Homework," *Washington Post*, April 27, 1984.
125. "working mothers": Mann, "Learning," *Washington Post*, March 30, 1983.
126. All Heyns's quotes from: Heyns, "Influence," pp. 249, 250.
127. All Pleck's quotes from: Joseph Pleck, "Husbands' and Wives' Family Work, Paid Work, and Adjustment," Working Paper no. 95, Wellesley College Center for Research on Women, Wellesley, pp. 3-3, 3-8.
128. Figures on time with children: "Time Allocation in American Households," as reported in "Interim Report to the Foundation for Child Development: Demographic Differences in Parents' and Children's Time Use," 1981, from the Home and School Institute's National Conference on Working Parents and Achieving Children, Washington, D.C., April 1984.

9. Day Care: The Demand

131. Statistics for children with working mothers: Marjorie Lueck, Ann C. Orr, and Martin O'Connell, "Trends in Child Care Arrangements of Working Mothers," Current Population Reports, Special Studies, Series P-23, no. 117, U.S. Department of Commerce, Bureau of the Census, June 1982, p. 1.

132. Quotes: Sandra Porter, telephone conversation, August 1984, and Elinor Guggenheimer, telephone conversation, winter 1982.

132. Employment statistics: "Table 15: Employment Status of Women," unpublished data, U.S. Department of Labor, Bureau of Labor Statistics, March 1984.

133. "Between 1947 and 1980": *Employed Parents and Their Children: A Data Book* (Washington, D.C.: Children's Defense Fund, 1982), p. 35.

133. "In just five years": Martin O'Connell and Carolyn C. Rogers, "Child Care Arrangements of Working Mothers: June 1982," Current Population Reports, Special Studies, Series P-23, no. 129, U.S. Department of Commerce, Bureau of the Census, November 1983, p. 3.

133. "A person is classified": Edward J. Welniak and Mary F. Henson, "Money Income of Households, Families, and Persons in the United States: 1982," Current Population Reports, Consumer Income, Series P-60, no. 142, U.S. Department of Commerce, Bureau of the Census, February 1984, p. 209.

134. Part-time statistics derived from: Bureau of Labor Statistics Table 15.

136. Statistics derived from: ibid.

136. Statistics derived from: ibid.

137. Income statistics: Welniak and Henson, "Money Income," p. 93.

137. Child support figures: Children's Defense Fund, telephone conversation, spring 1985.

138. $15,000 a year: Sandra Porter, phone conversation.

139. Statistics in Table I derived from: "Table F-11: Income of Wife by Income of Husband in 1983," unpublished data, Current Population Survey, U.S. Department of Commerce, Bureau of the Census, and Welniak and Henson, "Money Income," p. 97.

140. Figures in Table II from: "Table 17: Labor Force Status of Wife . . . by Income of Husband . . . and Age of Children," unpublished data, U.S. Department of Labor, Bureau of Labor Statistics, March 1983.

141. All figures and quotes: George Sternlieb and James W. Hughes, "Running Faster to Stay in Place: Family Income and the Baby Boom," special reprint of "Working Women," *American Demographics*.

142. Income figures from: "Tables 39, 40, 41: Number of Families with Own Children under 18 years, by Type of Family, Labor Force Status of Parents, and Family Income," unpublished data, U.S. Department of Labor, Bureau of Labor Statistics, March 1983.

10. Day Care: The Supply

147. Statistics on subsidy cuts: Marion W. Edelman, "The Testimony of the Children's Defense Fund Before the Select Committee on Children, Youth, and Families," April 4, 1984, p. 8.

147. Figures on children served: Helen Blank, "Children and Federal Child Care Cuts: A National Survey of the Impact of Federal Title XX Cuts on State Child Care Systems, 1981–1983," a Children's Defense Fund White Paper (Washington, D.C.: Children's Defense Fund, 1983), pp. 14–15.

148. Delaware and Michigan statistics: Edelman, "Testimony," p. 13.

148. Latchkey statistics: Blank, "Child Care Cuts," pp. 1, 8, 9.

149. "The [National Day Care Study] results": Raymond C. Collins, "Child Care and the States: The Comparative Licensing Study," *Young Children* 38, no. 5 (July 1983), p. 4.

151. Figures and quotations from: Emily Schrag, "Infant and Toddler Care in the States: The Comparative Licensing Study and Beyond," *Zero to Three* 4, no. 3, Bulletin of the National Center for Clinical Infant Programs (February 1984), pp. 8–11.

152. Staff-child ratios for four-year-olds: figures and quotations from Collins, "Child Care," pp. 3–11.

152. Children's Defense Fund figures and quotations from: Blank, "Child Care Cuts," pp. 27–28.

153. Figures and quotations from: Licensing Branch, Texas Department of Human Services, unpublished papers.

154. "It is awarded": Millie Almy, "Day Care and Early Childhood Education," in Edward F. Zigler and Edmund W. Gordon, eds., *Day Care: Scientific and Social Policy Issues* (Boston: Auburn House Publishing Co., 1982), p. 489.

155. Child care income figures: *Child Care Employee News* 2, no. 3 (Fall 1983), p. 1.

155. "Percentage increases": ibid., p. 2.

11. Paying for Day Care

159. Figure for center care cost: Marion W. Edelman, "The Testimony of the Children's Defense Fund Before the Select Committee on Children, Youth, and Families," April 4, 1984, p. 6.

159. "Women's unskilled work": Carol Hymowitz and Michaele Weissman, *A History of Women in America* (New York: Bantam Books, 1978), p. 239.

160. "Before the invention": ibid., pp. 303–304.

162. "There is a popular": Bettye Caldwell, "Confronting the Realities of Child Care," *Child Care Information Exchange*, special reprint, p. 13.

165. "Proprietary operators": Sharon L. Kagan and Theresa Glennon, "Considering Proprietary Child Care," in Edward F. Zigler and Edmund W. Gordon, eds., *Day Care: Scientific and Social Policy Issues* (Boston: Auburn House Publishing Co., 1982), p. 406.

165. Child care expenditures: ibid., p. 407.

166. Staff expenditures: ibid., p. 406.

166. Turnover rates: *Child Care Employee News* 3, no. 3 (Fall 1984), p. 2.

166. Bureau of Labor Statistics report: ibid., p. 1.

166. "cost-cutting methods": Kagan and Glennon, "Proprietary Child Care," p. 408.

167. "Centers were clean": ibid.

168. Strike information: *Child Care Employee News* 1, no. 4 (Winter 1982–83), p. 5, and *Child Care Employee News* 2, no. 3 (Fall 1983), p. 5.

169. "They're really at the bottom": *Toronto Clarion*, December 3, 1982, p. 7.

172. "In Morristown": Sandra S. Friedland, "More Companies Offering Day Care," *New York Times*, July 20, 1981.

172. Background information on business involvement in child care: Conversations with and papers by Dana Friedman, The Conference Board, New York.

174. "Most women get the message": Naomi Barko, "Corporate Etiquette," *Working Mother*, May 1984, p. 56.

175. "In spite of": Susan McHenry, "Advice for Corporations," *Ms.*, September 1984, p. 118.

175. History of child care legislation: Edward F. Zigler and Jody Goodman, "The Battle for Day Care in America: A View from the Trenches," in Zigler and Gordon, eds., *Day Care*, pp. 338–350.

176. "For example": W. Gary Winget, "The Dilemma of Affordable Child Care," in Zigler and Gordon, eds., *Day Care*, p. 360.

176. Delaware figures: Helen Blank, "Children and Federal Child Care Cuts: A National Survey of the Impact of Federal Title XX Cuts on State Child Care Systems, 1981–1983," a Children's Defense Fund White Paper (Washington, D.C.: Children's Defense Fund, 1983), appendices.

176. Title XX figures: ibid., p. 5.

177. "On the one hand": U.S. Commission on Civil Rights, publication no. 87, p. 20.

178. Congressional Budget Office figures: Blank, "Child Care Cuts," p. 2.

179. "the most effective": Winget, "Dilemma," p. 374.

12. The Politics of Day Care

185. "Let's look": "Demographic and Social Trends: Implications for Federal Support of Dependent-Care Services for Children and the Elderly," report of the Select Committee on Children, Youth, and Families of the House of Representatives, December 1983, p. 82.

186. "My pastoral advice is": Jerry Falwell, "Sex and God in American Politics," a symposium report in *Policy Review*, Summer 1984, p. 16.

186. "Where there's": Paul Weyrich, in ibid., p. 17.

186. "'profamily' interest groups": Rochelle Beck, "Beyond the Stalemate in Child Care Public Policy," in Edward F. Zigler and Edmund W. Gordon, eds., *Day Care: Scientific and Social Policy Issues* (Boston: Auburn House Publishing Co., 1982), p. 309.

187. "If a mother": Weyrich, "Sex and God," p. 17.

187. "The energies": Phyllis Schlafly, *The Power of the Positive Woman* (New York: Jobe Publications, 1978; originally published by Harcourt Brace Jovanovich, 1977), p. 203.

187. "Certainly one major drift": Chester E. Finn, Jr., "What Children Need," *Commentary*, May 1983, pp. 78–80.

188. Ideas about government involvement in child care: Connaught Marshner, interview, fall 1984.
190. "Whenever an adult": Dominique Browning, "Waiting for Mommy," *Texas Monthly*, February 1982, p. 189.
191. "Sometimes the State": Ellen Goodman, "The Real Daycare Problem: Not Enough of It," *Boston Globe*, January 13, 1983.

13. The Profamily Movement

194. "since God ordained": Phyllis Schlafly, *The Power of the Positive Woman* (New York: Jobe Publications, 1978; originally published by Harcourt Brace Jovanovich, 1977), p. 87.
196. "a system of moral norms": Connaught Marshner, *The New Traditional Woman* (Washington, D.C.: The Free Congress Research and Education Foundation, 1982), p. 4.
196. "The husband is": Connaught Marshner, interview, fall 1984.
197. "Come, leave your home": Schlafly, *Positive Woman*, p. 78.
197. "whether you wake up": ibid., p. 62.
197. "If you think": ibid., pp. 63, 57–60.
198. "attempt to substitute": Rita Kramer, *In Defense of the Family: Raising Children in America Today* (New York: Basic Books, 1983), p. 73.
198. "This speaks": ibid.
199. "First there were": Carol Hymowitz and Michaele Weissman, *A History of Women in America* (New York: Bantam Books, 1978), pp. 221, 223.
199. "The biggest problem": Schlafly, *Positive Woman*, pp. 73–75.
201. "I was able": Phyllis Schlafly, interview, summer 1984.
201. "Her daughter was practicing": Marabel Morgan, *The Total Woman* (New York: Pocket Books, 1973), pp. 210–211.
201. "When a close friend": ibid., p. 218.
202. "A mother can see": Schlafly, *Positive Woman*, p. 63.

14. The Women's Movement and Motherhood

204. "They baked": Betty Friedan, *The Feminine Mystique* (New York: Dell, 1974; originally published by W. W. Norton, 1963), p. 14.
207. "because the insurance companies": Dale Mezzacappa, "Congressional Leaders Vow to Block Sex Bias in Pensions, Insurance," *Philadelphia Inquirer*, January 28, 1983.
207. "If your husband": Deborah Rankin, "Check Up on Your Pension Rights, NOW!," *Woman's Day*, March 8, 1983, p. 60.
207. Thirty per cent figure on pensions from: "Pensions," *Chronicle of Higher Education*, March 2, 1983.
209. "recognize a woman's contribution": "WEAL Warns Against Further Cuts in Women's Low Social Security Benefits," *WEAL Washington Report* 12, no. 1 (February/March 1983), p. 5.
209. explanation of "earnings sharing": Maxine Forman, "What Will Your Candidate Do for Women? Ask About Earnings Sharing," *WEAL Washington Report* 13, no. 1 (February/March 1984), pp. 1–2.

209. "The feminists want": *The Phyllis Schlafly Report* 14, no. 9, section 1 (April 1981), p. 1.

209. "If we want": Judith B. Finn, *The Treatment of Women Under Social Security: A Critique of the Proposed Reforms* (Washington, D.C.: The Free Congress Research and Education Foundation, 1981), p. 14.

210. "The most important": ibid., p. 53.

210. "The old feminist ambivalence": Barbara Ehrenreich, "How to Get Housework out of Your System," *Ms*, October 1979, p. 48.

211. "Holidays and every day": Letty Cottin Pogrebin, *Family Politics: Love and Power on an Intimate Frontier* (New York: McGraw-Hill, 1983), p. 160.

211. "The point is": ibid., p. 167.

212. "The media, politicians": Catharine R. Stimpson, "I'm Not a Feminist But," *Ms*, July 1979, p. 64.

212. "The housewife's issues": Letty Cottin Pogrebin, interview, December 1984.

213. "As a working mother": Jean Curtis, *A Guide for Working Mothers: How to Be a Success as a Parent and in Your Job, Your Home, and Your Marriage* (New York: Touchstone/Simon and Schuster, 1975), p. 32.

215. "Articles that appear": Carol Tucker Foreman, letters to the editor, *Washington Monthly*, March 1982, p. 3.

216. "there is chilling evidence": Caroline Bird, *The Two-Paycheck Marriage* (New York: Rawson, Wade, 1979), pp. 36–37.

216. "not only is this": Pogrebin, *Family Politics*, p. 131.

217. Quotes from Jane Lazarre: Jane Lazarre, "Jane Broderick's Story," *Ms*, May 1977, pp. 53–84.

217. "9:50: Stopped to feed": Phyllis Rosser, "A Housewife's Log: What She REALLY Does All Day," *Ms*, March 1976, pp. 54, 87.

218. "It would seem to me": Betty Friedan, *The Second Stage* (New York: Summit Books, 1981), p. 260.